XNA® GAME STUDIO 4.0 FOR XBOX 360® DEVELOPERS

JONATHAN S. HARBOUR

Course Technology PTR
A part of Cengage Learning

COURSE TECHNOLOGY
CENGAGE Learning

Australia • Brazil • Japan • Korea • Mexico • Singapore • Spain • United Kingdom • United States

XNA® Game Studio 4.0 for Xbox 360® Developers
Jonathan S. Harbour

Publisher and General Manager, Course Technology PTR: Stacy L. Hiquet

Associate Director of Marketing: Sarah Panella

Manager of Editorial Services: Heather Talbot

Marketing Manager: Jordan Castellani

Acquisitions Editor: Heather Hurley

Project Editor: Kate Shoup

Technical Reviewer: James Perry

Copy Editor: Kate Shoup

Interior Layout Tech: MPS Limited, a Macmillan Company

Cover Designer: Mike Tanamachi

Indexer: Kelly Talbot Editing Services

Proofreader: Brad Crawford

Library of Congress Control Number: 2010933076

ISBN-13: 978-1-58450-537-2

ISBN-10: 1-58450-537-0

Course Technology, a part of Cengage Learning
20 Channel Center Street
Boston, MA 02210
USA

Cengage Learning is a leading provider of customized learning solutions with office locations around the globe, including Singapore, the United Kingdom, Australia, Mexico, Brazil, and Japan. Locate your local office at: **international.cengage.com/region**

Cengage Learning products are represented in Canada by Nelson Education, Ltd.

For your lifelong learning solutions, visit **courseptr.com**

Visit our corporate website at **cengage.com**

Printed in the United States of America
1 2 3 4 5 6 7 8 12 11

This book is dedicated to my good friend, Peter Blue.

ACKNOWLEDGMENTS

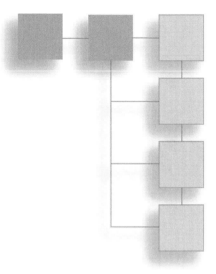

Thanks to Heather Hurley and Kate Shoup for their valiant efforts to get this book into print after many delays and two versions of XNA! Thanks to Jim Perry, who is a Microsoft MVP and XNA forum contributor, for his excellent technical review and helpful critique. Thanks to my wife, Jennifer, and my kids, Jeremiah, Kayleigh, Kourtney, and Kaitlyn, for not just their love and support but also their feedback. Thanks go out to Mark Simpson (Prinz Eugn at Gamedev.net) for the artwork used in the multiplayer game featured in the last chapter.

About the Author

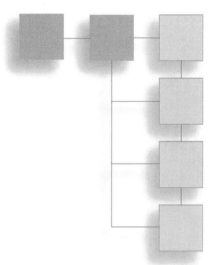

Jonathan S. Harbour has been programming video games since the 1980s. His first game system was an Atari 2600, which he played with disassembled on the floor of his room as a kid. He has written on numerous subjects such as C++, C#, Basic, Java, DirectX, Allegro, Lua, DarkBasic, Pocket PC, and game consoles. He is the author of the recent books *Visual C# Game Programming for Teens*; *Beginning Java Game Programming, 2nd Edition*; *Visual Basic Game Programming for Teens, Third Edition*; and *Multi-Threaded Game Engine Design*. He holds a master's degree in Information Systems Management. Visit his Web log and game-development forum at http://www.jharbour.com.

CONTENTS

INTRODUCTION

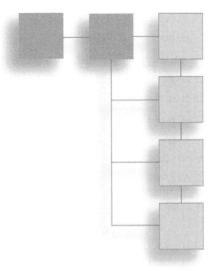

XNA Game Studio 4.0 for Xbox 360 Developers is an intermediate-level book with an emphasis on programming in the C# language and targeting primarily the Xbox 360 platform. XNA Game Studio is Microsoft's gift to game developers, of both the professional and hobby persuasion. Independent ("indie") developers make up a particularly large group that benefits from XNA Game Studio due to Microsoft's very appealing publishing royalty terms on the Xbox Live Indie Arcade (XBLIA) service, which makes their indie games available to the general public via Xbox Live.

This book was originally intended to be a comprehensive reference on the XNA Framework library. When XNA Game Studio 4.0 was announced in early 2010, work shifted from an XNA 3.1 reference to a more comprehensive *applied* book on XNA 4.0. Part II, "XNA Framework Library," is only a quick reference to the XNA Framework, with simple examples, not a large and complex one. Although the reference information is comprehensive—covering *every* namespace—it is not overly detailed. Not every overloaded method is listed. Constructors and method parameters are not expanded in detail; we have MSDN resources online for that. The purpose of this book, then, is to provide a quick reference of the XNA Framework as it applies to the Xbox 360, and for C# programmers primarily interested in creating games for this platform.

XNA GAME STUDIO 4.0

XNA Game Studio makes it possible to create games for the popular Xbox 360 video-game console system! This is the most significant platform of note. When

XNA Game Studio 1.0 was released to developers in 2006, it marked the first time a video-game–console manufacturer released development tools for their system *free* to the public, without requiring an expensive license agreement. XNA Game Studio also targets the Windows platform. This might seem like a no-brainer, a foregone conclusion, to those already experienced with XNA. But it's not at all common for a console-development tool to support both the console and the development PC platform! What this means is, you can compile and run your game code on your Windows PC *for* Windows or *for* Xbox 360, and then run it on either platform.

But that's not all! Not to sound like an infomercial, but the latest version of XNA Game Studio, which is now up to version 4.0, *also* supports the mobile platform called Windows Phone 7. This is a hot new device that's comparable to (and competitive with) Apple's iPhone and Google's Android mobile smart phones. Both Apple and Google provide free developer tools for the iPhone and Android, respectively, so Microsoft is on board with support for Windows Phone 7 in the new XNA Game Studio 4.0. Admittedly, this is the most significant reason for the new version, since XNA Game Studio 3.1 was released just about a year and a half earlier (in mid-2009), and 4.0 leverages Windows Phone 7 rather heavily. As a result of this new mobile device, the XNA team decided to sacrifice support for the Zune mobile media/music player. This is somewhat understandable, because Windows Phone 7 trumps Zune by supporting the same media playback capabilities *in addition* to smart-phone features comparable to the iPhone. There's no compelling reason on the technical side to abandon Zune, so it must have been an issue of marketing, branding, and product placement, as well as slagging sales for the Zune platform.

Although the code in this book in general will compile and run on all platforms, we do cover the specific features available only on the Xbox 360. These features (such as Xbox Live Avatars) are not available on the other platforms such as Windows Phone 7.

LICENSING AND MEMBERSHIPS

On the Xbox 360 platform, you *can* compile and run your code on a *retail* Xbox 360! This is extremely exciting for game developers and video-game fans! Imagine seeing your own game running on your friend's Xbox 360! Of course, there is a cost, because this is a huge benefit, but the cost is meager compared to the price of a full-blown Xbox Development Kit (XDK), which is used by professional game studios. To make this happen, you will need a membership for the XNA Creators

Club, which has been renamed to App Hub. The cost is approximately $100 per year. You will also want an Xbox Live Gold account for best results, which is an additional cost of approximately $60 per year. These prices might be high for a student, but they are more than reasonable for an indie developer since the development tools are *free!*

This membership fee gives you the ability to publish your game online for others to purchase using Microsoft Points—the same currency used to buy expansions and other downloadable content (DLC) on Xbox Live! As an App Hub developer, your game will be listed in a special section of the Xbox Live Arcade (XBLA) called the Xbox Live Indie Arcade (XBLIA). Anyone on Xbox Live can download your game, presumably first as a demo version, and if they like it, they will buy your full version at the price you set. (Typical cost for a quality indie game is about 400 points, or about $5.) This is a great way to share your games with the world and make a decent living at it—*if* you have the talent and technical know-how to make a great game. The former is up to you, but this book will certainly help you with the latter!

We don't get into account management, licensing terms, uploading games for review, and receiving royalties in this book, because frankly, the terms and conditions of those things change often. If you make your way to the last chapter and have a great idea for a game, then getting it up on XBLIA will be the easy part.

What Will You Learn?

This book teaches the beginning to intermediate C# programmer how to use XNA Game Studio 4.0 with Visual C# 2010 to create games primarily for the Xbox 360. Although most of the source code presented in these chapters can be adapted for the other platforms supported by XNA, the emphasis is on the Xbox 360 and Xbox Live. The first two chapters will help the reader get started with the new versions of these tools. Numerous chapters provide reference information for the XNA Framework. The latter chapters culminate in a networked multiplayer game called *Tank Battle*. This game, featured in the last chapter of the book, includes the networking code to allow two players to host or connect to each other (repeatedly) to drive their tanks around and shoot at each other. Granted, it's not a highly polished game, and could use quite a bit of creative souping up, but it's a good technical example of networking a sprite-based game with the most important features you will need to make your own game.

It's true that we don't spend much time on 3D rendering in this book. The reason is simple: We are focusing on the XNA Framework as a whole, and the Xbox 360 features in particular, which means coverage of the Xbox 360 controller, playing audio, and using features of Xbox Live—especially networking via system link and online. Chapter 12, "Avatars," shows how to render a gamer avatar, which is a 3D character representing the player online. We also explore the loading and rendering of meshes in Chapter 15, "Meshes," with the associated 3D camera and lighting code needed to make it work. These are very lightweight issues in rendering—just the absolute basics really—but then this book is not focused on rendering. Because XNA Game Studio 4.0 is based on DirectX 9, *any* book or reference on High Level Shader Language (HLSL) 3.0 will provide useful shader examples that will also work in XNA—including the same FX files.

There are scores of such books on DirectX 9 available. If you like this author's writing style, I recommend his *Multi-Threaded Game Engine Design* (Course Technology PTR, 2010). This book covers basic shader theory, per-pixel lighting, surface detail effects like bump mapping and specular reflection (which add realism to a textured surface), heightmap terrain, skyboxes, and more—and the FX files in this book will work in your XNA projects. If you are looking for additional references, see Appendix, "Resources for Further Study," for a list.

PREREQUISITES

The goal of this book is to teach you how to use the latest version of XNA Game Studio. You will benefit from a basic knowledge of Visual C# in advance, because we don't really cover the language at all. Programming a game for the Xbox 360 is a challenge for an experienced developer, let alone a beginner. But by paying attention and studying the examples, even a beginner should be able to get through the book without too much difficulty, because the examples are on the small side for the most part.

REQUIRED SOFTWARE

This book supports Visual C# 2010, which should be installed first—*before* XNA Game Studio 4.0. I recommend that you download the free version of Visual C# 2010 Express Edition. The URL is http://www.microsoft.com/express/Windows/. Because Web links change frequently, you may need to Google for "Visual C#

2010 Express download." There may still be links to the 2008 version as well, but 2010 is required for XNA Game Studio 4.0.

Tip

You may continue to use XNA 3.1 with Visual C# 2008 simultaneously with the newer tools without any problems. This may be desirable if you need to continue to support Zune projects.

Another option is to install the Windows Phone 7 developer tools, which include both Visual C# 2010 Express and XNA Game Studio 4.0. Although some extra tools are included that you may not need, such as Silverlight, these are good tools to have anyway should you wish to delve into Windows Phone 7 development. The URL is http://www.microsoft.com/express/Phone/.

DOWNLOADING THE SOURCES

My Web site is at http://www.jharbour.com. There is information about this book and links to the sources that you may download. Most visitors join the forum to discuss their game projects and ask questions. If you have any problems working through this book, stop by the forum to chat. Since the book ships without a CD, you will need to download the resource files, which includes the source code for all of the projects in the book. The URL is http://www.cengage.com/downloads. The aforementioned Web forum also provides links to the sources at http://www.jharbour.com/forum.

CONTENTS

The book is divided into three major parts:

- **Part I, "Introduction and Primer."** This part includes two chapters that will help get you started programming in XNA, with an introduction to the new features in XNA 4.0 as well as coverage of the XNA Framework and how to create new projects with Visual C# 2010. It includes the following chapters:

  - Chapter 1: "Introduction to XNA Game Studio 4.0"
  - Chapter 2: "Peeking Under the Hood"

- **Part II, "XNA Framework Library."** This part includes nine chapters that provide a reference for the XNA Framework with sample code to show how each namespace in the XNA Framework can be used in a game project. Chapters in this part are as follows:

- Chapter 3: "XNA Framework Overview"
- Chapter 4: "Audio"
- Chapter 5: "Content"
- Chapter 6: "GamerServices"
- Chapter 7: "Graphics"
- Chapter 8: "Input"
- Chapter 9: "Media"
- Chapter 10: "Net"
- Chapter 11: "Storage"

- **Part III, "Xbox Live."** This part includes six applied chapters covering the major features of Xbox Live that can be utilized in an XNA 4.0 project, including coverage of avatars and multiplayer networking. The final chapter culminates in a multiplayer *Tank Battle* game that demonstrates the networking capabilities of XNA and acts as a rudimentary networked game engine for your own projects. Chapters 12 and 15 both cover 3D programming, loading a mesh, and rendering it using a basic shader.

  - Chapter 12: "Avatars"
  - Chapter 13: "Guide"
  - Chapter 14: "Multiplayer Networking"
  - Chapter 15: "Meshes"
  - Chapter 16: "Sprites"
  - Chapter 17: "Multiplayer Game Engine"

CONVENTIONS USED IN THIS BOOK

Source code is presented in fixed-width font for easy readability.

```
// This is how source code will be formatted in the text
public void Hello()
{
  Console.WriteLine("Hello World");
}
```

The following styles are used in this book to highlight portions of text that are important. You will find note boxes here and there throughout the book.

Note

Notes offer additional pointers on the current subject being covered or additional details and information about a subject that should help the reader get the most out of the situation.

Sidebar

A sidebar is an often lengthy paragraph about a related but off-topic subject, set apart so as to avoid interrupting the flow of thought on the main thread of the chapter.

COMPANION WEB SITE DOWNLOADS

You may download the companion Web site files from www.courseptr.com/downloads. Please note that you will be redirected to our Cengage Learning site.

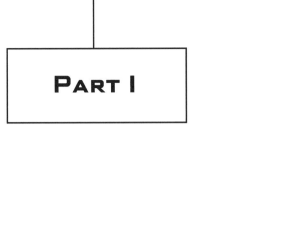

Part I

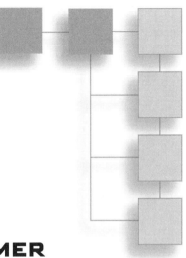

Introduction and Primer

The first part of the book provides a general introduction to XNA Game Studio 4.0, laying out the goals and project requirements for the reference- and project-based chapters. It also digs into the inner workings of XNA Game Studio to help the reader better understand the code presented in the book. Here are the chapters:

- Chapter 1: "Introduction to XNA Game Studio 4.0"
- Chapter 2: "Peeking Under the Hood"

CHAPTER 1

INTRODUCTION TO XNA GAME STUDIO 4.0

XNA Game Studio 4.0 is the latest version of the iconic multiplatform game-development tool from Microsoft. XNA Game Studio 4.0 makes it possible to build a game for Windows and Xbox 360—plus handheld devices—using essentially the same source code and media files. This chapter explores XNA from a high-altitude, bird's-eye view to give you a general feel for what XNA is, what you can do with it, what the licensing terms are, and how it can be used for commercial success. This is not a book for beginners; it is focused on the intermediate to advanced reader. It assumes that readers know the C# language. It also assumes readers can create their own Xbox Live Gold and XNA Creators Club/App Hub accounts, so it does not go over these steps. If you are unsure how to proceed, visit the XNA Creators Club/App Hub Web site at http://creators.xna.com or http://create.msdn.com to find out how to get started. Here's the rundown:

- A little history of XNA
- What XNA is
- What XNA isn't
- XNA platforms
- The XNA Framework
- XNA Creators Club

A LITTLE HISTORY OF XNA

The first version of XNA Game Studio was launched in the spring of 2006 as a preview build, with an official version 1.0 being somewhat informal. In other words, XNA is not itself a for-profit product vested with a large customer-service team. Rather, it is more of a gift to developers. Microsoft's business model for XNA is wrapped up in sales of games on the special area of Xbox Live Arcade called the Creators Club (recently renamed App Hub), reserved for developers who subscribe to the service for $100 per year (in addition to obtaining the required Gold membership account).

Note

Rumors abound, but three possible meanings for the "XNA" acronym are *XNA's Not Acronymed*, *Cross-platform Next-gen Architecture*, or *DirectX DNA*. Because XNA is intended only to be a hobby tool, I question the validity of the second meaning (implying that XNA itself is "next gen"), but it may be appropriate for the indie market.

When Visual Studio .NET 2002 was released with the infamous .NET Framework 1.0 (a library of programming tools for Windows programmers), this whole new environment not only required developers to learn the new system, but it rendered most existing Windows code obsolete. At the time, Visual Basic 6.0 was the most popular programming language and environment for Windows programmers. The popularity of Basic has waned a bit today, largely due to the new language presented for the first time with Visual Studio .NET 2002, known as C# (pronounced "see-sharp"). This is the language of XNA Game Studio; therefore, it is the language you will be using in this book.

Note

Fans of the classic Basic language will likely be interested in my book *Visual Basic Game Programming for Teens, Third Edition*. This book is based on the latest Visual Studio with an emphasis on role-playing game design and programming.

XNA is larger than just the Game Studio tool, which includes a plug-in modification to Visual Studio that links in the appropriate runtime library files for Windows, Xbox 360, or the handhelds, depending on your build target. Figure 1.1 shows how the XNA libraries and tools work together, with Game Studio being just one part of the suite.

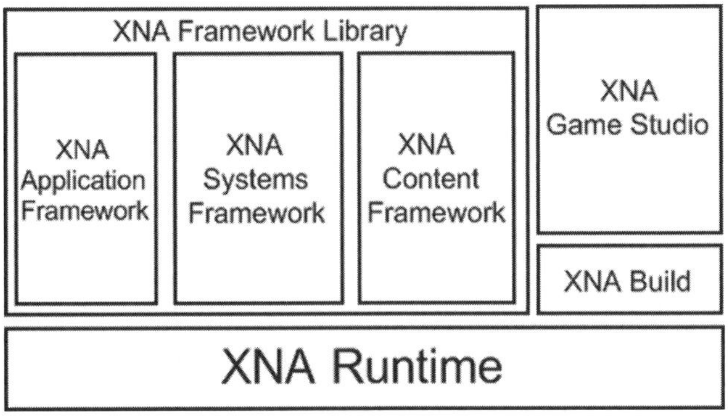

Figure 1.1
The libraries and tools of Microsoft XNA.

Note

All the licenses and software needed to get up and running with XNA Game Studio are found at the XNA Creators Club Web site at http://creators.xna.com. Note that due to a recent name change to correspond with the release of XNA Game Studio 4.0, Creators Club is now called App Hub.

WHAT XNA IS

First, let's see what XNA *is*, with regard to other products. XNA Game Studio is not a programming environment itself. Instead, it is a plug-in for Visual Studio. The first version, released in 2006, was installed as a plug-in of Visual Studio 2005 with custom project templates. To be more precise, it required a special version called Visual C# 2005 Express, and did not work with any of the commercially licensed versions of Visual Studio (Professional, Enterprise, etc). Because Visual Studio now has a robust plug-in system, you might call XNA simply an SDK—a Software Development Kit for cross-platform games. But XNA has taken a path of its own during its short lifetime, and is often mistaken for being a self-contained product. XNA is an SDK but also has the properties of a rudimentary game engine, albeit only in the sense that a timed loop is provided for you, but no rendering capabilities. Table 1.1 shows when each version of XNA Game Studio was released.

I like to think of XNA as a special version of DirectX, but even that is an insufficient comparison. XNA comes with much more than just DirectX SDK files; it includes a compiled Xbox Development Kit (XDK) library that makes it possible to compile standalone executable code that will run on a retail Xbox 360. Although I would like to append "no strings attached" to that statement, that is not the case.

Table 1.1 XNA Game Studio Version History

XNA Version	Year of Release
XNA Game Studio 1.0	2006
XNA Game Studio 2.0	2007
XNA Game Studio 3.0	2008
XNA Game Studio 3.1	2009
XNA Game Studio 4.0	2010

Even so, the XNA team has made an effort to make XNA as easy as possible so that even inexperienced programmers can see their code running on their very own retail Xbox 360 with only a few steps. That's right, you do *not* need an expensive Xbox Development Kit to make your own Xbox 360 games. Even if you *could* buy an XDK, they are very expensive—tens of thousands of dollars! The following memberships are required to test code on your Xbox 360:

■ Xbox Live Gold Account ($60)

■ XNA Creators Club Account ($100)

If all you want to do is learn XNA for Windows, no special membership account is needed. Just install XNA Game Studio and get started writing code. Because the most compelling feature of XNA is that it gives you the ability to write games that run on an Xbox 360, I assume you and I share that interest and will be taking that approach. Therefore, both a Gold account and Creators Club/App Hub account are needed, for an annual cost of about $160. What this gives you is the ability to compile your XNA code for Xbox 360 and actually *run it* on your own retail Xbox 360 console. The process is similar to that used for mobile-device development on most platforms; it's similar for Pocket PC (now obsolete), Zune HD, Java Wireless Toolkit, and Apple's iPhone, iPod, and iPad. A connection is made from XNA Game Studio (i.e. *Visual Studio*) to your retail Xbox 360, which must be on the same network as your development PC.

Note

Microsoft has made available a quick-start guide to setting up XNA Game Studio and creating Xbox Live and Creators Club accounts, including tutorials on connecting your PC to your Xbox 360 for live debugging on the console. See the guide here: http://create.msdn.com/en-US/home/getting_started.

WHAT XNA ISN'T

Now let's take a look at what XNA *isn't*, to form a comparison with other products. XNA is not a game engine. As mentioned earlier, it has a real-time loop with timing, which is a simple sort of engine (or, one might say, a *pump* in the sense that it does only rudimentary message handling). But XNA cannot render anything automatically, such as from a script file, like a real game engine can. XNA Game Studio comes with these project templates:

- Windows Phone Game (4.0)
- Windows Phone Game Library (4.0)
- Windows Game (4.0)
- Windows Game Library (4.0)
- Xbox 360 Game (4.0)
- Xbox 360 Game Library (4.0)
- Content Pipeline Extension Library (4.0)
- Empty Content Project (4.0)

The four platforms supported by XNA are as follows:

- Windows
- Xbox 360
- Zune/Zune HD
- Windows Phone 7

But there's a catch: Zune HD is no longer supported in XNA 4.0. To continue developing for Zune, you have to use XNA 3.1 (with Visual C# 2008). All these platforms are owned by Microsoft, but they are quite different in architecture and capabilities. This makes XNA a true cross-platform development tool. What makes this possible is the fact that Visual Studio is the development tool used for all of these platforms separately. Thus, incorporating support for them all in XNA for game development did not require a custom environment or tools, but rather project templates and custom options for the various compilers that bring Visual Studio projects to life.

Note

I have another recent book that may interest you: *Visual C# Game Programming for Teens*. Like its sister *For Teens* book, this one takes a special interest in role-playing games, but focuses on the dungeon hack-and-slash genre rather than the quest-based world.

How Does XNA Code Compare?

Understanding how XNA functions can help to make you a better XNA developer. Let's spend a little time examining how XNA works behind the scenes. I will show you a simple program that prints a message on the screen using three different tools: XNA, DirectX, and a custom game engine.

A Windows Game project looks very much like a C++ DirectX program, with a WinMain() function, a WinProc() message handler, and a while loop. Figure 1.2 shows these core functions. This program initializes Direct3D with the desired rendering options and screen properties. User input support is provided either by DirectInput or by the WinProc() function's ability to detect key and mouse events. A special library called XInput provides a Windows program with Xbox 360 controller input, if you want to use it. After Direct3D is initialized, but before the while loop begins running, the LoadContent() function is called from somewhere within WinMain() (see Figure 1.2). This is one of the main XNA functions provided in every new XNA project, and it is where we load game

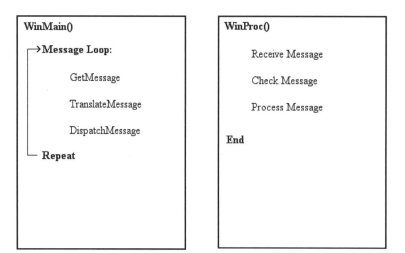

Figure 1.2
The innermost core of a Windows program.

assets (textures, sounds, meshes, etc). After initialization is complete, the while loop begins running, and two more XNA functions are called repeatedly.

First, the Update() function is called with a timing parameter that tells us how much time has passed since the last time the function was called. Update() has the potential to run at the CPU clock speed, but by default it is limited to 60 fps for consistency with our rendering code. The Draw() function is called from within a timed block of code set to always run at 60 fps. Unlike Update(), the frequency with which Draw() is called cannot be changed. Figure 1.3 shows an illustration of the main loop.

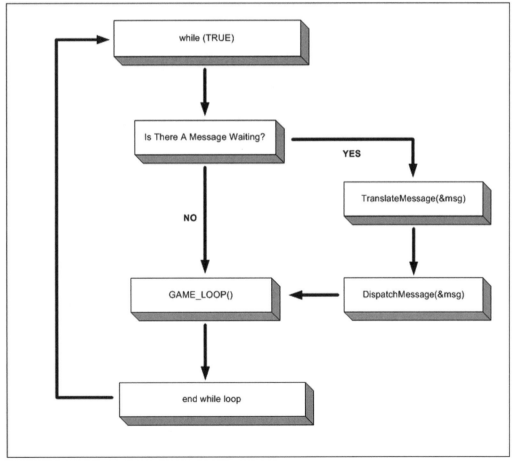

Figure 1.3
The primary loop of a Windows program.

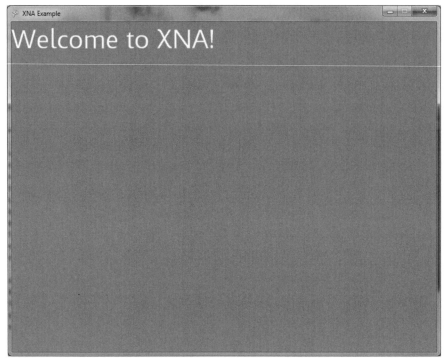

Figure 1.4
This simple XNA program just prints out a welcome message.

XNA Code

We're going to look at a simple XNA program first, and then look at a similar program written in C++ using DirectX, to help you get a feel for what's going on behind the scenes in XNA. First, let's take a look at the XNA example (see Listing 1.1). This program just prints "Welcome to XNA!" on the screen. Here is a sample program written in C# using XNA, with its output shown in Figure 1.4.

Listing 1.1   XNA Example

```
using System;
using System.Collections.Generic;
using System.Linq;
using Microsoft.Xna.Framework;
using Microsoft.Xna.Framework.Audio;
using Microsoft.Xna.Framework.Content;
using Microsoft.Xna.Framework.GamerServices;
```

```
using Microsoft.Xna.Framework.Graphics;
using Microsoft.Xna.Framework.Input;
using Microsoft.Xna.Framework.Media;
using Microsoft.Xna.Framework.Net;
using Microsoft.Xna.Framework.Storage;

namespace XNA_Example
{
    public class Game1 : Microsoft.Xna.Framework.Game
    {
        GraphicsDeviceManager graphics;
        SpriteBatch spriteBatch;
        SpriteFont spriteFont;

        public Game1()
        {
            graphics = new GraphicsDeviceManager(this);
            Content.RootDirectory = "Content";
        }

        protected override void Initialize()
        {
            base.Initialize();
        }

        protected override void LoadContent()
        {
            spriteBatch = new SpriteBatch(GraphicsDevice);
            spriteFont = Content.Load<SpriteFont>("SpriteFont1");
        }

        protected override void UnloadContent()
        {
        }

        protected override void Update(GameTime gameTime)
        {
            if (Keyboard.GetState().IsKeyDown(Keys.Escape)) this.Exit();
            base.Update(gameTime);
        }
```

```
        protected override void Draw(GameTime gameTime)
        {
            GraphicsDevice.Clear(Color.CornflowerBlue);
            spriteBatch.Begin();
            spriteBatch.DrawString(spriteFont, "Welcome to XNA!",
                new Vector2(0, 0), Color.White);
            spriteBatch.End();
            base.Draw(gameTime);
        }
    }
}
```

DirectX Code

Listing 1.2 contains a similar program that also prints a message on the screen, but this one uses C++ and DirectX. This is a complete Windows program with a WinMain() function that uses Direct3D to print a message on the screen. You

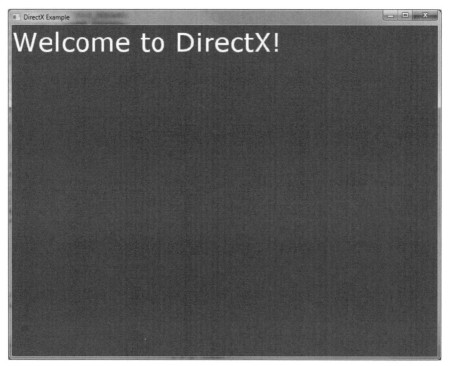

Figure 1.5
This DirectX program also prints out a welcome message.

will likely notice many similarities to the XNA sample program, such as the use of a `SpriteBatch` type object (which, in C++ terminology, is derived from `LPD3DXSPRITE`, which itself is derived from `ID3DXSprite`). In addition, you have the usual C++ header file includes, library file linker options, and project configuration complexity that has the potential to make a grown man cry like a baby. A good comparison here is often drawn from automobiles: Just because you can drive your Toyota Camry on the I-10 during rush hour, that doesn't put you in a league with NASCAR drivers. C# hides many of the details from us at the expense of performance. But then, who would want to commute to work and back in a custom-built 550-horsepower NASCAR race car? (Okay, so would I, but what I mean is, who would want to do that *every day*? Oh, never mind! Forget the whole analogy.) Figure 1.5 shows the output of the code listing that follows.

Listing 1.2   DirectX Example

```
#include <windows.h>
#include <d3d9.h>
#include <d3dx9.h>
#include <string>
using namespace std;
#pragma comment(lib,"d3d9.lib")
#pragma comment(lib,"d3dx9.lib")

//program settings
const string APPTITLE = "DirectX Example";
const int SCREENW = 816;
const int SCREENH = 638;

//Direct3D objects
LPDIRECT3D9 d3d = NULL;
LPDIRECT3DDEVICE9 d3ddev = NULL;
LPD3DXSPRITE spriteBatch = NULL;
LPD3DXFONT font = NULL;
HWND window = 0;
bool gameover = false;

//macro to detect key presses
#define KEY_DOWN(vk_code) ((GetAsyncKeyState(vk_code) & 0x8000) ? 1 : 0)
```

```
//function prototypes
bool Initialize();
void Update();
void Draw();

LRESULT WINAPI WinProc(HWND hWnd, UINT msg, WPARAM wParam, LPARAM lParam)
{
    switch( msg )
    {
        case WM_DESTROY:
            gameover = true;
            PostQuitMessage(0);
            return 0;
    }
    return DefWindowProc( hWnd, msg, wParam, lParam );
}

int WINAPI WinMain(HINSTANCE hInstance, HINSTANCE hPrevInstance,
    LPSTR lpCmdLine, int nCmdShow)
{
    //set the new window's properties
    WNDCLASSEX wc;
    wc.cbSize = sizeof(WNDCLASSEX);
    wc.style         = CS_HREDRAW | CS_VREDRAW;
    wc.lpfnWndProc   = (WNDPROC)WinProc;
    wc.cbClsExtra    = 0;
    wc.cbWndExtra    = 0;
    wc.hInstance     = hInstance;
    wc.hIcon         = NULL;
    wc.hCursor       = LoadCursor(NULL, IDC_ARROW);
    wc.hbrBackground = NULL;
    wc.lpszMenuName  = NULL;
    wc.lpszClassName = APPTITLE.c_str();
    wc.hIconSm       = NULL;
    RegisterClassEx(&wc);

    //create the program window
    window = CreateWindow( APPTITLE.c_str(), APPTITLE.c_str(),
        WS_OVERLAPPEDWINDOW, CW_USEDEFAULT, CW_USEDEFAULT,
        SCREENW, SCREENH, NULL, NULL, hInstance, NULL);
```

```
    //display the window
    ShowWindow(window, nCmdShow);
    UpdateWindow(window);

    //initialize Direct3D
    if (!Initialize()) return 0;

    //main message loop
    MSG message;
    while (!gameover)
    {
        if (PeekMessage(&message, NULL, 0, 0, PM_REMOVE))
        {
            TranslateMessage(&message);
            DispatchMessage(&message);
        }

        Update();
        Draw();
    }

    //free memory
    d3ddev->Release();
    d3d->Release();
    spriteBatch->Release();
    font->Release();

    return message.wParam;
}

bool Initialize()
{
    //initialize Direct3D
    d3d = Direct3DCreate9(D3D_SDK_VERSION);

    //set Direct3D presentation parameters
    D3DPRESENT_PARAMETERS d3dpp;
    ZeroMemory(&d3dpp, sizeof(d3dpp));
    d3dpp.Windowed = TRUE;
    d3dpp.SwapEffect = D3DSWAPEFFECT_DISCARD;
```

```
        d3dpp.BackBufferFormat = D3DFMT_X8R8G8B8;
        d3dpp.BackBufferCount = 1;
        d3dpp.BackBufferWidth = SCREENW;
        d3dpp.BackBufferHeight = SCREENH;
        d3dpp.hDeviceWindow = window;

        //create Direct3D device
        d3d->CreateDevice( D3DADAPTER_DEFAULT, D3DDEVTYPE_HAL, window,
            D3DCREATE_SOFTWARE_VERTEXPROCESSING, &d3dpp, &d3ddev);

        //create sprite batch object
        D3DXCreateSprite(d3ddev, &spriteBatch);

        //create a font object
        D3DXFONT_DESC desc = { 60, 0, 0, 0, false, DEFAULT_CHARSET,
            OUT_TT_PRECIS, CLIP_DEFAULT_PRECIS, DEFAULT_PITCH, "Verdana" };
        D3DXCreateFontIndirect(d3ddev, &desc, &font);

        return true;
}

void Update()
{
        if (KEY_DOWN(VK_ESCAPE)) gameover = true;
}

void Draw()
{
        d3ddev->Clear(0, NULL, D3DCLEAR_TARGET, D3DCOLOR_XRGB(70,70,255), 1.0f, 0);

        if (d3ddev->BeginScene())
        {
            spriteBatch->Begin(D3DXSPRITE_ALPHABLEND);

            string text = "Welcome to DirectX!";
            D3DCOLOR color = D3DCOLOR_XRGB(255,255,255);
            font->DrawText(spriteBatch, text.c_str(), text.length(), NULL,
                DT_LEFT, color);
```

```
        spriteBatch->End();

        d3ddev->EndScene();
        d3ddev->Present(NULL, NULL, NULL, NULL);
    }
}
```

The great thing about these two code listings is that they produce *identical* results! Both cover the background with a light blue color and *both* print a welcome message on the screen. Both the XNA and Direct3D versions of this program generate a texture upon which font characters are rendered (when the font object is created) and then used for the purpose of printing text on the screen. One difference is that our C++ Update() function has no parameter, while an XNA Update() function has a timing parameter. At any rate, it's an interesting comparison—the irony being that code very similar to this is found within the XNA libraries.

Take a look in Program Files, Microsoft XNA, v4.0, References folder and note the different files located here! That should give you an idea about how XNA works. Here are the Windows runtime files:

- Microsoft.Xna.Framework.Content.Pipeline.AudioImporters.dll

- Microsoft.Xna.Framework.Content.Pipeline.dll

- Microsoft.Xna.Framework.Content.Pipeline.EffectImporter.dll

- Microsoft.Xna.Framework.Content.Pipeline.FBXImporter.dll

- Microsoft.Xna.Framework.Content.Pipeline.TextureImporter.dll

- Microsoft.Xna.Framework.Content.Pipeline.VideoImporters.dll

- Microsoft.Xna.Framework.Content.Pipeline.XImporter.dll

- Microsoft.Xna.Framework.Content.Pipeline.xml

- Microsoft.Xna.Framework.dll

- Microsoft.Xna.Framework.Game.dll

- Microsoft.Xna.Framework.Game.xml

- Microsoft.Xna.Framework.xml

Interestingly enough, the XNA source-code example in Listing 1.1 tends to resemble XNA-style game code much more closely than it resembles DirectX code (ignoring the slight differences between C# and C++).

Engine Code

Octane is not a professional game engine; it's a "workbench" engine used for hobby projects, having evolved into a somewhat respectable engine in my DirectX book titled *Multi-Threaded Game Engine Design*. The main goal for this engine, shown in Listing 1.3, was to make it accessible to C++ programmers of all experience levels, because so many engines tend to be quite complex. Figure 1.6 shows the output of the listing.

N o t e

Visit www.jharbour.com/forum to learn more about Octane Engine, including information on how to access the complete source code for the engine and all examples.

Figure 1.6
This Octane program prints out a welcome message.

Listing 1.3   Octane Engine Code

```
#include "Engine.h"
using namespace std;
using namespace Octane;
Font *font=NULL;

bool game_preload()
{
    g_engine->setAppTitle("Octane Engine Example");
    g_engine->setScreen(800,600,32,false);
    g_engine->setBackdropColor(D3DCOLOR_XRGB(60,60,255));
    return true;
}

bool game_init(HWND hwnd)
{
    font = new Font("Arial",60);
    if (!font)
    {
        debug << "Error creating font" << endl;
        return false;
    }
    return true;
}

void game_update( float deltaTime ) { }

void game_render3d() { }

void game_end() { }

void game_render2d()
{
    font->Print(0,0,"Welcome to Octane!");
}

void game_event( IEvent* e )
{
    switch( e->getID() )
    {
```

```
        case EVENT_KEYPRESS:      break;
        case EVENT_KEYRELEASE:    break;
        case EVENT_MOUSEMOVE:     break;
        case EVENT_MOUSECLICK:    break;
        case EVENT_MOUSEMOTION:   break;
        case EVENT_MOUSEWHEEL:    break;
    }

}
```

MOBILE DEVICES

XNA Game Studio can also compile code for mobile devices! Currently, XNA supports three devices: the older Zune media player, Zune HD (shown in Figure 1.7), and Windows Phone 7. There are some limitations to the types of programs you can

Figure 1.7
Zune HD mobile media player and game device.

write for these mobile devices. XNA builds for Zune, for instance, can only render 2D graphics. The great thing about mobile-device support in XNA is that you can use our existing source code *almost* without change. However, Zune is no longer supported in XNA 4.0, although you can still use XNA 3.1 to compile for the Zune target.

The XNA team has worked hard to make the code base even more compatible across all platforms. The 3D capabilities of Windows Phone 7 (see Figure 1.8) mean you can use your existing Windows and Xbox 360 code for that mobile device. Obviously, no mobile device will have the same capabilities as a full-blown PC or console, but it can come close! Although some advanced rendering effects may not be possible, you can simulate them in various ways. For instance, you can simulate fog on a mobile device using alpha blending—an old technique.

Figure 1.8
Windows Phone 7 supports media playback and games.

Xᴃᴏx 360

I cannot show any real C++ code for an Xbox 360 game because any such code would fall under licensing restrictions and a non-disclosure agreement (NDA). Any hacked or reverse-engineered example would definitely attract the attention of Microsoft's legal department. But we can speculate based on what we know about Windows development in C++ and what we know about the Xbox 360 hardware. Early development systems for the Xbox 360 were most likely based on an Apple Mac system, because the Xbox 360's central processor is a PowerPC chip, like one of the older G5 dual-core chips. The Xbox 360 team would have prototyped code on that G5-like box, but would have needed to transition over to Windows as the development platform of choice for Xbox 360 development (for so many uncomfortable reasons, I don't even know where to start). Figure 1.9 shows the latest iteration of the Xbox 360, now a four-year old, mature, proven video-game console system!

Dare I suggest some sort of XboxMain() function being used? The actual function name is not important, because we are not doing any C++ programming

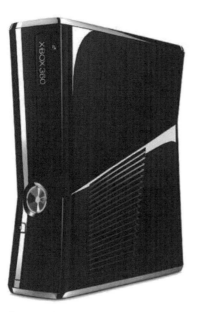

Figure 1.9
The ability to write your own Xbox 360 code without a dev kit is extraordinary!

here. Whatever the function is called, it likely has very little resemblance to WinMain() and the traditional Windows message-handling system. Perusing the Program Files, XNA Game Studio, v4.0, References, Xbox360 folder, we find these files:

- Microsoft.Xna.Framework.dll
- Microsoft.Xna.Framework.Game.dll
- Microsoft.Xna.Framework.Game.xml
- Microsoft.Xna.Framework.xml
- mscorlib.dll
- mscorlib.xml
- System.Core.dll
- System.Core.xml
- System.dll
- System.xml
- System.Xml.dll
- System.Xml.Linq.dll
- System.Xml.Linq.xml
- System.Xml.xml

We find a similar list of runtime files for Zune and Windows Phone 7, which is quite different from the Windows reference files. Why do you suppose that is? One file in particular, mscorlib.dll, is the granddaddy of the .NET Framework, containing the all-important System.Object class and other core framework classes. Interestingly, this file is not included in the Windows/x86 folder, because it's usually already installed on Windows systems and included in the XNA runtime redistributable package (which can be run on an end-user's PC if he or she does not have XNA Game Studio installed).

THE XNA FRAMEWORK

At the core of Microsoft XNA is a managed runtime environment that is based on the .NET framework (.NET compact framework on the Xbox 360 and mobile devices) and has been optimized for use by video games. There are currently three implementations of the XNA runtime (which we'll go over shortly). These allow games written for XNA to run on any Windows PC, Xbox 360, or supported mobile device with little or no modification to source code.

The XNA Framework Library

Sitting directly above the runtime is a cross-platform managed library called the XNA Framework library. The XNA Framework library consists of several namespaces, each focusing on a different area of game development and closely tied to the hardware of the supported platforms. These namespaces make game programming simpler by providing developers with a managed, high-level way to access and control the video-game hardware and user-input devices. Additionally, because XNA is built upon the .NET Framework, developers have access to most of the classes in the .NET Framework library for developing games. Although XNA is a managed library, much of it is implemented as a wrapper around the native DirectX 9 SDK. Because XNA is designed to be portable between any platforms that support the XNA Framework, some of the functionality provided by DirectX natively is hidden in Windows and may be difficult to access while using the XNA Framework library.

Note

Why doesn't XNA support DirectX 10 or 11? For maximum cross-platform compatibility, XNA supports only DirectX 9, mainly because the Xbox 360 does not support many of the features of DirectX 10 and 11 that came out after the console (born in 2006).

The XNA Application Framework

In addition to the namespaces, which focus on solving problems regularly faced by game programmers, the XNA Framework also contains a namespace that eliminates much of the boilerplate code often required within Windows games—the windowed or full-screen device for rendering with the default rendering options already set and a running `while` loop. This allows game programmers to get into gameplay quickly, without the hassle of creating a window, initializing the render device, handling input devices, and so on.

XNA Game Studio

Working in conjunction with the XNA Framework is XNA Game Studio, an integrated development environment (IDE) extension that installs itself alongside either Visual C# 2010 Express Edition or Visual Studio 2010. This development environment, along with the XNA Build system, gives game developers a complete development environment with which to manage their game assets as well as to write, deploy, and test their games. For those on a shoestring budget, the development environment is absolutely free. People intent on seeing their games published, however, will be conscious of the benefits afforded with a paid membership to the App Hub.

XNA Build and the Content Pipeline

XNA provides a customizable content framework that enables easy integration of third-party tools and file formats into your asset pipeline. Although it is possible to use the asset-compilation components at runtime, this is less frequently done because it requires the inclusion of more assemblies and removes the implicit performance benefits of pre-compiling game assets. An exception to this is when you are creating an external tool such as a world editor or automated build system. More frequently, a programmer will rely on the integrated build system within XNA Game Studio (XNA Build) to create the game assets at compile time and then package the runtime assets along with the game. Whatever method is used, the runtime component of the content framework allows assets such as textures, models, shaders, and fonts to be easily loaded and referenced within your game.

The Content Framework Pipeline

The asset pipeline, which connects an artist's or designer's work to the game engine, can be one of the most frustrating and complex areas of development. Constant changes in third-party content-creation tools, publisher requirements, and asset requirements due to changes in the game engine can require thousands of complete rebuilds of all game assets over the course of a project's lifetime. And those same changes that require a rebuild can often break the compatibility between the engine and the assets, preventing artwork and levels from being imported into the game. Microsoft created the XNA content pipeline to remedy this problem. The XNA content framework pipeline can be divided into two parts:

- A compile-time component, which is responsible for building game assets and preparing them for use by the game
- A runtime component, which is responsible for loading assets from disk and instantiating them within your game engine

The compile-time component of the XNA content framework pipeline begins with XNA Build, a synchronized build system based on MS Build and integrated into XNA Game Studio. Once assets have been added, XNA Build takes responsibility for making sure art assets are kept up to date (per platform) by running them through a two-part build process. The first part, the import phase, accepts third-party or custom file formats and uses an importer to load the file into memory. Once the asset is loaded into memory, it is run through the second stage, the processor, which creates a compact game-specific content object that can be easily loaded by the runtime component of the content pipeline framework.

Microsoft provides quite a few default importers and processors with XNA Game Studio; however, game developers and third-party content-creation–tool companies are welcome to provide their own. Having the ability to create customizable importers and processors that convert assets native to a specific content-creation tool to game-specific objects creates a layer of abstraction that can act as a safety net for game teams. This ultimately allows either the engine or game assets to vary independently without requiring significant changes to the other. Additionally, because only the importers and processors need to vary in order to switch from one file format to another, larger game companies that have multiple teams—each using a different set of content-creation tools—can still take advantage of shared engine code.

By default, XNA Game Studio provides importers and processors for the following types of asset formats:

- HLSL effects (FX)
- Models (FBX or X)

- SpriteFonts (BMP, SpriteFont, DDS, DIB, HDR, JPG, PFM, PNG, PPM, TGA)
- 2D textures (BMP, DDS, DIB, HDR, JPG, PFM, PNG, PPM, TGA)
- 3D textures (DDS)
- Cubic textures (DDS)

Note

For details and a complete working example of a custom content importer, see Chapter 5, "Content," wherein we learn to create a custom text file importer—which could be useful for adding script file support to a game project or any sort of data files.

XNA Creators Club

The central hub of activity for XNA development is Microsoft's Creators Club Web site, found online at http://creators.xna.com. From this hub, you can download the complete XNA Game Studio 4.0 and Visual C# 2010 Express, and access tutorials and sample projects galore. There is one caveat, however: Although it's possible to get into XNA development at no cost, there are limitations to a free Xbox 360 account (a so-called "Silver account"). You will be unable to run Xbox 360 code on your retail console, which *is* possible with a Gold account and a Creators Club membership. If you are serious about XNA development and you want to see your game running on Windows and Xbox 360 and *published*, then it goes without saying that you need both memberships. And, you get a lot for a meager annual fee of $160 ($60 for XBLA Gold plus $100 for XNA Creators Club). Figure 1.10 shows the Creators Club/App Hub Web site at the time of this writing.

If you are just getting started, then by all means wait until you're competent at writing XNA code in C# before spending the money on a membership to the Creators Club/App Hub. But there is one thing to consider: While you are learning, the App Hub can be a great asset. Many parts of the Web site are restricted to members only, including many articles, examples, and sample games. Take a look at the features available with each type of membership before

Figure 1.10
The XNA Creators Club/App Hub Web site home page.

deciding which one to use. Once you have created an App Hub account, you will have your own profile and will be able to post games you've created online for others to download and (hopefully) purchase! Microsoft offers a very respectable royalty rate for indie developers—70 percent at the time of this writing. So if you sell your game for $10 on the XNA App Hub and it is listed on Xbox Live Arcade (XBLA), then you pocket $7 of every sale.

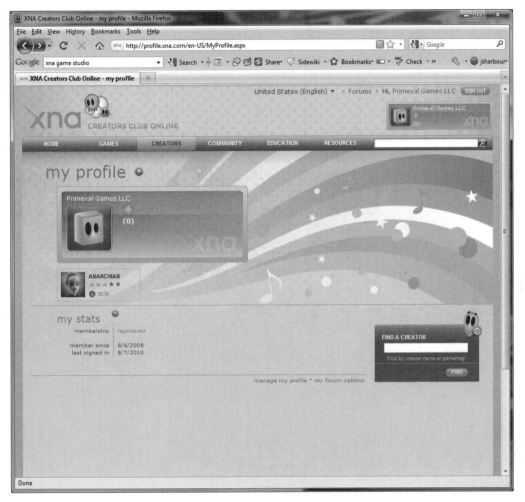

Figure 1.11
The old Creators Club account profile page—note the linked Xbox Live account name at the top right.

Figure 1.11 shows what the profile page looked like just prior to the launch of the new App Hub Web site (for historical comparison), while Figure 1.12 shows the new App Hub site. This will soon be your most commonly visited Web site while in the midst of a game-development project, as it is full of knowledge that you will find invaluable!

Figure 1.12
The new App Hub Web site for XNA developers.

SUMMARY

This chapter was a springboard for your efforts to get into XNA programming as quickly as possible, with a goal of getting productive rather than learning very much theory. You should have all the information you need to get XNA Game Studio 4.0 up and running on your development PC. You should also have an App Hub account (or plans to subscribe in the future). Because we'll be focusing quite a bit on Xbox 360, it goes without saying that you'll get the most out of future chapters *with* a membership, but I would say it is possible to get by without one if you are still on the learning curve and not quite ready to produce anything of your own yet. Let me reiterate that an App Hub account is *not* necessary for compiling Windows projects—it is only needed if you want to run and debug your code on a retail Xbox 360 (which is, however, the focus of this book).

CHAPTER 2

PEEKING UNDER THE HOOD

This chapter looks at a simple, complete game framework, which will be a point of reference as you explore the XNA framework. Even readers with experience programming games will find this chapter to be the first stepping stone on the path toward mastering XNA, so I do recommend reading this chapter before moving on. It covers the framework from a high-level perspective, showing how an XNA program works (both in front of and behind the scenes, so to speak); future chapters include detailed coverage of each component with the assumption that the basics are already understood. Think of this chapter as a good primer for XNA programming, without getting into the specifics of the C# language (because that is a known prerequisite). Let our intentions be known:

- Reverse engineering an example
- Understanding Using statements
- Examining the Game class
- The Frame Update Demo program
- Adjusting the Update() rate
- Using high-definition 720p mode

REVERSE ENGINEERING AN EXAMPLE

We're using Visual Studio 2010 with XNA Game Studio 4.0. There are two key ways to use the tools: either with the separate installers or with the complete package wrapped around the Windows Phone development tools (see Figure 2.1). The Windows Phone package includes additional tools with an intelligent installer that scans your system to figure out what to install; this is then installed automatically.

- Microsoft Visual Studio 2010 Express
- Microsoft Expression Blend 4
- Microsoft Silverlight
- Microsoft Windows Phone Developer Tools

Note

The nine chapters of Part II, "XNA Framework Library," cover each of the key components of the XNA Framework in detail.

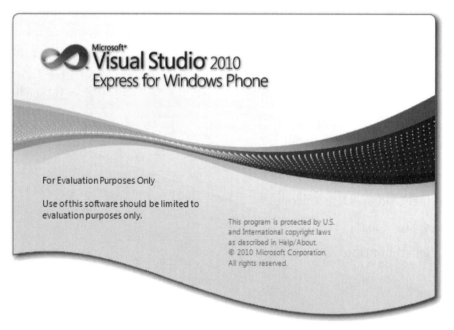

Figure 2.1
Visual Studio 2010 Express with Windows Phone development tools.

There is precedent for giving away the developer tools for a platform in which Microsoft has invested heavily. Back in the day, when Microsoft Pocket PC was a valid platform (between 2000 and 2004), the Embedded Visual Tools 3.0 product was also a free download with a zero-cost license, before any of the Express editions had been considered.

Let's just take a look at what information we can find out from XNA about running code without writing any of our own utility code up front. In other words, what properties does XNA give us out of the box, so to speak? We'll create a new project to study. I've called my example "Frame Update Demo," which is an XNA project that will simply display some properties on the screen about the running system (as much info as we can dig up). Listing 2.1 contains the default source code provided for us by the XNA project template. I've added a small amount of code to create a font and write a hello message to the screen. Otherwise, I've left the generated code largely as it appears when a new project is created (complete with wrapped lines).

Listing 2.1 Default Code in the XNA Project Template with Minor Additions

```
using System;
using System.Collections.Generic;
using System.Linq;
using Microsoft.Xna.Framework;
using Microsoft.Xna.Framework.Audio;
using Microsoft.Xna.Framework.Content;
using Microsoft.Xna.Framework.GamerServices;
using Microsoft.Xna.Framework.Graphics;
using Microsoft.Xna.Framework.Input;
using Microsoft.Xna.Framework.Media;

namespace Example
{
    /// <summary>
    /// This is the main type for your game
    /// </summary>
    public class Game1 : Microsoft.Xna.Framework.Game
    {
        GraphicsDeviceManager graphics;
        SpriteBatch spriteBatch;
        SpriteFont font1;
```

```csharp
public Game1()
{
    graphics = new GraphicsDeviceManager(this);
    Content.RootDirectory = "Content";
}


/// <summary>
/// Allows the game to perform any initialization it needs to before
starting to run.
/// This is where it can query for any required services and load any non-
graphic
/// related content.   Calling base.Initialize will enumerate through
any components
/// and initialize them as well.
/// </summary>
protected override void Initialize()
{
    // TODO: Add your initialization logic here

    base.Initialize();
}


/// <summary>
/// LoadContent will be called once per game and is the place to load
/// all of your content.
/// </summary>
protected override void LoadContent()
{
    // Create a new SpriteBatch, which can be used to draw textures.
    spriteBatch = new SpriteBatch(GraphicsDevice);
    font1 = Content.Load<SpriteFont>("font1");

    // TODO: use this.Content to load your game content here
}


/// <summary>
/// UnloadContent will be called once per game and is the place to unload
/// all content.
```

```
        /// </summary>
        protected override void UnloadContent()
        {
            // TODO: Unload any non ContentManager content here
        }


        /// <summary>
        /// Allows the game to run logic such as updating the world,
        /// checking for collisions, gathering input, and playing audio.
        /// </summary>
        /// <param name="gameTime">Provides a snapshot of timing values.</param>
        protected override void Update(GameTime gameTime)
        {
            // Allows the game to exit
            if(GamePad.GetState(PlayerIndex.One).Buttons.Back == ButtonState.
Pressed)
                this.Exit();

            // TODO: Add your update logic here

            base.Update(gameTime);
        }


        /// <summary>
        /// This is called when the game should draw itself.
        /// </summary>
        /// <param name="gameTime">Provides a snapshot of timing values.</pa-
ram>
        protected override void Draw(GameTime gameTime)
        {
            GraphicsDevice.Clear(Color.CornflowerBlue);

            spriteBatch.Begin();
            spriteBatch.DrawString(font1, "Hello World", new Vector2(0, 0),
Color.White);
            spriteBatch.End();

            base.Draw(gameTime);
        }
    }
}
```

Understanding Using Statements

Personally, I find the source-code–documenting feature to be a distraction, rendering the code *less* readable. So my first order of business is to delete all default comments. There's a noble purpose for the structure of the comments: They provide detailed information to IntelliSense to assist programmers who are using a component. The good thing about this is that it eliminates the need for extensive documentation. The first three using lines make available common System components.

```
using System;
using System.Collections.Generic;
using System.Linq;
```

For instance, System.Collections.Generic includes these container types:

- Dictionary
- HashSet
- List
- Queue
- Stack

The main System namespace contains the bulk of the .NET framework data types and classes, such as Integer, Double, Boolean, Math, Random, etc. It is therefore not unique to XNA or even C#, but common to all .NET languages. When code from a C# or Basic program is compiled, the resulting file is not an assembly or object file familiar to C++ programmers; instead, .NET code is compiled down to what's called *Common Intermediate Language* (CIL). You might think of C#, Basic, F#, J#, Fortran, and other .NET language variations as higher-level languages—perhaps not as high level as Lua or Python script, but close to it. Functionally, there is no difference between C# and Basic; both compile down to CIL code, which is then subsequently compiled using a compiler/linker for a specific platform. Thus, while our code looks the same for Windows, Xbox 360, Zune, and Windows Phone, and even compiles down to the same code at the CIL level, something much different happens at the next level down toward the binary executable.

A Windows build requires a component wrapped around the Windows SDK runtime library (mscorlib.dll) and Visual C++ runtime library (msvcr90.dll). An Xbox 360 build will have a library built with the Xbox Development Kit (XDK) wrapped in a component that can be linked with our CIL code. A similar thing happens when we target Zune or Windows Phone. Ultimately, regardless of the platform, it's a C++ library wrapped in a .NET component that gets linked in and does all the real work, while our .NET language of choice (C#) is quite a few layers above the hardware, cushioned by many layers of software in between.

The XNA Framework is included in the remaining `using` statements. What `using` does is make everything inside a named namespace visible to the program without the namespace being required. So, if you include `Microsoft.Xna.Framework`, every class found within is visible and can be used in variable or class definitions without spelling out the whole namespace.

```
using Microsoft.Xna.Framework;
using Microsoft.Xna.Framework.Audio;
using Microsoft.Xna.Framework.Content;
using Microsoft.Xna.Framework.GamerServices;
using Microsoft.Xna.Framework.Graphics;
using Microsoft.Xna.Framework.Input;
using Microsoft.Xna.Framework.Media;
using Microsoft.Xna.Framework.Net;
using Microsoft.Xna.Framework.Storage;
```

The preceding nine lines include all but two XNA Framework namespaces (see Figure 2.2): `Microsoft.Xna.Framework.Design` and `Microsoft.Xna.Framework.Game`. This is basic C# programming fare, but I wanted you to be aware of what is included and point out that you can make changes to the list of included components if you want. Think of the project template code as a *suggestion*, not a rule. *You* are in charge of your source code!

Examining the `Game` Class

`Microsoft.Xna.Framework.Game` is not in the `using` list because it is the parent class for our program.

```
public class Game1 : Microsoft.Xna.Framework.Game
```

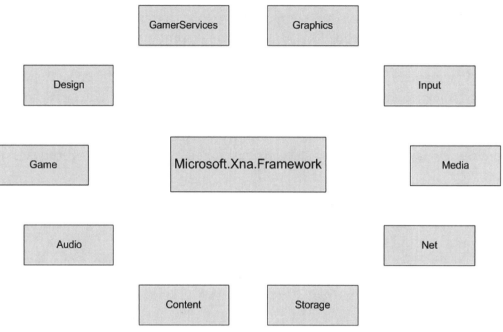

Figure 2.2
The 10 namespaces in the XNA Framework.

Every function in our program, Game1, has inherent access to everything in the parent class declared with protected or public scope.

Note

The XNA Framework is covered extensively in the next chapter, so we will gloss over specific details about each component for now and just use what we need.

Do you want to see the interface source code for Microsoft.Xna.Framework. Game? In the source-code file, right-click Game and choose Go to Definition in the menu that appears. With all the readability-destroying comments removed, the Game class interface is somewhat readable. You can see in Listing 2.2 that all functions are declared as virtual, which clues us in to the fact that we can override such functions in our own derived class. Any function not declared as virtual, such as the Tick() function, is called automatically and not available to us. You will even see how obsolete functions are handled: LoadGraphicsContent() and UnloadGraphicsContent() were functions in XNA 2.0 that have been renamed to `LoadContent()` and `UnloadContent()`, respectively. There are two new items added to `Game` in 4.0, highlighted in bold.

Listing 2.2   Game Class

```
public class Game : IDisposable
{
    public Game();
    public GameComponentCollection Components { get; }
    public ContentManager Content { get; set; }
    public GraphicsDevice GraphicsDevice { get; }
    public TimeSpan InactiveSleepTime { get; set; }
    public bool IsActive { get; }
    public bool IsFixedTimeStep { get; set; }
    public bool IsMouseVisible { get; set; }
    public LaunchParameters LaunchParameters { get; }
    public GameServiceContainer Services { get; }
    public TimeSpan TargetElapsedTime { get; set; }
    public GameWindow Window { get; }
    public event EventHandler Activated;
    public event EventHandler Deactivated;
    public event EventHandler Disposed;
    public event EventHandler Exiting;
    protected virtual bool BeginDraw();
    protected virtual void BeginRun();
    public void Dispose();
    protected virtual void Dispose(bool disposing);
    protected virtual void Draw(GameTime gameTime);
    protected virtual void EndDraw();
    protected virtual void EndRun();
    public void Exit();
    protected virtual void Initialize();
    protected virtual void LoadContent();
    protected virtual void OnActivated(object sender, EventArgs args);
    protected virtual void OnDeactivated(object sender, EventArgs args);
    protected virtual void OnExiting(object sender, EventArgs args);
    public void ResetElapsedTime();
    public void Run();
    public void RunOneFrame();
    protected virtual bool ShowMissingRequirementMessage(Exception exception);
```

```
    public void SuppressDraw();
    public void Tick();
    protected virtual void UnloadContent();
    protected virtual void Update(GameTime gameTime);
}
```

Note

This sort of quick obsolescence in the core attributes of a software product is common in products driven by marketing rather than engineering—which is a necessary reality for the App Hub business model (give away the tool, earn money on royalties). The really good news for anyone who has invested time into XNA is that the Xbox 360 has seen a revision this year rather than a replacement. Keeping up with the rapid pace of change in this industry can make a developer's head spin!

Because we will be spending most of our time in the Game class, I want to go over the properties and functions of the class in detail—to overturn every rock, so to speak.

Game Class: Public Properties

There are a number of public properties in the Game class that we can use. The Window property, for instance, is closely tied to the rendering device and provides access to properties such as ClientBounds (which returns the dimensions of the window or screen). Table 2.1 lists the public properties.

Game Class: Public Events

There are four public events in the Game class that can be triggered, each with an associated On function such as OnActivated. (See the upcoming table of protected functions.) These events are not absolutely necessary for a game to run properly, but they can be very helpful. For instance, if the game is running on an Xbox 360 and the player hits the jewel to bring up the mini-dashboard, that will trigger a Deactivated event, which is a cue that your game should pause itself. Similarly, a Windows build will trigger the Deactivated event whenever the game window loses focus. By responding intelligently to these events, we can make our game a fun experience for players. We don't need to call any of these functions ourselves; they are called automatically. Table 2.2 lists the public events.

Table 2.1 Public Properties

Property	Description
Components	Gets the collection of GameComponents owned by the game.
Content	Gets or sets the current ContentManager.
GraphicsDevice	Gets the current GraphicsDevice.
InactiveSleepTime	Gets or sets the time to sleep when the game is inactive.
IsActive	Indicates whether the game is currently the active application.
IsFixedTimeStep	Gets or sets a value indicating whether to use fixed time steps.
IsMouseVisible	Gets or sets a value indicating whether the mouse cursor should be visible.
LaunchParameters	Gets the startup parameters in LaunchParameters.
Services	Gets the GameServiceContainer holding all the service providers attached to the game.
TargetElapsedTime	Gets or sets the target time between calls to Update when IsFixedTimeStep is true.
Window	Gets the underlying operating-system window.

Table 2.2 Public Events

Event	Description
Activated	Raised when the game gains focus.
Deactivated	Raised when the game loses focus.
Disposed	Raised when the game is being disposed.
Exiting	Raised when the game is exiting.

Game Class: Protected Methods

The protected functions in the Game class are really the meat and potatoes of an XNA game. All of these functions can be declared in our derived class (usually called Game1). Although we see only a few of these functions in the code generated from the project template, they are all available to our application. The three most common functions featured in examples and tutorials will often be LoadContent(), Update(), and Draw(), as these are the three essential functions in any XNA game. Table 2.3 lists the protected methods.

Table 2.3 Protected Functions

Function	Description
BeginDraw	Starts the drawing of a frame. This method is followed by calls to Draw and EndDraw.
BeginRun	Called after all components are initialized but before the first update in the game loop.
Dispose	Releases all resources used by the Game class.
Draw	This is where gameplay objects may be drawn each frame.
EndDraw	Ends the drawing of a frame. This method is preceded by calls to Draw and BeginDraw.
EndRun	Called after the game loop has stopped running before exiting.
Initialize	Called after the Game and GraphicsDevice are created, but before LoadContent.
LoadContent	This is where gameplay assets may be loaded.
OnActivated	Raises the Activated event. Override this method to add code to handle when the game gains focus.
OnDeactivated	Raises the Deactivated event. Override this method to add code to handle when the game loses focus.
OnExiting	Raises an Exiting event. Override this method to add code to handle when the game is exiting.
ShowMissingRequirementMessage	This is used to display an error message if there is no suitable graphics device or sound card.
UnloadContent	Called when graphics resources need to be unloaded. Override this method to unload any game-specific graphics resources.
Update	This is where gameplay objects may be updated each frame.

Game Class: Public Methods

The public functions, listed in Table 2.4, will seldom be used. The exception is Exit(), which we use to end an XNA program (for instance, when the user presses the Back button or the Esc key).

Where Is the Game Object Created?

It seems that XNA programs do some things automatically before our code even gets a chance to run. For a C++ programmer, this can be a bit disconcerting—as if someone is keeping us from seeing what's going on in *our* program. (C++ coders tend to be control freaks.) You have to put aside your need to explore and just let XNA handle a few of these things for us—hard as that may be! But we can at least see how it all gets going, and this might even bring a smile to the face

Table 2.4 Public Methods

Function	Description
Dispose	Immediately releases the unmanaged resources used by this object.
Exit	Exits the game.
ResetElapsedTime	Resets the elapsed time counter.
Run	Call this method to initialize the game, begin running the game loop, and start processing events for the game. Reference page contains code sample.
RunOneFrame	Run the game through what would happen in a single tick of the game clock. This method is designed for debugging only.
SuppressDraw	Prevents calls to Draw until the next Update.
Tick	Updates the game's clock and calls Update and Draw.

of a control freak who would like to at least get their hands on the "pump" or "engine" that seems to start running without our permission. If you open up the Program.cs file in every XNA program, you'll find code like in Listing 2.3.

Listing 2.3 Program.cs Code

```
using System;

namespace Example
{
    static class Program
    {
        /// <summary>
        /// The main entry point for the application.
        /// </summary>
        static void Main(string[] args)
        {
            using (Game1 game = new Game1())
            {
                game.Run();
            }
        }
    }
}
```

Aha! We have a static void Main() function to play with. Yes, you can screw with it and render your XNA program unusable, but go ahead. Just be prepared to use

Undo to get it back to working order after you've messed around with it. Microsoft's code invokes an instance of Game1 within a using statement so that memory can be freed automatically in the event of an exception or untimely exit, because the game object will be destroyed automatically (in a way somewhat reminiscent of a std::auto_ptr in C++). Run() is one of the public functions, so we can't make changes to it. From this function, we get calls to Update() and Draw() in your derived class. Here's the summary comment:

> "Call this method to initialize the game, begin running the game loop, and start processing events for the game."

Although we can't see the code in Run(), because it's implemented differently for each of the target platforms and precompiled, we can speculate as to what the function looks like. XNA gives us quite a bit of control over what happens in Run(), so rewiring the function is unnecessary.

Note

Remember, the deeper you explore a software system, or the more highly efficient you try to make a system, the less maintainable the code becomes. When we give up some control over the way in which XNA runs, we may also give up responsibility for it and move on to more important things— like gameplay code.

Focus and Intent

Did you notice this comment in Program.cs?

```
/// The main entry point for the application.
```

The Wikipedia article at http://en.wikipedia.org/wiki/Application_software defines "application" as follows:

> "...computer software designed to help the user to perform singular or multiple related specific tasks. Examples include enterprise software, accounting software, office suites, graphics software and media players."

What's even more telling is the screen shot of OpenOffice included in the Wikipedia article as a *de facto* example of an application. A game is not an application, so this is a mislabeled comment. I feel it's absolutely critical to clearly define one's intentions in order to succeed! We are doing game programming here with a very complex, advanced, cross-platform development tool. We are not developing *applications*.

The Frame Update Demo Program

Our first really functional demo that *does something* will be focused on timing. You may be wondering, why be concerned about timing with XNA? After all, doesn't XNA handle the loop and timing for you? Yes, XNA does handle the loop and timing for you. But we *do* need to be concerned, because XNA has a clunky timing mechanism that needlessly wastes processor core cycles. This is something over which a C++ engine programmer, working with the full-blown XDK, would have full control. But we aren't using the XDK—and one very important factor to keep in mind is that XNA is essentially free. (The $100 fee for the App Hub is a negligible paperwork fee in this industry).

Although XNA has a property that will give us the current frame rate, it does not differentiate between `Update()` time and `Draw()` time, which is very important for us to know (in order to identify any slowdown in our code). To get the frame rate from XNA, assuming you're in the `Update()` function when doing so, use the `gameTime` parameter to retrieve the number of milliseconds since the last call to `Update()`:

```
gameTime.ElapsedGameTime.TotalMilliseconds
```

We can use this property to calculate the frame rate by dividing 1,000 by it:

```
double frames = 1000.0 / gameTime.ElapsedGameTime.TotalMilliseconds;
```

Unless some process is slowing down the program, this will always result in a number close to 60, which XNA attempts to run at—even during the `Update()` function, which really should not be under such a limitation. We really want all the processor cycles we can get our hands on! Listing 2.4 contains the Frame Update Demo program code. However, I prefer to do my own timing, thank you very much. Two sets of three variables each keep track of the `Update()` and `Draw()` timing.

Listing 2.4   Frame Update Demo Program

```
using System;
using System.Collections.Generic;
using System.Linq;
using Microsoft.Xna.Framework;
using Microsoft.Xna.Framework.Audio;
using Microsoft.Xna.Framework.Content;
```

```
using Microsoft.Xna.Framework.GamerServices;
using Microsoft.Xna.Framework.Graphics;
using Microsoft.Xna.Framework.Input;
using Microsoft.Xna.Framework.Media;
using System.Text;

namespace Frame_Update_Demo
{
    public class Game1 : Microsoft.Xna.Framework.Game
    {
        GraphicsDeviceManager graphics;
        SpriteBatch spriteBatch;
        SpriteFont font1;
        private bool p_paused;
        double drawCount = 0, drawTime=0, drawRate = 0;
        double updateCount = 0, updateTime=0, updateRate = 0;
        bool Use720HD = false;
        private Rectangle workBounds;

        public Game1()
        {
            graphics = new GraphicsDeviceManager(this);
            Content.RootDirectory = "Content";
            p_paused = false;

            //set the desired resolutions
            Vector2 screen = new Vector2(640, 480);
            if (Use720HD)
                screen = new Vector2(1280, 720);
            graphics.PreferredBackBufferWidth = (int)screen.X;
            graphics.PreferredBackBufferHeight = (int)screen.Y;
            graphics.ApplyChanges();

            //usable TV resolution is about 90 %
            int bx = (int)(screen.X * 0.05);
            int by = (int)(screen.Y * 0.05);
            workBounds = new Rectangle(bx, by,
                (int)screen.X - bx, (int)screen.Y - by);
        }
```

```csharp
protected override void Initialize()
{
    base.Initialize();
    IsFixedTimeStep = true;
    long ticks = 10000000L / 100L;
    TargetElapsedTime = new TimeSpan(ticks);
    IsMouseVisible = true;
}

protected override void LoadContent()
{
    spriteBatch = new SpriteBatch(GraphicsDevice);
    font1 = Content.Load<SpriteFont>("font1");
}

protected override void UnloadContent()
{
}

protected override void Update(GameTime gameTime)
{
    //calculate update fps
    updateCount++;
    if (Environment.TickCount > updateTime + 1000)
    {
        updateRate = updateCount;
        updateCount = 0;
        updateTime = Environment.TickCount;
    }

    if (GamePad.GetState(PlayerIndex.One).Buttons.Back == ButtonState.Pressed)
        this.Exit();
    if (Keyboard.GetState().IsKeyDown(Keys.Escape))
        this.Exit();
    if (GamePad.GetState(PlayerIndex.One).Buttons.A == ButtonState.Pressed)
        this.IsFixedTimeStep = !this.IsFixedTimeStep;
    if (Keyboard.GetState().IsKeyDown(Keys.A))
        this.IsFixedTimeStep = !this.IsFixedTimeStep;
```

```
        base.Update(gameTime);
    }

    public string TF(bool value)
    {
        return (value) ? "True" : "False";
    }

    protected override void Draw(GameTime gameTime)
    {
        //calculate draw fps
        drawCount++;
        if (Environment.TickCount > drawTime + 1000)
        {
            drawRate = drawCount;
            drawCount = 0;
            drawTime = Environment.TickCount;
        }

        GraphicsDevice.Clear(Color.CornflowerBlue);

        spriteBatch.Begin();
        StringBuilder labels = new StringBuilder();
        labels.AppendLine("Processor cores:");
        labels.AppendLine("Tick count:");
        labels.AppendLine("Reported frame rate:");
        labels.AppendLine("Update frame rate:");
        labels.AppendLine("Draw frame rate:");
        labels.AppendLine("");
        labels.AppendLine("Elapsed game time:");
        labels.AppendLine("Fixed time step:");
        labels.AppendLine("Target update time:");
        labels.AppendLine("Total game time");
        labels.AppendLine("Is running slowly:");
        labels.AppendLine("");
        labels.AppendLine("Screen device name:");
        labels.AppendLine("Window size:");
        labels.AppendLine("Window title:");
        labels.AppendLine("OS version:");
        labels.AppendLine("Library version:");
        labels.AppendLine("Paused:");
```

```
            StringBuilder values = new StringBuilder();
            values.AppendLine(Environment.ProcessorCount.ToString());
            values.AppendLine(Environment.TickCount.ToString());

            double frames = 1000.0 / gameTime.ElapsedGameTime.TotalMilli-
seconds;
            values.AppendLine(frames.ToString("N0"));
            values.AppendLine(updateRate.ToString("N0"));
            values.AppendLine(drawRate.ToString("N0"));
            values.AppendLine("");
            values.AppendLine(gameTime.ElapsedGameTime.Milliseconds.
ToString());
            values.AppendLine("[A] " + IsFixedTimeStep.ToString());
            values.AppendLine(TargetElapsedTime.ToString());
            values.AppendLine(gameTime.TotalGameTime.ToString());
            values.AppendLine(gameTime.IsRunningSlowly.ToString());
            values.AppendLine("");
            values.AppendLine(Window.ScreenDeviceName);
            string size = Window.ClientBounds.Width.ToString() +
                "," + Window.ClientBounds.Height.ToString();
            values.AppendLine(size);
            values.AppendLine(Window.Title);
            values.AppendLine(Environment.OSVersion.ToString());
            values.AppendLine(Environment.Version.ToString());
            values.Append(p_paused.ToString());

            //print labels
            int x = workBounds.Left;
            int y = workBounds.Top;
            spriteBatch.DrawString(font1, labels, new Vector2(x, y), Color.
White);

            //print values
            x = workBounds.X + 260;
            spriteBatch.DrawString(font1, values, new Vector2(x, y), Color.
White);

            spriteBatch.End();
            base.Draw(gameTime);
        }
```

```
protected override void OnActivated(object sender, EventArgs args)
{
    p_paused = false;
    base.OnActivated(sender, args);
}

protected override void OnDeactivated(object sender, EventArgs args)
{
    p_paused = true;
    base.OnDeactivated(sender, args);
}
    }
}
```

The Frame Update Demo program is shown running under Windows in Figure 2.3, and on an Xbox 360 in Figure 2.4. Note the number of processor cores reported on the console! That comes from the custom PowerPC processor equipped with three hardware-threaded cores (for a total of six).

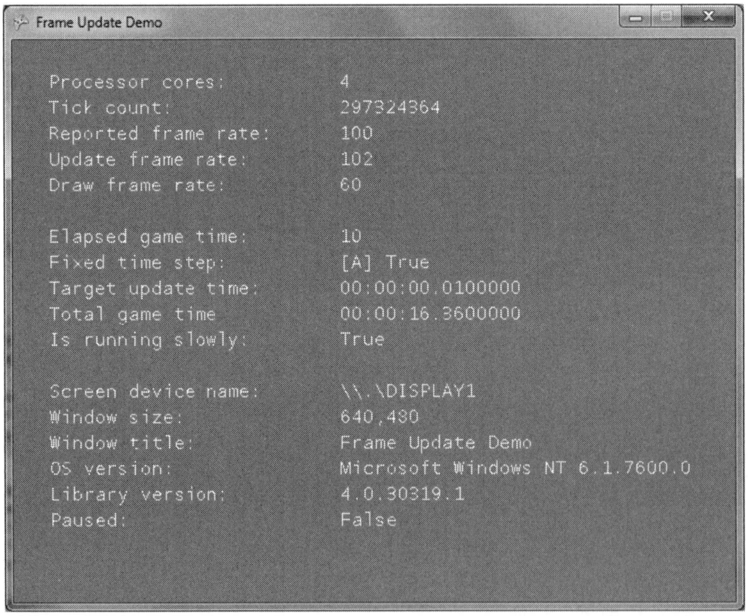

Figure 2.3
The Frame Update Demo program displays system information reported by XNA.

```
Processor cores:        6
Tick count:             10676487
Reported frame rate:    100
Update frame rate:      101
Draw frame rate:        61

Elapsed game time:      10
Fixed time step:        [A] True
Target update time:     00:00:00.0100000
Total game time:        00:00:23.1666418
Is running slowly:      True

Screen device name:     \\.\DISPLAY1
Window size:            1920,1080
Window title:           Game
OS version:             Xbox 2.360.0
Library version:        3.7.10112.0
Paused:                 False
```

Figure 2.4
The demo displays console-specific properties while running on an Xbox 360.

Capturing Screenshots from an Xbox 360

To capture a screenshot from your Xbox 360 through the network connection, use the XNA Game Studio Device Center tool (listed in the Tools menu of Visual Studio or Visual C# Express). Assuming you already have created the connection from your PC to your Xbox 360, right-click the Xbox 360 console icon in the Device Center and choose Take Screen Capture in the menu that appears (see Figure 2.5).

Adjusting the *Update()* Rate

We can take control over the rate at which Update() is called by setting two properties: IsFixedTimeStep and TargetElapsedTime. IsFixedTimeStep, despite being an apparent get or read-only property, is actually writeable (which makes no sense, but there you have it). Setting it to true will enable Update() timing control. The rate at which Update() is called can then be set using TargetElapsedTime with a TimeSpan value. You can use one of TimeSpan's overloaded sets of parameters, but the most common parameter to set is the int ticks parameter, ignoring overloads with hours, minutes, seconds, milliseconds, etc. When using the ticks parameter, you must keep in mind that a nanosecond value is

Figure 2.5
Capturing a screenshot from the remote Xbox 360.

expected. So, to target a certain frame rate, divide 10,000,000L (10 million nanoseconds) by the desired frame rate. Figure 2.6 shows the program running with the fixed time step turned off (which is the default in XNA).

```
//set Update() rate to 100 fps
IsFixedTimeStep = true;
long ticks = 10000000L / 100L;
TargetElapsedTime = new TimeSpan(ticks);
```

Using High-Definition 720p Mode

The default resolution that XNA uses, if we don't tell it otherwise, is 640 × 480, which is standard definition (SD) resolution. Of course, you can set any resolution you want when running in windowed mode under Windows, but on the Xbox 360, the resolution must be set to a specific value. The Xbox 360 supports 720p HD (high definition) natively, which means this is the internal screen format used. All other resolutions are a result of scaling from this standard resolution: 1280 × 720. Every TV is a bit different, but most sets need some breathing room around the edges, which is a non-technical way to refer to

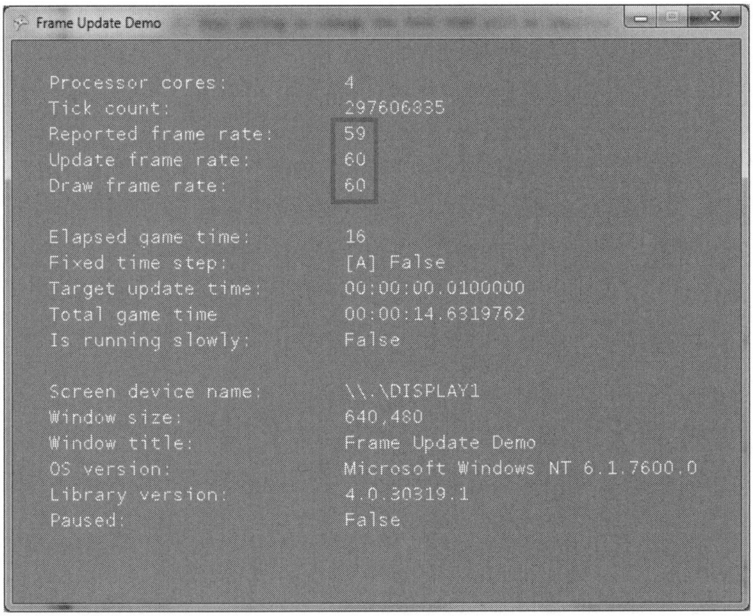

Figure 2.6
Hitting a stable 60 fps with fixed time step turned off.

the crop region around the edges of most TV sets. Newer LCD/plasma screens do not have this problem, but most older TVs do, especially the original boob-tube–style sets (seen frequently in *Fallout 3*). You might be able to get away with just using the full size of the screen (800 × 600 or 1280 × 720), but odds are that many potential customers who may buy your game on the XNA App Hub or Xbox Live Arcade will be using an older TV. It's up to you to decide whether to abandon that large customer base. I recommend a minimal border around the edge of 5 percent. For the lower resolution, that will be approximately 30 pixels around the edges; for the larger resolution, it will be about 60 pixels.

I have an older, projection-style HDTV, and it has a problem displaying the edges despite supporting 720p/1080i. I also have tested this code on my 46-inch LCD HDTV and a smaller 22-inch, both of which can do 1080p. Only a true 720p/1080p monitor will show every pixel perfectly. Use the following code as a guide; add it to the Game1 class constructor after the graphics object is created.

```
graphics.PreferredBackBufferWidth = 1280;
graphics.PreferredBackBufferHeight = 720;
graphics.ApplyChanges();
```

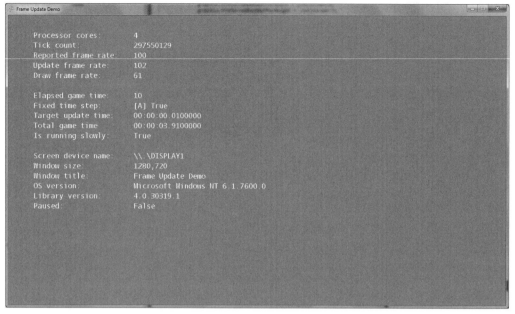

Figure 2.7
Running the demo in 720p HD (1280 × 720) mode.

Figure 2.7 shows a screenshot of the demo program running in 720p mode. As you can see, the text is barely legible because the font is so small. While this font looks just right at 800 × 600, it requires a magnifying glass at 720p. (Someone should mention this to BioWare; I felt like I needed a new eyeglass prescription after playing *Mass Effect 2*.)

SUMMARY

This chapter popped open the hood of an XNA example, so to speak, so we could examine the inner workings of XNA. We paid particular attention to timing, playing around with ways to adjust timing, which is something we'll do in later chapters with real benchmark code to see what happens when we try to take over more processing power than XNA would otherwise give us. At the very least, you now have a good feel for printing text on the screen. If you have an Xbox 360 and will be doing development work on it, I strongly recommend running these examples on your console as we go along. The Xbox 360 is what I'm primarily focusing on with the examples.

PART II

XNA Framework Library

This part focuses on exploring the XNA Framework library in detail. We will study every aspect of XNA 4.0 in this group of chapters which are part reference and part applied—never forgetting the ultimate goal: to learn how to write hard-core C# code using XNA. To get the most out of this environment and see the best results on the two primary platforms—Windows and Xbox 360—we need to know exactly what we're dealing with in XNA, not relying on rumor or discussion but on cold hard facts.

The reference chapters are not meant to be a dry read that you will immediately skip, flipping through them later when needed. On the contrary, the reference chapters are presented in a *quick reference* style that specifically *avoids* trying to be a complete reference to the XNA Framework library. Instead, what you'll find are short descriptions with lists of items contained within each namespace. These lists contain exactly the type of hands-on information that a fast-paced programmer needs, with return values and overloaded constructors on hand in a format you *will not* find in the XNA documentation or online on MSDN.

The chapters in this part are as follows:

- Chapter 3, "XNA Framework Overview"
- Chapter 4, "Audio"

- Chapter 5, "Content"
- Chapter 6, "GamerServices"
- Chapter 7, "Graphics"
- Chapter 8, "Input"
- Chapter 9, "Media"
- Chapter 10, "Net"
- Chapter 11, "Storage"

CHAPTER 3

XNA FRAMEWORK OVERVIEW

This chapter goes over the entire XNA Framework in detail to give you a clear understanding of what resources there are available within the XNA programming environment. A quick perusal of the entire XNA NetFX library—shorthand for ".NET Framework for XNA"—reveals hundreds of classes within a namespace structure that, in my opinion, makes no sense at all. (This isn't a value statement about the online documentation, it's just an observation—but then, most programmers are never quite satisfied with someone else's idea of a class structure.) NetFX is the core library that provides all services for game development in C# for Windows, Xbox 360, and the mobile devices, and you need to *master it*!

One of the most challenging aspects of working with a tool like XNA Game Studio—which has been on an insanely fast development track, going from a tentative release to version 4.0 in just four years—is the likelihood of things changing in the XNA Framework without much warning. You need to be fully exposed to the *entire* framework of namespaces and classes in order to really see what you can do in XNA Game Studio—especially on an Xbox 360, which is of primary focus in this book. You can use this chapter as a quick reference for NetFX. It's not quite a comprehensive reference, but a shorthand listing of the properties and methods of every important class. In other words, it's enough to show you what services are available. Let's see how the second option might work in this chapter with these topics:

- Perusing the XNA Framework
- XNA Framework classes
- XNA Framework structures
- XNA Framework enumerations

Perusing the XNA Framework

If you have invested a huge amount of time into a game project with tens of thousands of lines of code, the last thing you want to deal with is re-architecting the code when a new version of XNA Game Studio comes out. That has been a pretty common occurrence with this tool. It's challenging to build a tool like this with such an aggressive development schedule, supporting multiple plat-forms, and trying to keep users happy—especially because we technically minded people tend to be really critical! There are two ways to approach the problem of how to deal with the consistent nature of XNA Game Studio's frequent changes:

1. We can study each new version of XNA Game Studio after its release and incorporate those changes into our code base(s);

2. We can wrap the NetFX into our *own* framework in order to marginalize changes to our gameplay code as the tool evolves.

The good news is, even when we have our own framework, we can always write plain vanilla NetFX code if we want to.

There are 10 major namespaces in the current version of the XNA Framework (version 4.0), plus two additional sub-root namespaces. This chapter focuses on the root namespace, `Microsoft.Xna.Framework`, going over all the classes, structures, and enumerations in the namespace; later chapters take a somewhat less reference-style approach to cover the subsequent content with applied examples and incorporate the best items of each new framework into our own game library/engine.

Following is a list of the entire XNA Framework from a high-level view. The most oft-used namespace is the root, so it's important that we cover it in detail right away. This list includes some additional namespaces to be thorough, while Figure 3.1 shows just the primary high-level namespaces in the framework.

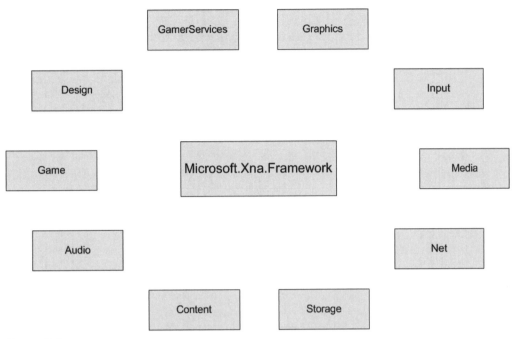

Figure 3.1
The major XNA Framework library namespaces.

Note

XNA is not the same as XNA Game Studio. XNA is the suite of tools used to build games for several platforms and the cross-platform Framework that makes it possible. But, for the sake of brevity, from this point forward I will use the term XNA alone to refer to the combination of XNA Game Studio *and* Visual Studio 2010, which together form the development environment. The term is incorrect, but the meaning is assumed already by most developers. Likewise, the term NetFX will be used henceforth when referring to the .NET Framework for XNA.

`Microsoft.Xna.Framework`	Provides commonly needed game classes such as timers and game loops.
`Microsoft.Xna.Framework.Audio`	Contains low-level application programming interface (API) methods that can load and manipulate XACT-created project and content files to play audio.
`Microsoft.Xna.Framework.Content`	Contains the run-time components of the Content Pipeline.
	(Continued)

`Microsoft.Xna.Framework.Design`	Provides a unified way of converting types of values to other types.
`Microsoft.Xna.Framework.GamerServices`	Contains classes that implement various services related to gamers. These services communicate directly with the gamer and the gamers' data, or otherwise reflect choices the gamer makes. Gamer services include input device and profile data APIs.
`Microsoft.Xna.Framework.Graphics`	Contains low-level application programming interface (API) methods that take advantage of hardware acceleration capabilities to display 3D objects.
`Microsoft.Xna.Framework.Graphics.PackedVector`	Represents data types with components that are not multiples of 8 bits.
`Microsoft.Xna.Framework.Input`	Contains classes to receive input from keyboard, mouse, and Xbox 360 controller devices.
`Microsoft.Xna.Framework.Input.Touch`	Contains classes that enable access to touch-based input on devices that support it.
`Microsoft.Xna.Framework.Media`	Contains classes to enumerate, play, and view songs, albums, playlists, and pictures.
`Microsoft.Xna.Framework.Net`	Contains classes that implement support for Xbox LIVE, multiplayer, and networking for XNA Framework games.
`Microsoft.Xna.Framework.Storage`	Contains classes that allow reading and writing of files.

MICROSOFT.XNA.FRAMEWORK

Let's start by examining the primary namespace of XNA: `Microsoft.Xna.Framework`. This namespace is implemented in several component DLL files, not just a single one. For instance, `Microsoft.Xna.Framework` is also derived by `Microsoft.Xna.Framework.Game`. A namespace can be defined by many source-code files and components, and C# will organize them all under the single namespace name. Even though `Microsoft.Xna.Framework` appears to be a parent for the other namespaces, it is not a parent in the same way that classes work. The apparent hierarchy of a namespace is just a way to organize software libraries. `Microsoft.Xna.Framework.Game` is a class within the namespace `Microsoft.Xna.Framework`. At the same level, `Microsoft.Xna.Framework.Audio` would seem to be another class like `Game`, but it is itself another namespace for organizing classes, structures, and properties.

Note

The terms method and function are synonymous and may be considered interchangeable in this book. That said, the term method is more commonly found in the XNA documentation. A method is usually associated with a class, while a function is usually associated with a library.

Because the hierarchy of namespaces and classes can lead to as much confusion as help, I often find it useful to spell out the entire namespace for a class when defining it—at least early on while working with an XNA namespace. There are some purists who prefer not to use the `using` statements at all and just explicitly define every construct in its entirety when creating new objects and variables. But at a certain point, you will either run out of patience with the purist approach or wear off the letters from your keyboard from too much typing—like half the keys on my keyboard are now! The `using` statements will make everything within a namespace (classes, structures, etc.) visible at the global level of your code.

Note

The chapters in Part 2, "XNA Framework Library," provide only a quick reference to the XNA Framework, not a comprehensive reference like what can be found in the Visual Studio Documentation and MSDN Online. One benefit to the quick references in this book is that return values and constructors are listed, while that information requires extra clicks in the online docs. Every class in the XNA Framework is derived from `Object`, which defines the shared methods `Equals()`, `GetHashCode()`, `GetType()`, and `ToString()`. Additionally, most classes define `op_Equality()` and `op_Inequality()`. Because these are common to every class, they will not be listed in the class references.

Classes

The following classes are found within the `Microsoft.Xna.Framework` namespace.

BoundingFrustum

Defines a frustum and helps determine whether other objects intersect with it.

Public Properties	
Bottom	Gets the bottom plane of the `BoundingFrustum`.
Far	Gets the far plane of the `BoundingFrustum`.
Left	Gets the left plane of the `BoundingFrustum`.

(Continued)

Matrix	Gets or sets the `Matrix` that describes this bounding frustum.
Near	Gets the near plane of the `BoundingFrustum`.
Right	Gets the right plane of the `BoundingFrustum`.
Top	Gets the top plane of the `BoundingFrustum`.

Public Methods

Contains	Checks whether the current `BoundingFrustum` contains a specified bounding volume.
GetCorners	Gets an array of points that make up the corners of the `BoundingFrustum`.
Intersects	Checks whether the current `BoundingFrustum` intersects a specified volume.

Curve

Stores an arbitrary collection of 2D `CurveKey` points and provides methods for evaluating features of the curve they define.

Public Properties

IsConstant	Gets a value indicating whether the curve is constant.
Keys	The points that make up the curve.
PostLoop	Specifies how to handle weighting values that are greater than the last control point in the curve.
PreLoop	Specifies how to handle weighting values that are less than the first control point in the curve.

Public Methods

Clone	Creates a copy of the `Curve`.
ComputeTangent	Computes the tangents for a specified `CurveKey` in this `Curve`.
ComputeTangents	Computes all tangents for all `CurveKeys` in the `Curve`.
Evaluate	Finds the value at a position on the `Curve`.

CurveKey

Represents a point in a multi-point curve.

Public Properties

CurveContinuity	Describes whether the segment between this point and the next point in the curve is discrete or continuous.
Position	Position of the `CurveKey` in the curve.
TangentIn	Describes the tangent when approaching this point from the previous point in the curve.

TangentOut	Describes the tangent when leaving this point to the next point in the curve.
Value	Describes the value of this point.
Public Methods	
Clone	Creates a copy of the CurveKey.
CompareTo	Compares this instance to another CurveKey and returns an indication of their relative values.

CurveKeyCollection

Contains the CurveKeys making up a Curve.

Public Properties	
Count	Gets the number of elements contained in the CurveKeyCollection.
IsReadOnly	Returns a value indicating whether the CurveKeyCollection is read-only.
Item	Gets or sets the element at the specified index.
Public Methods	
Add	Adds a CurveKey to the CurveKeyCollection.
Clear	Removes all CurveKeys from the CurveKeyCollection.
Clone	Creates a copy of the CurveKeyCollection.
Contains	Determines whether the CurveKeyCollection contains a specific CurveKey.
CopyTo	Copies the CurveKeys of the CurveKeyCollection to an array, starting at the array index provided.
GetEnumerator	Returns an enumerator that iterates through the CurveKeyCollection.
IndexOf	Determines the index of a CurveKey in the CurveKeyCollection.
Remove	Removes the first occurrence of a specific CurveKey from the CurveKeyCollection.
RemoveAt	Removes the CurveKey at the specified index.

DrawableGameComponent

A game component that is notified when it needs to draw itself.

Public Properties	
DrawOrder	Order in which the component should be drawn, relative to other components that are in the same GameComponentCollection.
GraphicsDevice	The GraphicsDevice with which the DrawableGameComponent is associated.
Visible	Indicates whether Draw should be called.

(Continued)

Public Methods

Dispose	Releases the resources used by the DrawableGameComponent class.
Draw	Called when the DrawableGameComponent needs to be drawn. Override this method with component-specific drawing code.
Initialize	Initializes the component. Override this method to load any non-graphics resources and query for any required services.

Protected Methods

LoadContent	Called when graphics resources need to be loaded. Override this method to load any component-specific graphics resources.
OnDrawOrderChanged	Called when the DrawOrder property changes. Raises the DrawOrderChanged event.
OnVisibleChanged	Called when the Visible property changes. Raises the VisibleChanged event.
UnloadContent	Called when graphics resources need to be unloaded. Override this method to unload any component-specific graphics resources.

Public Events

DrawOrderChanged	Raised when the DrawOrder property changes.
VisibleChanged	Raised when the Visible property changes.

FrameworkDispatcher

Implements the Windows-specific portion of a FrameworkDispatcher class.

Public Methods

Update	Updates the status of various framework components (such as power state and media), and raises related events.

Game

Provides basic graphics device initialization, game logic, and rendering code.

Public Properties

Components	Gets the collection of GameComponents owned by the game.
Content	Gets or sets the current ContentManager.
GraphicsDevice	Gets the current GraphicsDevice.
InactiveSleepTime	Gets or sets the time to sleep when the game is inactive.
IsActive	Indicates whether the game is currently the active application.
IsFixedTimeStep	Gets or sets a value indicating whether to use fixed time steps.
IsMouseVisible	Gets or sets a value indicating whether the mouse cursor should be visible.

LaunchParameters	Gets the startup parameters in `LaunchParameters`.
Services	Gets the `GameServiceContainer` holding all the service providers attached to the `Game`.
TargetElapsedTime	Gets or sets the target time between calls to `Update` when `IsFixedTimeStep` is true.
Window	Gets the underlying operating-system window.

Public Methods

Dispose	Immediately releases the unmanaged resources used by this object.
Exit	Exits the game.
ResetElapsedTime	Resets the elapsed time counter.
Run	Call this method to initialize the game, begin running the game loop, and start processing events for the game.
RunOneFrame	Run the game through what would happen in a single tick of the game clock; this method is designed for debugging only.
SuppressDraw	Prevents calls to `Draw` until the next `Update`.
Tick	Updates the game's clock and calls `Update` and `Draw`.

Protected Methods

BeginDraw	Starts the drawing of a frame. This method is followed by calls to `Draw` and `EndDraw`.
BeginRun	Called after all components are initialized but before the first update in the game loop.
Draw	Called when the game determines it is time to draw a frame.
EndDraw	Ends the drawing of a frame. This method is preceded by calls to `Draw` and `BeginDraw`.
EndRun	Called after the game loop has stopped running before exiting.
Finalize	Allows a `Game` to attempt to free resources and perform other cleanup operations before garbage collection reclaims the `Game`.
Initialize	Called after the `Game` and `GraphicsDevice` are created, but before `LoadContent`.
LoadContent	Called when graphics resources need to be loaded.
OnActivated	Raises the `Activated` event. Override this method to add code to handle when the game gains focus.
OnDeactivated	Raises the `Deactivated` event. Override this method to add code to handle when the game loses focus.
OnExiting	Raises an `Exiting` event. Override this method to add code to handle when the game is exiting.
ShowMissingRequirementMessage	This is used to display an error message if there is no suitable graphics device or sound card.
UnloadContent	Called when graphics resources need to be unloaded. Override this method to unload any game-specific graphics resources.
Update	Called when the game has determined that game logic needs to be processed.

Public Events

Activated	Raised when the game gains focus.
Deactivated	Raised when the game loses focus.
Disposed	Raised when the game is being disposed.
Exiting	Raised when the game is exiting.

GameComponent

Base class for all XNA Framework game components.

Public Properties

Enabled	Indicates whether GameComponent.Update should be called when Game.Update is called.
Game	Gets the Game associated with this GameComponent.
UpdateOrder	Indicates the order in which the GameComponent should be updated relative to other GameComponent instances. Lower values are updated first.

Public Methods

Dispose	Immediately releases the unmanaged resources used by this object.
Initialize	Called when the GameComponent needs to be initialized.
Update	Called when the GameComponent needs to be updated. Override this method with component-specific update code.

Protected Methods

Finalize	Allows a GameComponent to attempt to free resources and perform other cleanup operations before garbage collection reclaims the GameComponent.
OnEnabledChanged	Called when the Enabled property changes. Raises the EnabledChanged event.
OnUpdateOrderChanged	Called when the UpdateOrder property changes. Raises the UpdateOrderChanged event.

Public Events

Disposed	Raised when the GameComponent is disposed.
EnabledChanged	Raised when the Enabled property changes.
UpdateOrderChanged	Raised when the UpdateOrder property changes.

GameComponentCollection

A collection of game components that inherits from `Collection`.

Public Events	
ComponentAdded	Raised when a component is added to the `GameComponentCollection`.
ComponentRemoved	Raised when a component is removed from the `GameComponentCollection`.

GameComponentCollectionEventArgs

Arguments used with events from the `GameComponentCollection`.

Public Properties	
GameComponent	The game component affected by the event.

GameServiceContainer

A collection of game services.

Public Methods	
AddService	Adds a service to the `GameServiceContainer`.
GetService	Gets the object providing a specified service.
RemoveService	Removes the object providing a specified service.

GameTime

Snapshot of the game timing state expressed in values that can be used by variable-step (real time) or fixed-step (game time) games.

Public Properties	
ElapsedGameTime	The amount of elapsed game time since the last update.
IsRunningSlowly	Gets a value indicating that the game loop is taking longer than its `TargetElapsedTime`. In this case, the game loop can be considered to be running too slowly and should do something to catch up.
TotalGameTime	The amount of game time since the start of the game.

GameWindow

The system window associated with a Game.

Public Properties

AllowUserResizing	Specifies whether to allow the user to resize the game window.
ClientBounds	The screen dimensions of the game window's client rectangle.
CurrentOrientation	Gets the current display orientation.
Handle	Gets the handle to the system window.
ScreenDeviceName	Gets the device name of the screen the window is currently in.
Title	Gets and sets the title of the system window.

Public Methods

BeginScreenDeviceChange	Starts a device transition (windowed to full screen or vice versa).
EndScreenDeviceChange	Completes a device transition.

Protected Methods

OnActivated	Called when the GameWindow gets focus.
OnClientSizeChanged	Called when the size of the client window changes. Raises the ClientSizeChanged event.
OnDeactivated	Called when the GameWindow loses focus.
OnOrientationChanged	Called when the GameWindow display orientation changes.
OnPaint	Called when the GameWindow needs to be painted.
OnScreenDeviceNameChanged	Called when the GameWindow is moved to a different screen. Raises the ScreenDeviceNameChanged event.
SetSupportedOrientations	Sets the supported display orientations.
SetTitle	Sets the title of the GameWindow.

Public Events

ClientSizeChanged	Raised when the size of the GameWindow changes.
OrientationChanged	Raised when the display orientation of the GameWindow changes.
ScreenDeviceNameChanged	Raised when the GameWindow moves to a different display.

GraphicsDeviceInformation

Holds the settings for creating a graphics device on Windows.

Public Properties

Adapter	Specifies the graphics adapter on which to create the device.
GraphicsProfile	Gets the graphics profile, which determines the graphics feature set.
PresentationParameters	Specifies the presentation parameters to use when creating a graphics device.

GraphicsDeviceManager

Handles the configuration and management of the graphics device.

Public Fields

DefaultBackBufferHeight	Specifies the default minimum back-buffer height.
DefaultBackBufferWidth	Specifies the default minimum back-buffer width.

Public Properties

GraphicsDevice	Gets the GraphicsDevice associated with the GraphicsDeviceManager.
GraphicsProfile	Gets the graphics profile, which determines the graphics feature set.
IsFullScreen	Gets or sets a value that indicates whether the device should start in full-screen mode.
PreferMultiSampling	Gets or sets a value that indicates whether to enable a multisampled back buffer.
PreferredBackBufferFormat	Gets or sets the format of the back buffer.
PreferredBackBufferHeight	Gets or sets the preferred back-buffer height.
PreferredBackBufferWidth	Gets or sets the preferred back-buffer width.
PreferredDepthStencilFormat	Gets or sets the format of the depth stencil.
SupportedOrientations	Gets or sets the supported display orientations.
SynchronizeWithVerticalRetrace	Gets or sets a value that indicates whether to sync to the vertical trace (vsync) when presenting the back buffer.

Public Methods

ApplyChanges	Applies changes to device-related properties, changing the graphics device as necessary.
ToggleFullScreen	Toggles between full-screen and windowed mode.

Protected Methods

CanResetDevice	Determines whether the given GraphicsDeviceInformation is compatible with the existing graphics device.
Dispose	Releases the unmanaged resources used by the GraphicsDeviceManager and optionally releases the managed resources.
FindBestDevice	Finds the best device configuration that is compatible with the current device preferences.
OnDeviceCreated	Called when a device is created. Raises the DeviceCreated event.
OnDeviceDisposing	Called when a device is being disposed. Raises the DeviceDisposing event.
OnDeviceReset	Called when the device has been reset. Raises the DeviceReset event.

(Continued)

OnDeviceResetting	Called when the device is about to be reset. Raises the `DeviceResetting` event.
OnPreparingDeviceSettings	Called when the `GraphicsDeviceManager` is changing the `GraphicsDevice` settings (during reset or re-creation of the `GraphicsDevice`). Raises the `PreparingDeviceSettings` event.
RankDevices	Ranks the given list of devices that satisfy the given preferences.

Public Events

DeviceCreated	Raised when a new graphics device is created.
DeviceDisposing	Raised when the `GraphicsDeviceManager` is being disposed.
DeviceReset	Raised when the `GraphicsDeviceManager` is reset.
DeviceResetting	Raised when the `GraphicsDeviceManager` is about to be reset.
Disposed	Raised when the `GraphicsDeviceManager` is disposed.
PreparingDeviceSettings	Raised when the `GraphicsDeviceManager` is changing the `GraphicsDevice` settings (during reset or re-creation of the `GraphicsDevice`).

LaunchParameters

The startup parameters for launching a Windows Phone or Windows game, inherited from `Dictionary`.

MathHelper

Contains commonly used pre-calculated values.

Public Fields

E	Represents the mathematical constant e.
Log10E	Represents the log base 10 of e.
Log2E	Represents the log base 2 of e.
Pi	Represents the value of pi.
PiOver2	Represents the value of pi divided by 2.
PiOver4	Represents the value of pi divided by 4.
TwoPi	Represents the value of pi times 2.

Public Methods

Barycentric	Returns the Cartesian coordinate for one axis of a point that is defined by a given triangle and two normalized barycentric (areal) coordinates.
CatmullRom	Performs a Catmull-Rom interpolation using the specified positions.
Clamp	Restricts a value to be within a specified range.
Distance	Calculates the absolute value of the difference of two values.
Hermite	Performs a Hermite spline interpolation.
Lerp	Linearly interpolates between two values.
Max	Returns the greater of two values.
Min	Returns the lesser of two values.
SmoothStep	Interpolates between two values using a cubic equation.
ToDegrees	Converts radians to degrees.
ToRadians	Converts degrees to radians.
WrapAngle	Reduces a given angle to a value between π and $-\pi$.

PreparingDeviceSettingsEventArgs

Arguments for the `GraphicsDeviceManager.PreparingDeviceSettings` event.

Public Properties

GraphicsDeviceInformation	Information about the `GraphicsDevice`.

TitleContainer

Provides file-stream access to the title's default storage location.

Public Methods

OpenStream	Returns a stream to an existing file in the default title storage location.

Microsoft.Xna.Framework Structures

The following structures are used by the properties and methods of the `Microsoft.Xna.Framework` namespace.

BoundingBox

Defines an axis-aligned box-shaped 3D volume.

Public Fields

CornerCount	Specifies the total number of corners (eight) in the BoundingBox.
Max	The maximum point the BoundingBox contains.
Min	The minimum point the BoundingBox contains.

Public Methods

Contains	Tests whether the BoundingBox overlaps another bounding volume.
CreateFromPoints	Creates the smallest BoundingBox that will contain a group of points.
CreateFromSphere	Creates the smallest BoundingBox that will contain the specified BoundingSphere.
CreateMerged	Creates the smallest BoundingBox that contains the two specified BoundingBox instances.
GetCorners	Gets an array of points that make up the corners of the BoundingBox.
Intersects	Checks whether the current BoundingBox intersects with another bounding volume.

BoundingSphere

Defines a sphere.

Public Fields

Center	The center point of the sphere.
Radius	The radius of the sphere.

Public Methods

Contains	Checks whether the current BoundingSphere contains a specified bounding volume.
CreateFromBoundingBox	Creates the smallest BoundingSphere that can contain a specified BoundingBox.
CreateFromFrustum	Creates the smallest BoundingSphere that can contain a specified BoundingFrustum.
CreateFromPoints	Creates a BoundingSphere that can contain a specified list of points.
CreateMerged	Creates a BoundingSphere that contains the two specified BoundingSphere instances.
Intersects	Checks whether the current BoundingSphere intersects another bounding volume.
Transform	Translates and scales the BoundingSphere using a given Matrix.

Color

Represents a four-component color using red, green, blue, and alpha data.

Public Properties

A	Gets or sets the alpha component value.
B	Gets or sets the blue component value of this `Color`.
G	Gets or sets the green component value of this `Color`.
R	Gets or sets the red component value of this `Color`.

Public Methods

FromNonPremultiplied	Converts a non-premultipled alpha color to a color that contains premultiplied alpha.
Lerp	Linearly interpolate a color.
Multiply	Multiply each color component by the scale factor.
op_Multiply	Multiply operator.
ToVector3	Gets a three-component vector representation for this object.
ToVector4	Gets a four-component vector representation for this object.

Matrix

Defines a matrix.

Public Fields

M11	Value at row 1 column 1 of the matrix.
M12	Value at row 1 column 2 of the matrix.
M13	Value at row 1 column 3 of the matrix.
M14	Value at row 1 column 4 of the matrix.
M21	Value at row 2 column 1 of the matrix.
M22	Value at row 2 column 2 of the matrix.
M23	Value at row 2 column 3 of the matrix.
M24	Value at row 2 column 4 of the matrix.
M31	Value at row 3 column 1 of the matrix.
M32	Value at row 3 column 2 of the matrix.
M33	Value at row 3 column 3 of the matrix.
M34	Value at row 3 column 4 of the matrix.
M41	Value at row 4 column 1 of the matrix.
M42	Value at row 4 column 2 of the matrix.
M43	Value at row 4 column 3 of the matrix.
M44	Value at row 4 column 4 of the matrix.

(Continued)

Public Properties

Backward	Gets and sets the backward vector of the Matrix.
Down	Gets and sets the down vector of the Matrix.
Forward	Gets and sets the forward vector of the Matrix.
Identity	Returns an instance of the identity matrix.
Left	Gets and sets the left vector of the Matrix.
Right	Gets and sets the right vector of the Matrix.
Translation	Gets and sets the translation vector of the Matrix.
Up	Gets and sets the up vector of the Matrix.

Public Methods

Add	Adds a matrix to another matrix.
CreateBillboard	Creates a spherical billboard that rotates around a specified object position.
CreateConstrainedBillboard	Creates a cylindrical billboard that rotates around a specified axis.
CreateFromAxisAngle	Creates a new Matrix that rotates around an arbitrary vector.
CreateFromQuaternion	Creates a rotation Matrix from a Quaternion.
CreateFromYawPitchRoll	Creates a new rotation matrix from a specified yaw, pitch, and roll.
CreateLookAt	Creates a view matrix.
CreateOrthographic	Builds an orthogonal projection matrix.
CreateOrthographicOffCenter	Builds a customized, orthogonal projection matrix.
CreatePerspective	Builds a perspective projection matrix.
CreatePerspectiveFieldOfView	Builds a perspective projection matrix based on a field of view.
CreatePerspectiveOffCenter	Builds a customized, perspective projection matrix.
CreateReflection	Creates a Matrix that reflects the coordinate system about a specified Plane.
CreateRotationX	Creates a matrix that can be used to rotate a set of vertices around the x-axis.
CreateRotationY	Creates a matrix that can be used to rotate a set of vertices around the y-axis.
CreateRotationZ	Creates a matrix that can be used to rotate a set of vertices around the z-axis.
CreateScale	Creates a scaling Matrix.
CreateShadow	Creates a Matrix that flattens geometry into a specified Plane as if casting a shadow from a specified light source.
CreateTranslation	Creates a translation Matrix.
CreateWorld	Creates a world matrix.
Decompose	Extracts the scalar, translation, and rotation components from a 3D scale/rotate/translate (SRT) Matrix.

Determinant	Calculates the determinant of the matrix.
Divide	Divides a matrix by a scalar value or the components of another matrix.
Invert	Calculates the inverse of a matrix.
Lerp	Linearly interpolates between the corresponding values of two matrices.
Multiply	Multiplies a matrix by a scalar value or another matrix.
Negate	Negates individual elements of a matrix.
op_Addition	Adds a matrix to another matrix.
op_Division	Divides a matrix by a scalar value or the components of another matrix.
op_Multiply	Multiplies a matrix by a scalar value or another matrix.
op_Subtraction	Subtracts matrices.
op_UnaryNegation	Negates individual elements of a matrix.
Subtract	Subtracts matrices.
Transform	Transforms a `Matrix` by applying a `Quaternion` rotation.
Transpose	Transposes the rows and columns of a matrix.

Plane

Defines a plane.

Public Fields	
D	The distance of the `Plane` along its normal from the origin.
Normal	The normal vector of the `Plane`.
Public Methods	
Dot	Calculates the dot product of a specified `Vector4` and this `Plane`.
DotCoordinate	Returns the dot product of a specified `Vector3` and the `Normal` vector of this `Plane` plus the D constant value of the `Plane`.
DotNormal	Returns the dot product of a specified `Vector3` and the `Normal` vector of this `Plane`.
Intersects	Checks whether a `Plane` intersects a bounding volume.
Normalize	Changes the coefficients of the `Normal` vector of a `Plane` to make it of unit length.
Transform	Transforms a normalized `Plane` by a `Matrix` or `Quaternion`.

Point

Defines a point in 2D space.

Public Fields	
X	Specifies the x-coordinate of the `Point`.
Y	Specifies the y-coordinate of the `Point`.
Public Properties	
Zero	Returns the point (0,0).

Quaternion

Defines a four-dimensional vector (x,y,z,w), which is used to efficiently rotate an object about the (x, y, z) vector by the angle theta, where $w = \cos(\text{theta}/2)$.

Public Fields	
W	Specifies the rotation component of the quaternion.
X	Specifies the x-value of the vector component of the quaternion.
Y	Specifies the y-value of the vector component of the quaternion.
Z	Specifies the z-value of the vector component of the quaternion.
Public Properties	
Identity	Returns a `Quaternion` representing no rotation.
Public Methods	
Add	Adds two `Quaternion`s.
Concatenate	Concatenates two `Quaternion`s; the result represents the first rotation followed by the second rotation.
Conjugate	Calculates the conjugate of a `Quaternion`.
CreateFromAxisAngle	Creates a `Quaternion` from a vector and an angle to rotate about the vector.
CreateFromRotationMatrix	Creates a `Quaternion` from a rotation `Matrix`.
CreateFromYawPitchRoll	Creates a new `Quaternion` from specified yaw, pitch, and roll angles.
Divide	Divides a `Quaternion` by another `Quaternion`.
Dot	Calculates the dot product of two `Quaternion`s.
Inverse	Returns the inverse of a `Quaternion`.
Length	Calculates the length of a `Quaternion`.
LengthSquared	Calculates the length squared of a `Quaternion`.
Lerp	Linearly interpolates between two quaternions.
Multiply	Multiplies a quaternion by a scalar or another quaternion.
Negate	Flips the sign of each component of the quaternion.

Normalize	Divides each component of a quaternion by the length of the quaternion.
op_Addition	Adds two Quaternions.
op_Division	Divides a Quaternion by another Quaternion.
op_Multiply	Multiplies a quaternion by a scalar or another quaternion.
op_Subtraction	Subtracts a quaternion from another quaternion.
op_UnaryNegation	Flips the sign of each component of the quaternion.
Slerp	Interpolates between two quaternions, using spherical linear interpolation.
Subtract	Subtracts a quaternion from another quaternion.

Ray

Defines a ray.

Public Fields

Direction	Unit vector specifying the direction the Ray is pointing.
Position	Specifies the starting point of the Ray.

Rectangle

Defines a rectangle.

Public Fields

Height	Specifies the height of the rectangle.
Width	Specifies the width of the rectangle.
X	Specifies the x-coordinate of the rectangle.
Y	Specifies the y-coordinate of the rectangle.

Public Properties

Bottom	Returns the y-coordinate of the bottom of the rectangle.
Center	Gets the Point that specifies the center of the rectangle.
Empty	Returns a Rectangle with all its values set to 0.
IsEmpty	Gets a value that indicates whether the Rectangle is empty.
Left	Returns the x-coordinate of the left side of the rectangle.
Location	Gets or sets the upper-left value of the Rectangle.
Right	Returns the x-coordinate of the right side of the rectangle.
Top	Returns the y-coordinate of the top of the rectangle.

(Continued)

Public Methods

Contains	Determines whether this Rectangle contains a specified point or Rectangle.
Inflate	Pushes the edges of the Rectangle out by the horizontal and vertical values specified.
Intersect	Creates a Rectangle defining the area where one rectangle overlaps another rectangle.
Intersects	Determines whether a specified Rectangle intersects with this Rectangle.
Offset	Changes the position of the Rectangle.
Union	Creates a new Rectangle that exactly contains two other rectangles.

Vector2

Defines a vector with two components.

Public Fields

X	Gets or sets the x-component of the vector.
Y	Gets or sets the y-component of the vector.

Public Properties

One	Returns a Vector2 with both its components set to one.
UnitX	Returns the unit vector for the x-axis.
UnitY	Returns the unit vector for the y-axis.
Zero	Returns a Vector2 with all its components set to 0.

Public Methods

Add	Adds two vectors.
Barycentric	Returns a Vector2 containing the 2D Cartesian coordinates of a point specified in 2D barycentric (areal) coordinates.
CatmullRom	Performs a Catmull-Rom interpolation using the specified positions.
Clamp	Restricts a value to be within a specified range.
Distance	Calculates the distance between two vectors.
DistanceSquared	Calculates the distance between two vectors squared.
Divide	Divides a vector by a scalar or another vector.
Dot	Calculates the dot product of two vectors. If the two vectors are unit vectors, the dot product returns a floating-point value between -1 and 1 that can be used to determine some properties of the angle between two vectors. For example, it can show whether the vectors are orthogonal, parallel, or have an acute or obtuse angle between them.
Hermite	Performs a Hermite spline interpolation.
Length	Calculates the length of the vector.
LengthSquared	Calculates the length of the vector squared.
Lerp	Performs a linear interpolation between two vectors.

Max	Returns a vector that contains the highest value from each matching pair of components.
Min	Returns a vector that contains the lowest value from each matching pair of components.
Multiply	Multiplies a vector by a scalar or another vector.
Negate	Returns a vector pointing in the opposite direction.
Normalize	Creates a unit vector from the specified vector. The result is a vector 1 unit in length pointing in the same direction as the original vector.
op_Addition	Adds two vectors.
op_Division	Divides a vector by a scalar or another vector.
op_Multiply	Multiplies a vector by a scalar or another vector.
op_Subtraction	Subtracts a vector from a vector.
op_UnaryNegation	Returns a vector pointing in the opposite direction.
Reflect	Determines the reflect vector of the given vector and normal.
SmoothStep	Interpolates between two values using a cubic equation.
Subtract	Subtracts a vector from a vector.
Transform	Transforms one or more Vector2s by a Matrix or Quaternion.
TransformNormal	Transforms a vector normal or array of vector normals by a matrix.

Vector3

Defines a vector with three components.

Public Fields

X	Gets or sets the x-component of the vector.
Y	Gets or sets the y-component of the vector.
Z	Gets or sets the z-component of the vector.

Public Properties

Backward	Returns a unit Vector3 designating backward in a right-handed coordinate system (0, 0, 1).
Down	Returns a unit Vector3 designating down (0, −1, 0).
Forward	Returns a unit Vector3 designating forward in a right-handed coordinate system (0, 0, −1).
Left	Returns a unit Vector3 designating left (−1, 0, 0).
One	Returns a Vector2 with both its components set to 1.
Right	Returns a unit Vector3 pointing to the right (1, 0, 0).
UnitX	Returns the unit vector for the x-axis.
UnitY	Returns the unit vector for the y-axis.
UnitZ	Returns the unit vector for the z-axis.

(Continued)

Up	Returns a unit vector designating up (0, 1, 0).
Zero	Returns a `Vector3` with all its components set to 0.

Public Methods

Add	Adds two vectors.
Barycentric	Returns a `Vector3` containing the 3D Cartesian coordinates of a point specified in 3D barycentric (areal) coordinates.
CatmullRom	Performs a Catmull-Rom interpolation using the specified positions.
Clamp	Restricts a value to be within a specified range.
Cross	Calculates the cross product of two vectors.
Distance	Calculates the distance between two vectors.
DistanceSquared	Calculates the distance between two vectors squared.
Divide	Divides a vector by a scalar or another vector.
Dot	Calculates the dot product of two vectors. If the two vectors are unit vectors, the dot product returns a floating-point value between −1 and 1 that can be used to determine some properties of the angle between two vectors. For example, it can show whether the vectors are orthogonal, parallel, or have an acute or obtuse angle between them.
Hermite	Performs a Hermite spline interpolation.
Length	Calculates the length of the vector.
LengthSquared	Calculates the length of the vector squared.
Lerp	Performs a linear interpolation between two vectors.
Max	Returns a vector that contains the highest value from each matching pair of components.
Min	Returns a vector that contains the lowest value from each matching pair of components.
Multiply	Multiplies a vector by a scalar or another vector.
Negate	Returns a vector pointing in the opposite direction.
Normalize	Creates a unit vector from the specified vector. The result is a vector 1 unit in length pointing in the same direction as the original vector.
op_Addition	Adds two vectors.
op_Division	Divides a vector by a scalar or another vector.
op_Multiply	Multiplies a vector by a scalar or another vector.
op_Subtraction	Subtracts a vector from a vector.
op_UnaryNegation	Returns a vector pointing in the opposite direction.
Reflect	Determines the reflect vector of the given vector and normal.
SmoothStep	Interpolates between two values using a cubic equation.
Subtract	Subtracts a vector from a vector.
Transform	Transforms one or more `Vector3`s by a `Matrix` or `Quaternion`.
TransformNormal	Transforms a vector normal or array of vector normals by a matrix.

Vector4

Defines a vector with four components.

Public Fields

W	Gets or sets the w-component of the vector.
X	Gets or sets the x-component of the vector.
Y	Gets or sets the y-component of the vector.
Z	Gets or sets the z-component of the vector.

Public Properties

One	Returns a Vector4 with all its components set to 1.
UnitW	Returns the Vector4 (0, 0, 0, 1).
UnitX	Returns the Vector4 (1, 0, 0, 0).
UnitY	Returns the Vector4 (0, 1, 0, 0).
UnitZ	Returns the Vector4 (0, 0, 1, 0).
Zero	Returns a Vector4 with all its components set to 0.

Public Methods

Add	Adds two vectors.
Barycentric	Returns a Vector4 containing the 4D Cartesian coordinates of a point specified in 4D barycentric (areal) coordinates.
CatmullRom	Performs a Catmull-Rom interpolation using the specified positions.
Clamp	Restricts a value to be within a specified range.
Distance	Calculates the distance between two vectors.
DistanceSquared	Calculates the distance between two vectors squared.
Divide	Divides a vector by a scalar or another vector.
Dot	Calculates the dot product of two vectors. If the two vectors are unit vectors, the dot product returns a floating-point value between −1 and 1 that can be used to determine some properties of the angle between two vectors. For example, it can show whether the vectors are orthogonal, parallel, or have an acute or obtuse angle between them.
Hermite	Performs a Hermite spline interpolation.
Length	Calculates the length of the vector.
LengthSquared	Calculates the length of the vector squared.
Lerp	Performs a linear interpolation between two vectors.
Max	Returns a vector that contains the highest value from each matching pair of components.
Min	Returns a vector that contains the lowest value from each matching pair of components.
Multiply	Multiplies a vector by a scalar or another vector.
Negate	Returns a vector pointing in the opposite direction.

(Continued)

Normalize	Creates a unit vector from the specified vector. The result is a vector 1 unit in length pointing in the same direction as the original vector.
op_Addition	Adds two vectors.
op_Division	Divides a vector by a scalar or another vector.
op_Multiply	Multiplies a vector by a scalar or another vector.
op_Subtraction	Subtracts a vector from a vector.
op_UnaryNegation	Returns a vector pointing in the opposite direction.
SmoothStep	Interpolates between two values using a cubic equation.
Subtract	Subtracts a vector from a vector.
Transform	Transforms one or more `Vector4`s by a `Matrix` or `Quaternion`.

Microsoft.Xna.Framework Enumerations

The following enumerations support the properties and methods in the `Microsoft.Xna.Framework` namespace.

ContainmentType

Indicates the extent to which bounding volumes intersect or contain one another.

Contains	Indicates that one bounding volume completely contains the other.
Disjoint	Indicates there is no overlap between the bounding volumes.
Intersects	Indicates that the bounding volumes partially overlap.

CurveContinuity

Defines the continuity of `CurveKeys` on a `Curve`.

Smooth	Interpolation can be used between this `CurveKey` and the next.
Step	Interpolation cannot be used between this `CurveKey` and the next. Specifying a position between the two points returns this point.

CurveLoopType

Defines how the value of a `Curve` will be determined for positions before the first point on the `Curve` or after the last point on the `Curve`.

Constant	The Curve will evaluate to its first key for positions before the first point in the Curve and to the last key for positions after the last point.
Cycle	Positions specified past the ends of the curve will wrap around to the opposite side of the Curve.
CycleOffset	Positions specified past the ends of the curve will wrap around to the opposite side of the Curve. The value will be offset by the difference between the values of the first and last CurveKey multiplied by the number of times the position wraps around. If the position is before the first point in the Curve, the difference will be subtracted from its value; otherwise, the difference will be added.
Linear	Linear interpolation will be performed to determine the value.
Oscillate	Positions specified past the ends of the Curve act as an offset from the same side of the Curve toward the opposite side.

CurveTangent

Specifies different tangent types to be calculated for CurveKey points in a Curve.

Linear	A Linear tangent at a CurveKey is equal to the difference between its Value and the Value of the preceding or succeeding CurveKey.
Smooth	A Smooth tangent smoothes the inflection between a TangentIn and TangentOut by taking into account the values of both neighbors of the CurveKey.

DisplayOrientation

Defines the display orientation.

Default	The default display orientation.
LandscapeLeft	The display is rotated counterclockwise 90 degrees into a landscape presentation, where the width is greater than the height.
LandscapeRight	The display is rotated clockwise 90 degrees into a landscape presentation, where the width is greater than the height.
Portrait	The orientation is a portrait presentation, where the height is greater than the width.

PlaneIntersectionType

Describes the intersection between a plane and a bounding volume.

Back	There is no intersection, and the bounding volume is in the negative half-space of the Plane.
Front	There is no intersection, and the bounding volume is in the positive half-space of the Plane.
Intersecting	The Plane is intersected.

PlayerIndex

Specifies the game controller associated with a player.

One	The first controller.
Two	The second controller.
Three	The third controller.
Four	The fourth controller.

SUMMARY

The XNA Framework is a very thorough, comprehensive collection of classes, structures, and enumerations that makes it much easier for a programmer to get productive very quickly. Most game programmers have traditionally had to write most of the code in the XNA Framework from scratch, and usually separately for each new game project. This chapter covered the primary or root namespace of the framework, while subsequent chapters will focus on a more applied approach to covering the remaining namespaces in the framework.

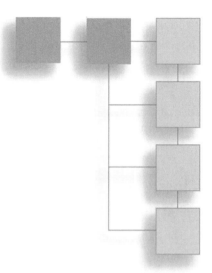

CHAPTER 4

AUDIO

The audio system in XNA makes it possible to reproduce sound effects and music in two different ways. First, we can play audio clips directly from audio files loaded at runtime, with support for the most common audio file formats. Second, we can use Microsoft's Cross-Platform Audio Creation Tool, also known as XACT, which is more often used for complex games with many audio files. The first approach involves loading and managing audio objects in our own code. The second approach leaves the details largely up to classes provided for working with XACT resources built at compile time and then made available from a container of objects. I'm going to cover the audio system in the `Microsoft.Xna.Framework.Audio` namespace in detail, followed by examples showing how to use the simple audio system and the full-blown XACT interface in XNA. These are the likely culprits in this lineup:

- `Microsoft.Xna.Framework.Audio` reference
- Simple audio playback
- Cross-Platform Audio Creation Tool (XACT)

MICROSOFT.XNA.FRAMEWORK.AUDIO REFERENCE

The XNA audio system is found in the `Microsoft.Xna.Framework.Audio` namespace, and the core class that we use to create audio objects is called `AudioEngine`. For simple audio playback, we can use `SoundEffect` and `SoundEffectInstance`, but for a more comprehensive audio solution we need to look at the rest of the classes. This reference to the audio system will be useful as you consider building the audio component of your own games.

Note

Because every class has common methods like `Dispose` and `Finalize` involved in object logistics, these common method names are intentionally left out of this reference in order to highlight the more relevant methods. This policy also applies to properties and methods derived from the base `Object` class.

Classes

Following are the classes found within this namespace.

AudioEmitter

Represents a 3D audio emitter.

Public Properties	
DopplerScale	Gets or sets a scalar applied to the level of Doppler effect calculated between this and any `AudioListener`.
Forward	Gets or sets the forward orientation vector for this emitter.
Position	Gets or sets the position of this emitter.
Up	Gets or sets the upward orientation vector for this emitter.
Velocity	Gets or sets the velocity vector of this emitter.

AudioEngine

Represents the audio engine. Applications use the methods of the audio engine to instantiate and manipulate core audio objects.

Public Fields	
ContentVersion	Specifies the current content version.
Public Properties	
RendererDetails	Gets a collection of audio renderers.
Public Methods	
GetCategory	Gets an audio category.
GetGlobalVariable	Gets the value of a global variable.
SetGlobalVariable	Sets the value of a global variable.
Update	Performs periodic work required by the audio engine.

AudioListener

Represents a 3D audio listener. This object, used in combination with an AudioEmitter, can simulate 3D audio effects for a given Cue or SoundEffect-Instance.

Public Properties

Forward	Gets or sets the forward orientation vector for this listener.
Position	Gets or sets the position of this listener.
Up	Gets or sets the upward orientation vector for this listener.
Velocity	Gets or sets the velocity vector of this listener.

Cue

Defines methods for managing the playback of sounds. Cues are what programmers use to play sounds. Cues are typically played when certain game events occur, such as footsteps or gunshots. A cue is composed of one or more sounds, so when the cue is triggered, the set of associated sounds is heard. A sound specifies how one or more waves should be played. A sound also has specific properties such as volume and pitch. The sound designer can adjust these properties. The advantage to using the Audio API to reference cues rather than specific sounds is that an audio designer can reassign sounds to a cue in the sound bank without programmer intervention. For example, a sound designer can try various gunshot waves associated with a particular game event without requiring the programmer to change code or rename sounds. Cues and sounds are referenced through SoundBank objects. The waves that compose a sound are referenced through WaveBank objects.

Public Properties

IsCreated	Returns whether the cue has been created.
IsPaused	Returns whether the cue is currently paused.
IsPlaying	Returns whether the cue is playing.
IsPrepared	Returns whether the cue is prepared to play.
IsPreparing	Returns whether the cue is preparing to play.
IsStopped	Returns whether the cue is currently stopped.
IsStopping	Returns whether the cue is stopping playback.
Name	Returns the friendly name of the cue.

Public Methods	
Apply3D	Calculates the 3D audio values between an AudioEmitter and an AudioListener object, and applies the resulting values to this Cue.
GetVariable	Gets a cue-instance variable value based on its friendly name.
Pause	Pauses playback.
Play	Requests playback of a prepared or preparing Cue.
Resume	Resumes playback of a paused Cue.
SetVariable	Sets the value of a cue-instance variable based on its friendly name.
Stop	Stops playback of a Cue.

DynamicSoundEffectInstance

Provides properties, methods, and events for playback of the audio buffer.

Public Properties	
IsLooped	Indicates whether the audio playback of the DynamicSoundEffectInstance object is looped.
PendingBufferCount	Returns the number of audio buffers in the queue awaiting playback.
Public Methods	
GetSampleDuration	Returns the sample duration based on the specified size of the audio buffer.
GetSampleSizeInBytes	Returns the size of the audio buffer required to contain audio samples based on the specified duration.
Play	Begins or resumes audio playback.
SubmitBuffer	Submits an audio buffer for playback.

InstancePlayLimitException

The exception thrown when there is an attempt to concurrently play more than 16 SoundEffectInstance sounds. All properties and methods are inherited from Exception and ExternalException.

Microphone

Provides properties, methods, and fields and events for capturing audio data with microphones.

Public Fields	
Name	Returns the friendly name of the microphone.
Public Properties	
All	Returns the collection of all currently available microphones.
BufferDuration	Gets or sets audio capture buffer duration of the microphone.
Default	Returns the default attached microphone.
IsHeadset	Determines if the microphone is a wired headset or a Bluetooth device.
SampleRate	Returns the sample rate at which the microphone is capturing audio data.
MicrophoneState	Returns the recording state of the Microphone object.
Public Methods	
GetData	Gets the latest recorded data from the microphone.
GetSampleDuration	Returns the duration of audio playback based on the size of the buffer.
GetSampleSizeInBytes	Returns the size of the byte array required to hold the specified duration of audio for this microphone object.
Start	Starts microphone audio capture.
Stop	Stops microphone audio capture.
Public Events	
BufferReady	Event that occurs when the audio capture buffer is ready to be processed.

NoAudioHardwareException

The exception thrown when no audio hardware is present, or when audio hardware is installed but the device drivers for the audio hardware are not present or enabled. All properties and methods are inherited from Exception and ExternalException.

NoMicrophoneConnectedException

The exception thrown when Microphone API calls are made on a disconnected microphone. All properties and methods are inherited from Exception.

SoundBank

Represents a sound bank, which is a collection of cues.

Public Properties	
IsInUse	Returns whether the sound bank is currently in use.
Public Methods	
GetCue	Gets a cue from the sound bank.
PlayCue	Plays a cue.

SoundEffect

Provides a loaded sound resource. A SoundEffect contains the audio data and metadata (such as wave data and loop information) loaded from a sound file. You can create multiple SoundEffectInstance objects and play them from a single SoundEffect. These objects share the resources of that SoundEffect. You can create a SoundEffect by calling ContentManager.Load. When you make that call, use the type SoundEffect and the asset name of an audio file. The audio file must be part of the content project. Be sure to use the SoundEffect-XNA Framework content processor. The only limit to the number of loaded Sound-Effect objects is memory. A loaded SoundEffect will continue to hold its memory resources throughout its lifetime. All SoundEffectInstance objects created from a SoundEffect share memory resources. When a SoundEffect object is destroyed, all SoundEffectInstance objects previously created by that SoundEffect will stop playing and become invalid.

Public Properties

DistanceScale	Gets or sets a value that adjusts the effect of distance calculations on the sound (emitter).
DopplerScale	Gets or sets a value that adjusts the effect of Doppler calculations on the sound (emitter).
TimeSpan Duration	Gets the duration of the SoundEffect.
MasterVolume	Gets or sets the master volume that affects all SoundEffectInstance sounds.
Name	Gets or sets the asset name of the SoundEffect.
SpeedOfSound	Returns the speed of sound: 343.5 meters per second.

Public Methods

CreateInstance	Creates a new SoundEffectInstance for this SoundEffect.
FromStream	Creates a SoundEffect object based on the specified data stream.
GetSampleDuration	Returns the sample duration based on the specified sample size and sample rate.
GetSampleSizeInBytes	Returns the size of the audio sample based on duration, sample rate, and audio channels.
Play	Plays a sound.

SoundEffectInstance

Provides a single playing, paused, or stopped instance of a `SoundEffect` sound. You can create a `SoundEffectInstance` by calling `SoundEffect.CreateInstance`. Initially, the `SoundEffectInstance` is created as stopped, but you can play it by calling `Play`. You can modify the volume, panning, and pitch of the `SoundEffectInstance` by setting the `Volume`, `Pitch`, and `Pan` properties. On Windows, there is no hard limit, but playing too many instances can lead to performance degradation. On Xbox 360, the limit is 300 sound-effect instances loaded or playing at a time.

Public Properties	
IsLooped	Gets a value that indicates whether looping is enabled for the `SoundEffectInstance`.
Pan	Gets or sets the panning for the `SoundEffectInstance`.
Pitch	Gets or sets the pitch adjustment for the `SoundEffectInstance`.
State	Gets the current state (playing, paused, or stopped) of the `SoundEffectInstance`.
Volume	Gets or sets the volume of the `SoundEffectInstance`.
Public Methods	
Apply3D	Applies 3D position to the sound.
Pause	Pauses a `SoundEffectInstance`.
Play	Plays or resumes a `SoundEffectInstance`.
Resume	Resumes playback for a `SoundEffectInstance`.
Stop	Stops playing a `SoundEffectInstance`.

WaveBank

Represents a wave bank, which is a collection of wave files.

Public Properties	
IsInUse	Returns whether the wave bank is currently in use.
IsPrepared	Returns whether the wave bank is prepared to play.

Structures

Following are the structures found within this namespace.

AudioCategory

Represents a particular category of sounds.

Public Properties	
Name	Specifies the friendly name of this category.
Public Methods	
Pause	Pauses all sounds associated with this category.
Resume	Resumes all paused sounds associated with this category.
SetVolume	Sets the volume of all sounds associated with this category.
Stop	Stops all sounds associated with this category.

RendererDetail

Represents an audio renderer, which is a device that can render audio to a user.

Public Properties	
FriendlyName	Gets the human-readable name for the renderer.
RendererId	Specifies the string that identifies the renderer.

Enumerations

Following are the enumerations found within this namespace.

AudioChannels

Defines the number of channels in the audio data.

Mono	Indicates audio data is contained in one channel.
Stereo	Indicates audio data contains two channels.

AudioStopOptions

Controls how Cue objects should stop when Stop is called.

AsAuthored	Indicates the cue should stop normally, playing any release phase or transition specified in the content.
Immediate	Indicates the cue should stop immediately, ignoring any release phase or transition specified in the content.

MicrophoneState

Current state of the Microphone audio capture (started or stopped).

Started	The Microphone audio capture has started.
Stopped	The Microphone audio capture has stopped.

SoundState

Current state (playing, paused, or stopped) of a SoundEffectInstance.

Paused	The SoundEffectInstance is paused.
Playing	The SoundEffectInstance is playing.
Stopped	The SoundEffectInstance is stopped.

SIMPLE AUDIO PLAYBACK

There is one very easy way to get audio to play in an XNA project: by using the SoundEffect class. There are some drawbacks to using SoundEffect rather than XACT, however. These include the tendency for the content project to become cluttered with many asset files. Even so, the SoundEffect class is convenient and easy to use for simple audio playback. (Refer to the reference information on this class earlier in this chapter.)

Adding Audio Content to the Project

Before we can play an audio clip, we have to add it to the content system. Right-click Content in Solution Explorer, choose Add, then choose Existing Item, as shown in Figure 4.1. This opens the Add Existing File dialog box. Locate the audio file you want to add to the project.

The following audio file types can be added to an XNA project for use with the SoundEffect class:

- XAP
- WAV
- WMA
- MP3

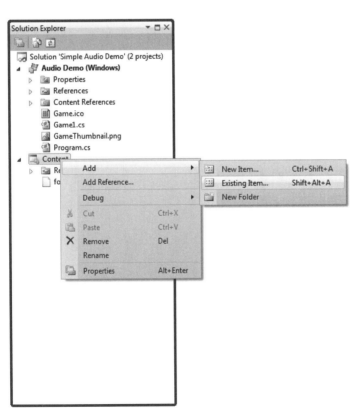

Figure 4.1
Adding an existing audio file to the project via the content system.

Loading the Audio Clip

We can create an instance of the SoundEffect class with a variable declared in the globals section at the top of the class as follows:

```
SoundEffect heartBeat;
```

The SoundEffect object is loaded in the LoadContent() function:

```
protected override void LoadContent()
{
    spriteBatch = new SpriteBatch(GraphicsDevice);
    font = Content.Load<SpriteFont>("Arial");
    heartBeat = Content.Load<SoundEffect>("heartbeat");
}
```

Note

When you add content to one platform project (such as Windows), the content item is also automatically added to the other platform projects (such as Xbox 360). You do not need to manage assets individually—a real time saver.

Playing the Audio Clip

The audio clip can be played back using the SoundEffect.Play() method. There is a simple version of Play() and an overloaded version, which gives us control over the Volume, Pitch, and Pan properties. Here is an example:

```
protected override void Update(GameTime gameTime)
{
    GamePadState gamepad = GamePad.GetState(PlayerIndex.One);
    KeyboardState keyboard = Keyboard.GetState();

    //Escape or Back to end program
    if (gamepad.Buttons.Back == ButtonState.Pressed) this.Exit();
    if (keyboard.IsKeyDown(Keys.Escape)) this.Exit();

    //A button or key plays sound effect
    if (gamepad.Buttons.A == ButtonState.Pressed)

        heartBeat.Play();
    if (Keyboard.GetState().IsKeyDown(Keys.A))
        heartBeat.Play();

    base.Update(gameTime);
}
```

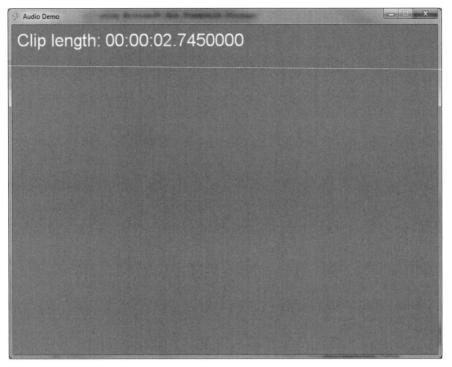

Figure 4.2
The Simple Audio Demo program.

Audio Clip Length

There is really only one useful property in the SoundEffect class: Duration. This property gives us the length of the audio clip in seconds. In the Draw() function of our sample program (Simple Audio Demo), we can print out the length of the audio clip, as shown in Listing 4.1. In fact, this class is not very helpful at all. What we need is a class with more functionality. Figure 4.2 shows the program running.

Listing 4.1   Simple Audio Demo Program

```
protected override void Draw(GameTime gameTime)
{
    GraphicsDevice.Clear(Color.CornflowerBlue);
    spriteBatch.Begin();

    string text = "Audio length: " + heartBeat.Duration.ToString();
```

```
    print(10, 10, text, Color.White);

    spriteBatch.End();
    base.Draw(gameTime);
}
void print(int x, int y, string text, Color color)
{
    spriteBatch.DrawString(font, text,

        new Vector2((float)x, (float)y), color);
}
```

SoundEffectInstance

The `SoundEffectInstance` class enhances the basic functionality of `SoundEffect` with additional properties and methods that make it more useful in a real-world game. (Refer to the class reference earlier in the chapter.) After loading the `SoundEffect` in `LoadContent()`, we can create an instance of the `SoundEffect-Instance` class from its `CreateInstance()` method:

```
heartBeat = Content.Load<SoundEffect>("heartbeat");
heartBeatInst = heartBeat.CreateInstance();
```

This class makes available several useful methods: `Play()`, `Stop()`, `Pause()`, and `Resume()`. And, the `Volume`, `Pitch`, and `Pan` properties have been moved from parameters into real class properties, which we can modify outside of the `Play()` method. In addition, we can cause an audio clip to loop during playback with the `IsLooping` property.

CROSS-PLATFORM AUDIO CREATION TOOL (XACT)

The XACT program is found in the Program Files folder, under XNA Game Studio 4.0, Tools. This is a separate program that runs outside of Visual C# Express or Visual Studio. When you start XACT, it will begin with an empty project. Use the File menu to create a new XACT project with the name of your choice.

Creating a New Audio Project

To configure a new audio project, follow these steps:

1. Under XACT Project, right-click Wave Banks and choose New Wave Bank. The default name, "Wave Bank," works fine for our purposes. If,

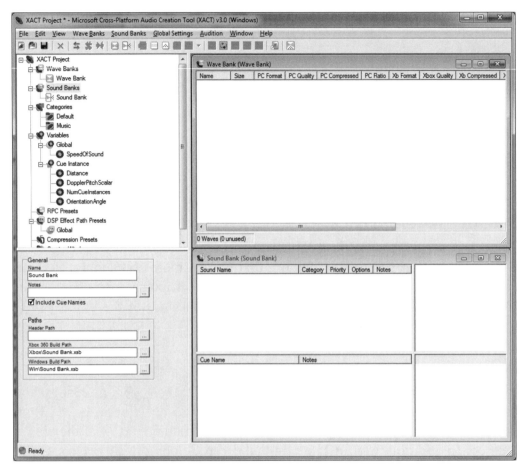

Figure 4.3
A new XACT project showing the wave banks and sound banks.

however, you intend to have multiple groups of sounds, then you would
want to rename this to an appropriate name.

2. Right-click Sound Banks and choose New Sound Bank. Figure 4.3 shows
   the two windows that have been opened: Wave Bank and Sound Bank.

3. Locate the audio files (usually just waves) you want to use for your
   game. You can add the audio files individually and even open up the
   project at a later time to manipulate the audio collection for a particular
   project.

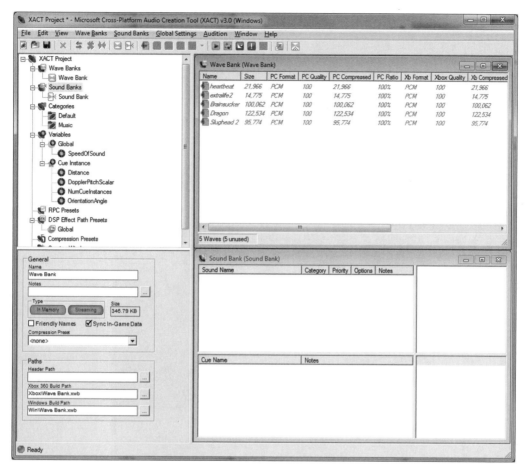

Figure 4.4
Adding audio files to the wave bank.

4. Right-click the Wave Bank window and choose Insert Wave File(s). Several wave files are added (see Figure 4.4).

5. Drag the file(s) from the wave bank into the cue list of the sound bank (the bottom list). The audios will be added to the sound list automatically. (Note: If you manually add them to the sound list and cue list, there will be double entries in the sound list.) Figure 4.5 shows the result.

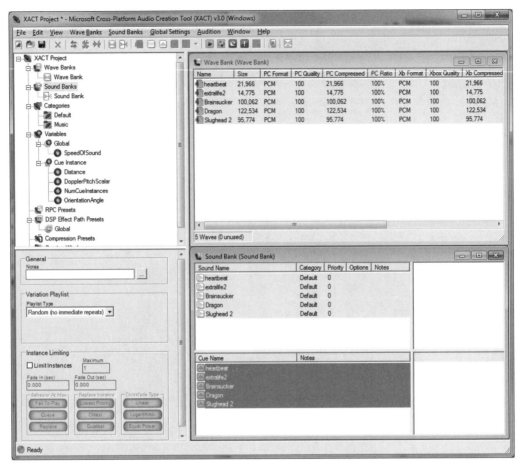

Figure 4.5
Creating cues and sounds from the audio files in the wave bank.

Building the Audio Project

Save the project by choosing File, Save, or by clicking the Save button in the toolbar. Then, build the project by choosing File, Build, or clicking the Build icon. The resulting file will have an extension of .xap. This file must be added to your XNA project along with the audio files (WAV, MP3, etc.).

Note

If the Build Project dialog box appears, just leave the Report option on None and click Finish.

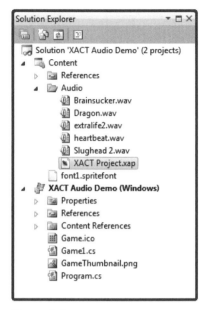

Figure 4.6
The audio files and XACT project file have been added.

Assuming you have built an XACT project into an XAP file, right-click the Content item in your XNA project's Solution Explorer and choose Add, Existing Item. Then choose the XAP file built from your XACT project. Your XAP file should appear in the list under Content.

You must also add all the audio files themselves into the project. The XAP file is actually just a text file describing what needs to be built, not a compiled binary containing audios. Because the list of assets under Content can become quite messy, I recommend putting audio files into an organizing folder called Audio (see Figure 4.6).

While you're copying files, grab the three files found inside the .\Win folder where your XAP project file is located. XACT creates the .\Win and .\Xbox folders wherever the XAP project file is located and outputs a global settings file with an .xgs extension and both the sound bank and wave bank files. All three are required by the project in order for it to work, so just copy them all into Content\Audio.

Now, we haven't written any code yet to work with the XACT project, but if you build it now, you'll see the C# compiler parse the XAP file, with output something like what appears in Listing 4.2. (Note that lengthy paths and namespaces were truncated for space.) There are two files being processed in this output.

Listing 4.2   XAP File Output

```
Building Audio\Brainsucker.wav -> C:\...\Content\Audio\Brainsucker.xnb
Rebuilding because asset is new
Importing Audio\Brainsucker.wav

  with Microsoft.Xna.Framework.Content.Pipeline.WavImporter
Processing Audio\Brainsucker.wav with
  Microsoft.Xna.Framework.Content.Pipeline.Processors.SoundEffectProcessor
Compiling C:\...\Content\Audio\Brainsucker.xnb

Building Audio\Dragon.wav -> C:\...\Content\Audio\Dragon.xnb
Rebuilding because asset is new
Importing Audio\Dragon.wav with
  Microsoft.Xna.Framework.Content.Pipeline.WavImporter
Processing Audio\Dragon.wav with

  Microsoft.Xna.Framework.Content.Pipeline.Processors.SoundEffectProcessor
Compiling C:\...\Content\Audio\Dragon.xnb
```

Once the files have been processed, the intelligent compiler will not rebuild them again unless the source file has changed—just the way it works with source-code files, with a date/time stamp.

Playing Sounds from an XACT Project

Now let's look at some code to load and play these sound clips out of the XACT project. Create three variables from AudioEngine, SoundBank, and WaveBank:

```
AudioEngine engine;
SoundBank soundBank;
WaveBank waveBank;
```

Create the objects either in Initialize() or LoadContent(), making sure of course to use your own filenames:

```
engine = new AudioEngine("Content\\Audio\\XACT Project.xgs");
soundBank = new SoundBank(engine, "Content\\Audio\\Sound Bank.xsb");
waveBank = new WaveBank(engine, "Content\\Audio\\Wave Bank.xwb");
```

The `SoundBank.PlayCue()` function is used to play sounds built into the XACT project, so we use the same `SoundBank` object to play all the sounds by name. I've used button and key-press events again to generate the audio effects. Here is the key code, found in `Update()`, that triggers the playback of the sounds.

```
GamePadState gamepad = GamePad.GetState(PlayerIndex.One);
KeyboardState keyboard = Keyboard.GetState();

//play sounds with controller buttons
if (gamepad.Buttons.A == ButtonState.Pressed)

    soundBank.PlayCue("Brainsucker");
if (gamepad.Buttons.B == ButtonState.Pressed)
    soundBank.PlayCue("Dragon");
if (gamepad.Buttons.X == ButtonState.Pressed)
    soundBank.PlayCue("extralife2");
if (gamepad.Buttons.Y == ButtonState.Pressed)
    soundBank.PlayCue("heartbeat");
if (gamepad.Buttons.Start == ButtonState.Pressed)
    soundBank.PlayCue("Slughead 2");

//play sounds with keys
if (keyboard.IsKeyDown(Keys.A))
    soundBank.PlayCue("Brainsucker");
if (keyboard.IsKeyDown(Keys.B))
    soundBank.PlayCue("Dragon");
if (keyboard.IsKeyDown(Keys.X))
    soundBank.PlayCue("extralife2");
if (keyboard.IsKeyDown(Keys.Y))
    soundBank.PlayCue("heartbeat");
if (keyboard.IsKeyDown(Keys.Enter))
    soundBank.PlayCue("Slughead 2");
```

This example doesn't display any dynamic data on the screen, just instructions, as shown in Figure 4.7.

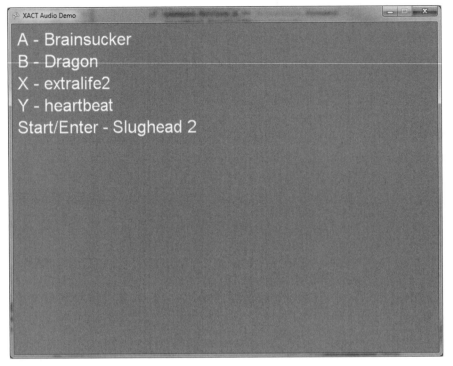

Figure 4.7
The XACT Audio Demo plays five different sounds.

Summary

We have now fully covered the XNA audio system with not just a quick reference (for future use) but also with two examples. One simple example is for quick or small clips, and a more complex example uses XACT. XACT is more appropriate when a game has a large number of audio clips, especially when both sound effects and music are needed.

CHAPTER 5

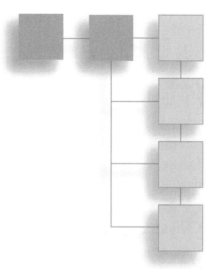

CONTENT

The Content Pipeline in XNA is a significant part of XNA Game Studio development, on par with the XNA Framework in terms of value and importance. The Content Pipeline handles asset management, including the freeing of memory, so we don't need to be overly concerned with cleanup after shutting down a game. The real power of the Content Pipeline, though, is in its ability to pre-process gameplay assets during *build time*, making them available to an XNA game at *runtime* in the most convenient format for a game. Furthermore, the Content Pipeline is *extendable*, meaning we can add our own custom assets to the Content Pipeline and have them converted to XNA format like the native file types (meshes, textures, etc.). As you will learn in this chapter, we can create a custom Content Pipeline extension library to convert any file into a managed asset—any file at all! If you have the specifications for 3DS Max or Maya native binary files, then it's possible to write an extension to convert such a file to the XNA format without the need for a third-party or custom conversion tool. The importance of scripting in a game project is also paramount! The ability to import a gameplay script file into XNA is extremely important, so we will learn how to create such an extension in this chapter. Here's the important stuff:

- Content reference
- Loading known asset types
- Loading custom assets and data with a Content Pipeline extension

- Creating a text file content importer
- Building text files as content

Microsoft.Xna.Framework.Content Reference

We don't need to go over all the classes in this namespace because they are used internally by XNA to manage assets that we tell it to load, and we will not need to use any class other than `ContentManager`. Here are the classes and their descriptions for completeness.

Classes

Following are the classes found within this namespace.

ContentLoadException

Used to report errors from the `ContentManager.Load` method. All the properties and methods are inherited from `Exception`.

ContentManager

The runtime component that loads managed objects from the binary files produced by the design-time Content Pipeline. It also manages the lifespan of the loaded objects. Disposing of the content manager will also dispose of any assets that are themselves `IDisposable`.

Public Properties	
RootDirectory	Gets or sets the root directory associated with this `ContentManager`.
ServiceProvider	Gets the service provider associated with the `ContentManager`.
Public Methods	
Load	Loads an asset that has been processed by the Content Pipeline.
Unload	Disposes all data that was loaded by this `ContentManager`.
Protected Methods	
OpenStream	Opens a stream for reading the specified asset. Derived classes can replace this to implement pack files or asset compression.
ReadAsset	Low-level worker method that reads asset data.

ContentReader

A worker object that implements most of `ContentManager.Load`. A new `ContentReader` is constructed for each asset loaded. Most of the properties and methods are derived from `BinaryReader`.

Public Properties	
AssetName	Gets the name of the asset currently being read by this `ContentReader`.
ContentManager	Gets the `ContentManager` associated with the `ContentReader`.
Public Methods	
ReadColor	Reads a `Color` value from the currently open stream.
ReadDouble	Reads a double value from the currently open stream.
ReadExternalReference	Reads a link to an external file.
ReadMatrix	Reads a `Matrix` value from the currently open stream.
ReadObject	Reads a single managed object from the current stream as an instance of the specified type. If a base class of the actual object type is specified, only data from the base type will be read.
ReadSharedResource	Reads a shared resource ID and records it for subsequent fix-up.
ReadSingle	Reads a float value from the currently open stream.
ReadVector2	Reads a `Vector2` value from the current stream.
ReadVector3	Reads a `Vector3` value from the current stream.
ReadVector4	Reads a `Vector4` value from the current stream.

ContentSerializerAttribute

A custom `Attribute` that marks a field or property to control how it is serialized or to indicate that protected or private data should be included in serialization.

Public Properties	
AllowNull	Gets or sets a value indicating whether this member can have a null value (default=true).
CollectionItem Name	Gets or sets the XML element name for each item in a collection (default = "Item").
ElementName	Gets or sets the XML element name (default=name of the managed type member).

`FlattenContent`	Gets or sets a value indicating whether to write member contents directly into the current XML context rather than wrapping the member in a new XML element (default=false).
`HasCollection ItemName`	Indicates whether an explicit `CollectionItemName` string is being used or the default value.
`Optional`	Indicates whether to write this element if the member is null and skip past it if not found when deserializing XML (default=false).
`SharedResource`	Indicates whether this member is referenced from multiple parents and should be serialized as a unique ID reference (default=false).

ContentSerializerCollectionItemNameAttribute

A custom `Attribute` that marks a collection class to specify the XML element name for each item in the collection.

Public Properties	
`CollectionItemName`	Gets the name that will be used for each item in the collection.

ContentSerializerIgnoreAttribute

A custom `Attribute` that marks public fields or properties to prevent them from being serialized. All properties and methods are inherited from `Attribute`.

ContentSerializerRuntimeTypeAttribute

A custom `Attribute` that specifies the corresponding runtime type of this object.

Public Properties	
`RuntimeType`	Gets the runtime type for the object.

ContentSerializerTypeVersionAttribute

A custom `Attribute` that specifies the corresponding runtime type version of this object.

Public Properties	
`TypeVersion`	Gets the runtime type version for the object.

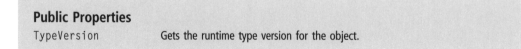

ContentTypeReader

Worker for reading a specific managed type from a binary format. Derive from this class to add new data types to the Content Pipeline system.

Public Properties	
CanDeserializeInto ExistingObject	Determines if deserialization into an existing object is possible.
TargetType	Gets the type handled by this reader component.
TypeVersion	Gets a format version number for this type.
Protected Methods	
Initialize	Retrieves and caches nested type readers. Called by the framework at creation time.
Read	Reads a strongly typed object from the current stream.

ContentTypeReaderManager

A manager that constructs and keeps track of type reader objects.

Public Methods	
GetTypeReader	Looks up a reader for the specified type.

ResourceContentManager

Subclass of ContentManager, which is specialized to read from RESX resource files rather than directly from individual files on disk. Most of the properties and methods are inherited from ContentManager.

Protected Methods	
OpenStream	Opens a stream for reading the specified resource. Derived classes can replace this to implement pack files or asset compression.

LOADING KNOWN ASSET TYPES

We can load an asset as a known type with the Content.Load() method by passing the content class name to the templated Load method like so:

```
Content.Load<SpriteFont>("font1");
```

The following types of files may be imported by the content processor:

- Model (FBX, X)
- Effect (FX)
- SpriteFont (BMP, SPRITEFONT, DDS, DIB, HDR, JPG, PFM, PNG, PPM, TGA)
- Texture (BMP, DDS, DIB, HDR, JPG, PFM, PNG, PPM, TGA)
- Texture2D (same extensions as Texture)
- TextureCube (DDS)

After an asset file has been imported by the content processor at compile time, the imported file will have an extension of .xnb. XNA does not load asset files from their native formats, such as WAV and BMP; it loads only from imported files. Once loaded, it's up to your code to do something with the asset. XNA is not a game engine. Although XNA has a collection of drawable objects, you have to inherit from a `DrawableComponent` class to take advantage of the collection. Even then, there's no control over the object at runtime, such as the ability to move and manipulate it.

The good news is, we can add new types of assets to an XNA project by extending the Content Pipeline with a new library of our own.

LOADING CUSTOM ASSETS AND DATA WITH A CONTENT PIPELINE EXTENSION

XNA makes it possible for you to add your own types of assets to the content manager so they can be built in the project like the known assets, and still loaded using `Content.Load()`. This ability is really helpful in more ways than mere asset loading. You could, for instance, write a custom content loader that returns the data for a *class* as a loaded object filled with data, rather than a traditional asset like texture, mesh, etc. A new content type is added to an XNA project, identified as "Content Pipeline Extension Library" in the list of project templates. Because this is a lot more work than just loading a file directly, it is not recommended for unique file types, only files that are common in a game project.

To give it a try yourself, add a new project to an existing XNA solution and choose this type of template to add a new extension to your solution, and we'll then see how to use it. After creating the new extension project, a source code file called ContentProcessor1.cs will be added with this code. Just remove this default file because we'll be adding our own from a template.

Creating a Text File Content Importer

To demonstrate how to create a custom Content Pipeline extension library, I will go over a simple extension that teaches XNA how to import a normal text file. Although simple in premise, there are actually quite far-reaching uses for a text file importer, not least of which is the ability to load a Lua or Python script file and process it!

Three classes are required to build a Content Pipeline extension importer, which has the job of reading a file in a native format and converting it to an XNA file with an extension of .xnb. You can store anything you want in the XNB file, because both text and binary data can be stored. The three classes needed to convert a file are as follows: Importer, Processor, and Writer. An additional class must be added to a secondary library project in order to load the asset from its XNB file into memory: Reader.

It's also up to you to write the XNB reader for your custom file so it can be read in by the game. It's a bit of a workaround process—importing, exporting, and then reading—but the result is that we can import any native file format (such as a 3DS Max or Maya file) and then have XNA process it during build time. Some studios prefer to build tools that process the native files into a proprietary format that the studio's game engines use. Either way, a custom importer makes the whole process run very smoothly. Also, this allows artists and designers to work with the native files. By simply saving them in their XNA content folders, those files can be built into the project without any intermediate steps.

Working with a Content Pipeline extension library can be *extremely* frustrating if you try to do it with just two projects—the extension library and your game. To resolve circular references and namespace problems, I recommend using a *third* project (itself a library) to act as a data share between the extension library and your game. If you have a game engine, then it's natural to use your engine project for that purpose.

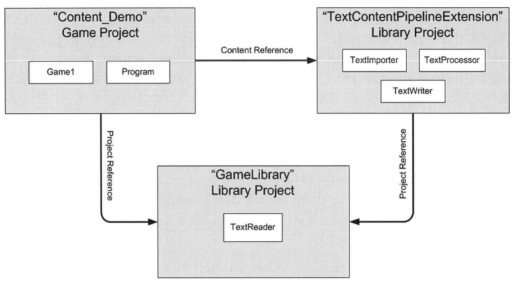

Figure 5.1
A Content Pipeline extension project works best with a helper library.

For this example, we need three projects: a primary game project, a Content Pipeline extension project, and a working data library project to help the two communicate effectively. Figure 5.1 shows how the three projects work together.

Importer (Extension Project)

Add a new file to the Content Pipeline extension project using the Project, Add New Item menu command. The Add New Item dialog box opens. Click XNA Game Studio 4.0 under Visual C# Items in the left column; then click Content Importer, as shown in Figure 5.2.

Following is the source code for the importer class, called TextImporter in this example. The purpose of this class is threefold:

- To describe the type of file to be processed using the file extension
- To specify how that asset file is to be processed
- To read the asset file into memory

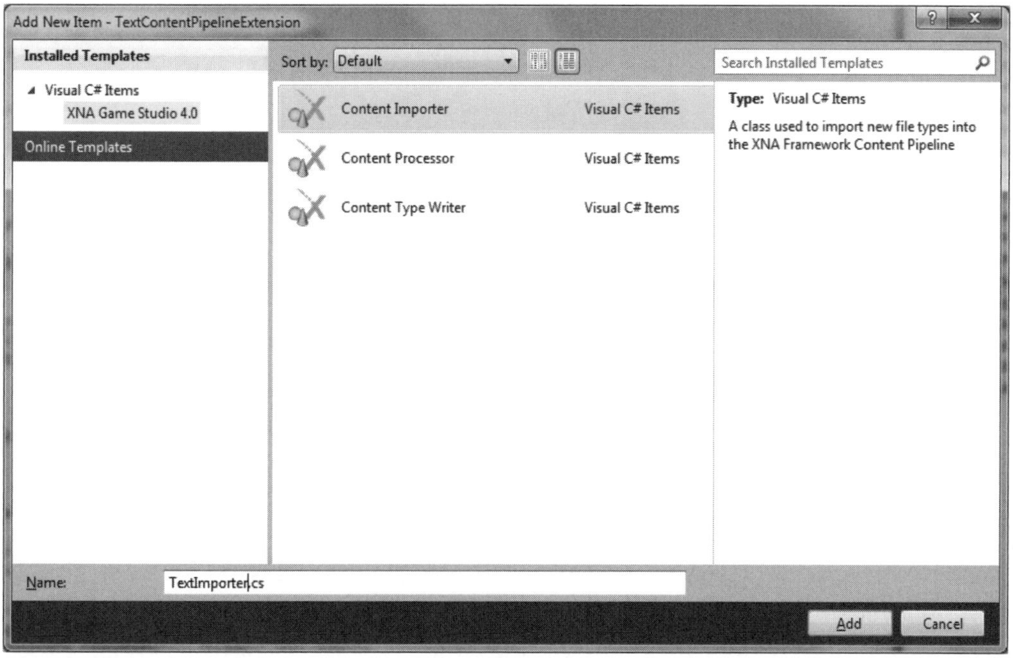

Figure 5.2
Adding the Content Importer class to the Content Pipeline extension project.

In the case of your text file importer, only one line of code is needed to read the entire text file into a string variable in memory. Note the namespace used in these classes: TextContentPipelineExtension.

```
using Microsoft.Xna.Framework;
using Microsoft.Xna.Framework.Content.Pipeline;

using TImport = System.String;

namespace TextContentPipelineExtension
{
    [ContentImporter(".txt", DisplayName = "Text File Importer",
        DefaultProcessor = "TextProcessor")]
    class TextImporter : ContentImporter<TImport>
    {
        public override TImport Import(string filename,
            ContentImporterContext context)
```

```
    {
        return System.IO.File.ReadAllText(filename);
    }
  }
}
```

Processor *(Extension Project)*

The next class we need in the extension library project is the Processor, which has the job of converting the input data from the Importer into whatever format needed in the resulting XNB file (which will be written using the Writer class). You need a new class for the Processor, so add it via the Project, Add New Item menu command. The Add New Item dialog box opens. Click XNA Game Studio 4.0 under Visual C# Items in the left column; then click Content Processor, as shown in Figure 5.3.

Here is the source code for the sample TextProcessor class. This very simple class just passes the string read in from the text file to Writer. Normally, you would need to do some processing on the input data to make it palatable within the XNA game. For instance, an image file loader would need to convert the read

Figure 5.3
Adding the Content Processor class to the project.

bytes into data compatible with a `Texture` or `Texture2D` class. In the interest of keeping this example simple, I'm just working with character data.

```
using Microsoft.Xna.Framework;
using Microsoft.Xna.Framework.Content.Pipeline;
using Microsoft.Xna.Framework.Content.Pipeline.Processors;

using TInput = System.String;
using TOutput = GameLibrary.MyData;

namespace TextContentPipelineExtension
{
    [ContentProcessor(DisplayName = "Text File Processor")]
    public class TextProcessor : ContentProcessor<TInput, TOutput>
    {
        public override TOutput Process(TInput input,
            ContentProcessorContext context)
        {
            GameLibrary.MyData data = new GameLibrary.MyData();
            data.MyString = input;
            return data;
        }
    }
}
```

Writer (Extension Project)

Now we have the `Writer` class. After the `Processor` class manipulates data read in by `Importer` into whatever format we need to use, the `Writer` class writes the data passed to it from `Processor` out to an XNA file with an extension of .xnb. To add a `Writer` class, run the Project, Add New Item menu command. The Add New Item dialog box opens; click XNA Game Studio 4.0 under Visual C# Items in the left column; then click Content Writer, as shown in Figure 5.4.

The source code for the `TextWriter` class is shown in Listing 5.1. Normally, there would be more than one line of code to write out the data for a custom asset file, but because we're just working with text data, we only need to write out the string to a text file. This is kept simple to demonstrate how the project works. After you've learned how to create a Content Pipeline extension, you will be able to work with more complex file types.

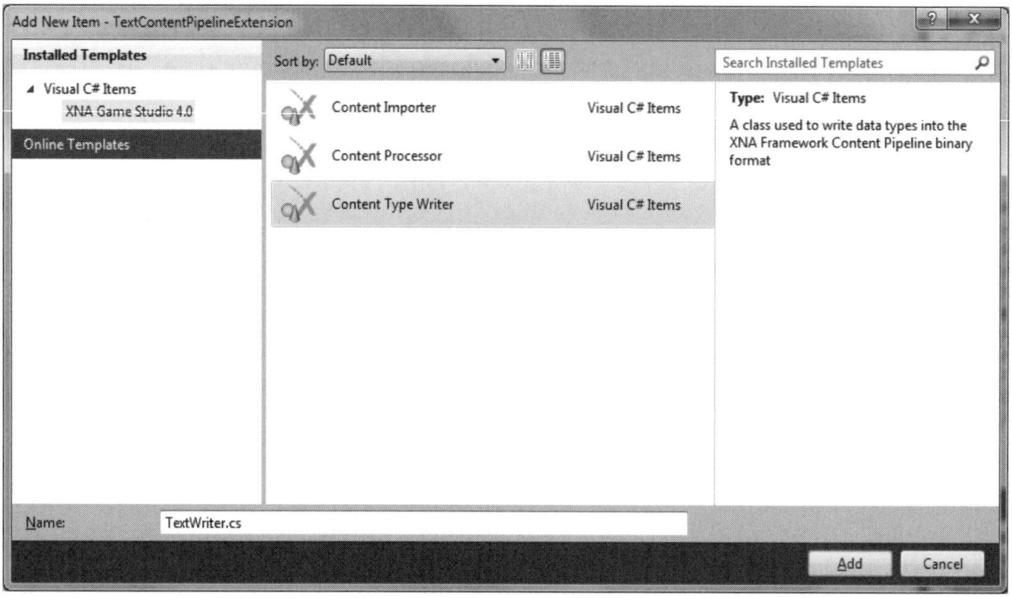

Figure 5.4
Adding the Content Type `Writer` class to the project.

Listing 5.1   The `TextWriter` Class

```csharp
using Microsoft.Xna.Framework;
using Microsoft.Xna.Framework.Content.Pipeline;
using Microsoft.Xna.Framework.Content.Pipeline.Processors;
using Microsoft.Xna.Framework.Content.Pipeline.Serialization.Compiler;

using TWrite = GameLibrary.MyData;

namespace TextContentPipelineExtension
{
    [ContentTypeWriter]
    public class TextWriter : ContentTypeWriter<TWrite>
    {
        protected override void Write(ContentWriter output, TWrite value)
        {
            //write the .xnb file
            output.Write(value.MyString);
        }
```

```
        public override string GetRuntimeReader(TargetPlatform target
Platform)
        {
            return "GameLibrary.TextReader, GameLibrary";
        }
    }
}
```

Reader (GameLibrary Project)

The Reader class is not part of the Content Pipeline, but is instead a class in the game project. The Reader is responsible for reading the XNB file that has been pre-processed by the custom Content Pipeline extension library (see Listing 5.2). The reason this class is not found in the Content Pipeline extension project is because that library *does not exist* at runtime! The content importer is not even part of the XNA Framework used at runtime, so you cannot put any class into the extension library project that you need to use at runtime. For that purpose, we have a second library that reads the XNA file and makes it available to Content.Load. This new class is called TextReader (note the namespace). See Figure 5.5.

Listing 5.2   The Reader Class

```
using System;
using Microsoft.Xna.Framework;
using Microsoft.Xna.Framework.Content;
using Microsoft.Xna.Framework.Graphics;

using TRead = GameLibrary.MyData;

namespace GameLibrary
{
    public struct MyData
    {
        public string MyString;
    }

    public class TextReader : ContentTypeReader<TRead>
    {
```

Figure 5.5
Adding a Content Reader class to the secondary library project.

```
protected override TRead Read(ContentReader input,
    TRead existingInstance)
{
    //read the .xnb file
    GameLibrary.MyData data = new GameLibrary.MyData();
    data.MyString = input.ReadString();
    return data;
}
    }
}
```

Building Text Files as Content

When the project is built, XNA processes any files with the extensions specified in the TextImporter class, running the code in our importer to process the input file (sample text file.txt), and writing out the output file (sample text file.xnb). Our code has full control over what, exactly, goes into the XNB file. That happens in the TextWriter class. When a text file is added to the project, XNA

Figure 5.6
The content manager recognizes this new asset file type (a text file).

should recognize it (by file type) and associate it with the new text file extension library. Per the descriptions in the TextImporter, the file is associated with the "Text File Importer" and "Text File Processor" (as you can see in Figure 5.6).

```
Building sample text file.txt -> C:\...\Content Demo\
  Content Demo\bin\x86\Debug\Content\sample text file.xnb
Rebuilding because asset is new
Importing sample text file.txt
  with TextContentPipelineExtension.TextImporter
Processing sample text file.txt
  with TextContentPipelineExtension.TextProcessor
Compiling C:\...\Content Demo\Content Demo\
  bin\x86\Debug\Content\sample text file.xnb
```

Building the project is just the first step, which produces the XNB files. The next step is to read the XNB file at runtime as a content item with Content.Load. The data should already be processed and simply provided to the function (via the TextReader class, which has the simple job of just passing the data along to Content.Load). But, errors can occur here. The most common error occurs when the wrong content type strings are specified in the writer class (TextWriter in this example). Here is the source code for the Content Demo program that puts these pieces together. The result is shown in Figure 5.7, which displays the contents of the file "sample text file.txt."

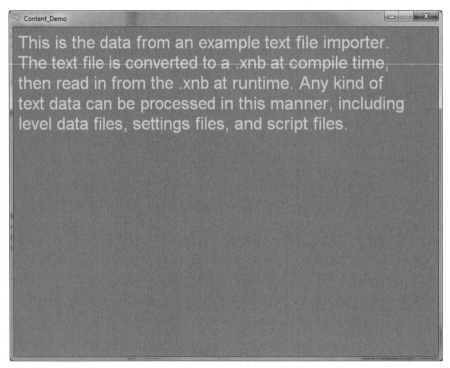

Figure 5.7
The Content Demo program shows how the Content Pipeline extension library works.

```
public class Game1 : Microsoft.Xna.Framework.Game
{
    GraphicsDeviceManager graphics;
    SpriteBatch spriteBatch;
    SpriteFont font;
    string textData;

    public Game1()
    {
```

```
    graphics = new GraphicsDeviceManager(this);
    Content.RootDirectory = "Content";
}

protected override void Initialize()
{
    base.Initialize();
    this.IsMouseVisible = true;
}

protected override void LoadContent()
{
    spriteBatch = new SpriteBatch(GraphicsDevice);
    font = Content.Load<SpriteFont>("Arial");

    //load custom content text file
    GameLibrary.MyData mydata;
    mydata = Content.Load<GameLibrary.MyData>("sample text file");
    textData = mydata.MyString;
}

protected override void UnloadContent()
{
}
protected override void Update(GameTime gameTime)
{
    GamePadState gamepad = GamePad.GetState(PlayerIndex.One);
    KeyboardState keyboard = Keyboard.GetState();
    if (gamepad.Buttons.Back == ButtonState.Pressed) this.Exit();
    if (keyboard.IsKeyDown(Keys.Escape)) this.Exit();
    base.Update(gameTime);
}
protected override void Draw(GameTime gameTime)
{
    GraphicsDevice.Clear(Color.CornflowerBlue);
    spriteBatch.Begin();

    //print string read from text file
    print(10, 10, textData, Color.Yellow);
```

```
        spriteBatch.End();
        base.Draw(gameTime);
    }

    void print(int x, int y, string text, Color color)
    {
        spriteBatch.DrawString(font, text, new Vector2((float)x,
            (float)y), color);
    }
}
```

Summary

This chapter was a bit more than just a reference of the content manager in XNA; it was a full tutorial on how to write a Content Pipeline extension! This capability gives us a great deal of control over the types of asset files we can use in our XNA games, above and beyond the default assets supported by XNA.

CHAPTER 6

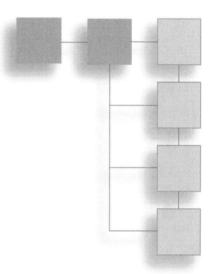

GAMERSERVICES

The GamerServices namespace within Microsoft.Xna.Framework is one of the most, er, *entertaining* collections of classes available in XNA. It gives you access to the Xbox Live avatar, friends, and player settings! Because this action-packed namespace has so much to offer, we will spend quite a bit of time here and cover every detail. First, this chapter has a quick reference to the GamerServices namespace with all of its great classes, structures, and enumerations. Then, we jump into the code and experiment with these great features!

As a side note, most of the features covered in this chapter require an Xbox Live Gold account, and it goes without saying that you need to have your Xbox 360 connected to the Net in order to retrieve the information provided by these features in the GamerServices namespace. If you don't have your Xbox 360 online, most of the examples in this chapter will not work. As for the Windows version of the examples, these features don't make much sense on Windows, so there will likely be some null values and connectivity failures even though the code will still compile for the Windows platform. This chapter is primarily focused on the Xbox 360. Here's what I'll be covering:

- GamerServices classes
- GamerServices interfaces
- GamerServices structures

- `GamerServices` enumerations

- `GamerProfile` Demo program

Microsoft.Xna.Framework.GamerServices Reference

`GamerServices` is one of the largest namespaces in the XNA Framework. This namespace provides information about the gamer profile, which is basically an Xbox Live membership account with all the stored data about that player's experiences on Xbox Live, such as games played, achievements, friends, avatar, gamer profile picture, game rank leaderboards, and related information. There's a lot of information to cover in this chapter, which begins with a quick reference to the most important details first, followed by a sample program.

Note

Microsoft disclaims the availability of the `GamerServices` features on the Windows platform with this comment: "Games for Windows Live is unavailable to finished games. This functionality is not included in the redistributable version of the XNA Framework. A game that attempts to use these components without XNA Game Studio installed will result in a GamerServicesNotAvailableException."

Classes

Following are the classes found within the `GamerServices` namespace.

Achievement

`public sealed class Achievement`

Describes a single achievement, including the achievement name, description, picture, and whether it has been achieved by the currently signed-in gamer. Unfortunately, you can't use achievements in indie games unless they have been officially published on Xbox Live (which involves a contract with Microsoft).

Note

Microsoft disclaimer: "This class and all related methods and properties will only retrieve a calculated result for titles approved to access Xbox Live services through the Xbox Live Registered Developer Program. For Xbox Live Indie games, the properties in this class will not return a calculated result and related methods will report a NotSupportedException."

Public Properties

Description	Gets the localized achievement description string.
DisplayBeforeEarned	Gets whether this achievement should be displayed before it is earned.
EarnedDateTime	Gets the date at which this achievement was earned.
EarnedOnline	Gets whether this achievement was earned while online.
GamerScore	Gets the amount of gamer score awarded for earning this achievement.
HowToEarn	Gets the localized description of the steps necessary to earn the achievement.
IsEarned	Gets whether the current player has earned this achievement.
Key	Gets the achievement key string.
Name	Gets the localized achievement name string, for display to the user.

Public Methods

GetPicture	Gets the image associated with this achievement.

AchievementCollection

Collection holding the achievements belonging to a signed-in gamer.

Note

Microsoft disclaimer: "For Xbox Live Indie games, the properties in this class will not return a calculated result and related methods will report a NotSupportedException."

Public Properties

Count	Gets the number of objects in the collection.
Item	Properties that retrieve an achievement from the collection.

Public Methods

GetEnumerator	Gets an enumerator that can iterate through this Achievement Collection.

AvatarAnimation

Provides methods and properties for animating an avatar using standard animations (for example, celebrate).

Public Properties

BoneTransforms	Gets the current position of the bones at the time specified by CurrentPosition.
CurrentPosition	Gets or sets the current time position in the animation.

(Continued)

Expression	Gets the expression of the related animation at the current time position.
IsDisposed	Gets the disposed state of the avatar animation.
Length	Gets the length of the current animation.
Public Methods	
Update	Updates the current time position of the avatar animation.

AvatarDescription

Provides access to the methods and properties of the description data for an avatar.

Public Properties	
BodyType	Gets the body type of the avatar based on the description data.
Description	Internal description buffer of the avatar, stored as a byte buffer.
Height	Height of the avatar, from the feet to the top of the head.
IsValid	Determines whether the internal data buffer is valid.
Public Methods	
BeginGetFromGamer	Begins the process of getting an AvatarDescription object for a specified gamertag.
CreateRandom	Creates an AvatarDescription object with random gender, features, and clothing.
EndGetFromGamer	Ends the process of getting an AvatarDescription object for a specified gamertag.
Public Events	
Changed	Occurs when a gamer's avatar changes.

AvatarRenderer

Provides properties and methods for rendering a standard avatar.

Public Fields	
BoneCount	Number of bones in the avatar model.
Public Properties	
AmbientLightColor	Gets or sets the color of the ambient light used by the avatar renderer.
BindPose	Gets the collection of bind pose positions for each bone of the avatar model.
IsLoaded	Gets the loaded state of the avatar.
LightColor	Gets or sets the color of the directional light used by the avatar renderer.
LightDirection	Gets or sets the direction of the directional light used by the avatar renderer.

ParentBones	Collection of the parent indices for each bone in the related BindPose collection.
Projection	Gets or sets the projection matrix for the avatar.
State	Gets the state of the avatar.
View	Gets or sets the view matrix for the avatar.
World	Gets or sets the world matrix for the avatar.
Public Methods	
Draw	Draws the avatar to the current render target.

FriendCollection

Represents the complete friends list of a local gamer.

Public Properties	
Count	Gets the number of elements contained in the ReadOnlyCollection <(Of <(T>)>) instance.
Item	Gets the element at the specified index.
Protected Properties	
Items	Returns the IList that the ReadOnlyCollection wraps.
Public Methods	
GetEnumerator	Returns a strongly typed GamerCollection. GamerCollectionEnumerator structure that can iterate through a GamerCollection.

FriendGamer

Provides the presence information of a friend of the local gamer.

Public Properties	
DisplayName	Gets the display name string for the gamer.
FriendRequest-ReceivedFrom	Gets whether the local gamer who requested the friends list has received a friend request from this gamer.
FriendRequestSentTo	Gets whether the local gamer who requested the friends list has sent a friend request to this gamer.
Gamertag	Gets the gamertag string.
HasVoice	Gets whether this friend currently has voice capability.
InviteAccepted	Gets whether this friend has accepted an invitation from the local gamer who requested the friends list.

(Continued)

InviteReceivedFrom	Gets whether the local gamer who requested the friends list has received an invitation from this friend.
InviteRejected	Gets whether this friend has rejected an invitation from the local gamer who requested the friends list.
InviteSentTo	Gets whether the local gamer who requested the friends list has sent an invitation to this friend.
IsAway	Gets whether this friend is currently away from the computer or console.
IsBusy	Gets whether this friend is currently busy.
IsJoinable	Gets whether this friend is currently in a public session that can be joined.
IsOnline	Gets whether this friend is currently online.
IsPlaying	Gets whether this friend is currently playing a game.
LeaderboardWriter	Gets an object that can be used to write leaderboard statistics for this gamer.
Presence	Gets a presence string describing what this friend is currently doing.
Tag	Gets or sets a custom object that can be used to attach arbitrary user-defined data to the gamer.

Public Methods

BeginGetProfile	Starts an asynchronous profile read operation.
EndGetProfile	Ends an asynchronous profile read operation.
GetProfile	Reads profile data for this gamer.

GameDefaults

Describes a gamer's preferred settings.

Public Properties

AccelerateWith-Buttons	Gets whether the gamer prefers to use controller buttons to accelerate in racing games.
AutoAim	Gets whether the title should automatically correct the gamer's aim.
AutoCenter	Gets whether the title should automatically center the view when the gamer moves.
BrakeWithButtons	Gets whether the gamer prefers to use controller buttons to brake in racing games.
Controller Sensitivity	Gets the preferred controller sensitivity setting for this gamer.
GameDifficulty	Gets the preferred difficulty setting for this gamer.
InvertYAxis	Gets whether the gamer prefers to invert the y-axis input of the controller.
ManualTransmission	Gets whether the gamer prefers to drive a manual shift transmission in racing games.
MoveWithRight ThumbStick	Gets whether the gamer prefers to move using the right thumbstick.
PrimaryColor	Gets the preferred color for the player character.

| RacingCameraAngle | Gets the gamer's preferred camera angle for racing games. |
| SecondaryColor | Gets a secondary color selection for the player character. |

Gamer

Abstract base class for types that represent game players (profiles that have an associated gamertag). The concrete types SignedInGamer and NetworkGamer derive from this. For the NetworkGamer class, see Chapter 10, "Net."

Public Properties

DisplayName	Gets the display name string for the gamer.
Gamertag	Gets the gamertag string.
LeaderboardWriter	Gets an object that can be used to write leaderboard statistics for this gamer.
SignedInGamers	Represents a collection of all gamers on the local system.
Tag	Gets or sets a custom object that can be used to attach arbitrary user-defined data to the gamer.

Public Methods

BeginGetFrom Gamertag	Begins the process of getting a Gamer object for a specified gamertag.
BeginGetPartner Token	Begins the asynchronous process of getting the partner token for this gamer.
BeginGetProfile	Starts an asynchronous profile read operation.
EndGetFrom Gamertag	Ends the process of getting a Gamer object for a specified gamertag.
EndGetPartner Token	Retrieves the results from an asynchronous request for the partner token for this gamer.
EndGetProfile	Ends an asynchronous profile read operation.
GetFromGamertag	Returns a Gamer object for the specified gamertag.
GetPartnerToken	Gets the partner token for this gamer.
GetProfile	Reads profile data for this gamer.

GamerCollection

Represents a collection of gamers. This collection cannot be modified and is updated automatically during the call to Update(). This class inherits from ReadOnlyCollection and uses the GamerCollectionEnumerator structure, but exposes no new properties or methods of its own.

GamerPresence

Provides properties to set the rich presence state for a locally signed-in gamer profile.

Public Properties	
PresenceMode	Gets or sets the current presence mode for this gamer.
PresenceValue	Gets or sets a custom presence value.

GamerPrivilegeException

Thrown if a gamer services or multiplayer API is called without a valid, signed-in profile. This class exposes no new properties or methods beyond its base class.

GamerPrivileges

Describes what operations a gamer is allowed to perform. GamerPrivileges can be defined by parental control settings, and will also be set automatically in response to things like age, region, and whether the gamer has a Live Gold or Live Silver account. Games do not need to explicitly check privileges because a GamerPrivilegeException will be thrown if they try to perform an unsupported operation, but these privilege bits may be useful to detect that an operation is unavailable before calling it so the relevant menu option can be grayed out.

Public Properties	
Allow-Communication	Checks whether this gamer is allowed to send and receive communications using voice, text, messaging, or game invites.
AllowOnlineSessions	Checks whether this gamer is allowed to play in online multiplayer sessions.
AllowPremium-Content	Checks whether this gamer is allowed to access premium content.
AllowProfile-Viewing	Checks whether this gamer is allowed to view the profiles of other gamers.
AllowPurchase-Content	Checks whether this gamer is allowed to purchase content from Live Marketplace.
AllowTradeContent-	Checks whether this gamer is allowed to trade content with other gamers.
AllowUser-CreatedContent	Checks whether this gamer is allowed to access user content that was created by other gamers.

GamerProfile

Profile settings describing information about a gamer such as the gamer's motto, reputation, and picture. This data is accessible for both locally signed-in profiles and remote gamers that you are playing with in a multiplayer session.

Public Properties

GamerScore	Gets the GamerScore of this gamer.
GamerZone	Gets the GamerZone setting.
Motto	Gets the gamer motto string.
Region	Gets the region of this gamer.
Reputation	Gets the gamer reputation, as a number of stars ranging 0 to 5.
TitlesPlayed	Gets the number of titles this gamer has played.
TotalAchievements	Gets the total number of achievements this gamer has obtained.

Public Methods

GetGamerPicture	Gets the gamer picture associated with this profile.

GamerServicesComponent

Wraps the functionality of the GamerServicesDispatcher.

Public Methods

Initialize	Initializes the GamerServicesDispatcher.
Update	Updates the GamerServicesDispatcher.

GamerServicesDispatcher

Implements the Windows-specific portion of a GamerServicesDispatcher class.

Public Properties

IsInitialized	Determines whether Initialize has been called.
WindowHandle	Gets or sets the handle to the underlying game window.

Public Methods

Initialize	Initializes gamer-services functionality for the game, automatically choosing the most appropriate gamer-service type for the platform.
Update	Updates the status of gamer services and raises related events.

GamerServicesNotAvailableException

Thrown if the gamer services system cannot be successfully initialized.

GameUpdateRequiredException

The exception thrown when a game (title) update is required in order to use Xbox Live.

Guide

Provides access to the Guide user interface.

Public Properties

IsScreenSaverEnabled	Gets or sets the current state of the screen saver.
IsTrialMode	Determines whether the game is running in limited trial mode.
IsVisible	Determines whether a Guide user-interface screen is active.
NotificationPosition	Determines where notifications appear on the screen.
SimulateTrialMode	Allows titles to simulate trial mode restrictions when testing using the development configuration.

Public Methods

BeginShowKeyboardInput	Overloads for showing the software keyboard interface asynchronously.
BeginShowMessageBox	Begins the process of displaying a message box with the specified parameters.
DelayNotifications	Delays system notifications for the specified amount of time.
EndShowKeyboardInput	Ends the display of the keyboard input dialog box.
EndShowMessageBox	Ends the display of a message box.
ShowComposeMessage	Shows the Compose Message user interface.
ShowFriendRequest	Shows the Friend Request user interface.
ShowFriends	Shows the Friends user interface.
ShowGameInvite	Overloads to display the Game Invitation user interface.
ShowGamerCard	Shows the Gamer Card user interface.
ShowMarketplace	Displays the Marketplace user interface.
ShowMessages	Shows the Messages user interface.
ShowParty	Shows the Xbox Live Party screen.
ShowPartySessions	Shows the Play with Party Member screen.
ShowPlayerReview	Shows the Player Review user interface.
ShowPlayers	Shows the Players user interface.
ShowSignIn	Shows the user interface a gamer uses for signing into Xbox Live.

GuideAlreadyVisibleException

Thrown if an attempt is made to display a component of the Guide user interface when a Guide component is already displayed.

InviteAcceptedEventArgs

Represents the arguments passed to an InviteAccepted event.

Public Properties	
Gamer	The signed-in gamer who is accepting the game invitation.
IsCurrentSession	Indicates if the invitation is for the current local session.

LeaderboardEntry

Class representing a single row of a leaderboard, holding all the information a specific gamer has uploaded to the board.

Public Properties	
Columns	Provides access to the columns for this leaderboard entry.
Gamer	Provides access to gamer information for this leaderboard entry.
Rating	Provides access to the rating associated with this leaderboard entry.

LeaderboardReader

Reads data from leaderboards.

Public Properties	
CanPageDown	Provides information about whether there are more leaderboard entries after the current page of entries.
CanPageUp	Provides information about whether there are more leaderboard entries before the current page of entries.
Entries	Gets the collection of leaderboard entries for the leaderboard.
LeaderboardIdentity	The identity of the leaderboard.
PageStart	Gets the index of the leaderboard entry at the start of the current page.
TotalLeaderboardSize	Provides information about the total number of entries in the leaderboard.

(Continued)

Public Methods

BeginPageDown	Begins an asynchronous read of the page of leaderboard data after the current page.
BeginPageUp	Begins an asynchronous read of the page of leaderboard data before the current page.
BeginRead	Methods for reading a leaderboard asynchronously.
EndPageDown	Checks the result of an asynchronous PageDown operation.
EndPageUp	Checks the result of an asynchronous PageUp operation.
EndRead	Checks the result of an asynchronous Read operation.
PageDown	Reads the next page of leaderboard data synchronously.
PageUp	Reads the previous page of leaderboard data synchronously.
Read	Method for synchronous reading of leaderboard data.

LeaderboardWriter

Records leaderboard data for players in a NetworkSession. Data can be written at any time during gameplay, but is only flushed to the server when the host calls EndGame. Data may be written for both local and remote gamers using the following rules:

- Ranked sessions can write to both arbitrated and non-arbitrated leaderboards.

- Other session types can only write to non-arbitrated leaderboards.

- Arbitrated statistics should be written by all machines for all gamers.

- Non-arbitrated statistics should only be written by their local machine.

- In ranked sessions, all machines should report TrueSkill for all gamers.

- In other session types, only the host should report TrueSkill data.

- Leaderboards can only be written while in a NetworkSession, and while in the gameplay state rather than in the lobby. To write scores from a single-player game, create a session using NetworkSessionType. LocalWithLeaderboards.

Public Methods

GetLeaderboard	Gets a leaderboard entry that can be used to write to a specified leaderboard.

NetworkException

Thrown if there is a network-communications failure.

NetworkNotAvailableException

Thrown if a network connection is unavailable.

PropertyDictionary

Holds a set of properties used to define presence states or leaderboard column values.

Public Properties	
Count	Gets the number of elements contained in this PropertyDictionary.
Item	Gets or sets the element with the specified key.
Public Methods	
ContainsKey	Determines whether the PropertyDictionary contains an element with the specified key.
GetEnumerator	Returns an enumerator that iterates through a collection of key/value pairs that represent elements in the PropertyDictionary.
GetValueDateTime	Gets the value of the property with the specified key, as a System.DateTime.
GetValueDouble	Gets the value of the property with the specified key, as a System.Double.
GetValueInt32	Gets the value of the property with the specified key, as a System.Int32.
GetValueInt64	Gets the value of the property with the specified key, as a System.Int64.
GetValueOutcome	Gets the value of the property with the specified key, as a LeaderboardOutcome.
GetValueSingle	Gets the value of the property with the specified key, as a System.Single.
GetValueStream	Gets the value of the property with the specified key, as a System.IO.Stream.
GetValueString	Gets the value of the property with the specified key, as a System.String.
GetValueTimeSpan	Gets the value of the property with the specified key, as a System.TimeSpan.
SetValue	Method to set the value of the property with the specified key.
TryGetValue	Determines if a value for the specified key exists in the PropertyDictionary.

SignedInEventArgs

Represents the arguments passed to a SignedIn event.

Public Properties	
Gamer	Gets the gamer who just signed in.

SignedInGamer

Represents a gamer (a profile that has an associated gamertag) on the local system. This class inherits from the abstract Gamer class, so refer to that class for more details.

Public Properties	
GameDefaults	Describes a gamer's preferred settings.
IsGuest	Determines whether the gamer is the guest of an Xbox Live–enabled profile.
IsSignedInToLive	Determines whether the gamer has an Xbox Live–enabled profile.
PartySize	Gets the current party size.
PlayerIndex	Gets the index of the gamer.
Presence	Gets an object that may be used to set the rich presence state for this gamer.
Privileges	Describes what operations a gamer is allowed to perform.
Public Methods	
BeginAwardAchievement	Starts an asynchronous operation to award an achievement to a locally signed-in gamer.
BeginGetAchievements	Starts an asynchronous achievement query operation.
EndAwardAchievement	Ends an asynchronous achievement award operation.
EndGetAchievements	Ends an asynchronous achievement query operation.
GetAchievements	Returns the collection of all achievements that may be earned by this gamer.
GetFriends	Reads the friends list of this local gamer. This includes both the gamertags of the friends and their current presence information.
IsFriend	Queries whether the specified gamer is a friend of this local gamer.
IsHeadset	Determines if the microphone associated with this signed-in gamer is a headset.
Public Events	
SignedIn	Occurs when a new gamer signs into the local system.
SignedOut	Occurs when a gamer signs out on the local system.

SignedInGamerCollection

Represents a collection of gamers on the local system.

Public Properties

Item	Gets a specific `SignedInGamer` object.

SignedOutEventArgs

Represents the arguments passed to a `SignedOut` event.

Public Properties

Gamer	Gets the gamer that just signed out.

Interfaces

The following interface is found in the `GamerServices` namespace.

IAvatarAnimation

Provides methods and properties for animating an avatar using custom animations.

Public Properties

BoneTransforms	Gets the current position of the bones at the time specified by `CurrentPosition`.
CurrentPosition	Gets or sets the current time position in the animation.
Expression	Gets the expression of the related animation at the current time position.
Length	Gets the length of the current animation.

Public Methods

Update	Updates the current time position of the avatar animation.

Structures

The following structures are found in the `GamerServices` namespace.

AvatarExpression

Contains the various components of the avatar's face, such as the left and right eyebrows.

Public Properties

LeftEye	Gets or sets the current texture for the avatar's left eye.
LeftEyebrow	Gets or sets the current texture for the avatar's left eyebrow.
Mouth	Gets or sets the current texture for the avatar's mouth.
RightEye	Gets or sets the current texture for the avatar's right eye.
RightEyebrow	Gets or sets the current texture for the avatar's right eyebrow.

GamerCollection.GamerCollectionEnumerator

Provides the ability to iterate through the gamers in a GamerCollection.

Public Properties

Current	Gets the current element in the GamerCollection.

Public Methods

MoveNext	Advances the enumerator to the next element of the GamerCollection.

LeaderboardIdentity

Contains leaderboard identity information for a particular leaderboard.

Public Properties

GameMode	Provides access to the game mode for this leaderboard identity.
Key	The key string associated with this leaderboard identity.

Public Methods

Create	Creates a leaderboard identity.

Enumerations

Following are the enumerations in the GamerServices namespace.

AvatarAnimationPreset

Defines standard animations for avatars. Note that additional animations can be downloaded from the XNA Web site as a collection, as can a sample bone structure mesh for use in creating your own custom avatar animations.

Celebrate	Gender-neutral, celebrating.
Clap	Gender-neutral, applauding.
FemaleAngry	Female, angry.
FemaleConfused	Female, confused.
FemaleCry	Female, cry.
FemaleIdleCheckNails	Female, checking nails.
FemaleIdleFixShoe	Female, fixing shoe.
FemaleIdleLookAround	Female, looking around.
FemaleIdleShiftWeight	Female, shifting weight from one foot to another.
FemaleLaugh	Female, laughing.
FemaleShocked	Female, shocked or surprised.
FemaleYawn	Female, yawning.
MaleAngry	Male, angry.
MaleConfused	Male, confused.
MaleCry	Male, crying.
MaleIdleCheckHand	Male, checking hand.
MaleIdleLookAround	Male, looking around.
MaleIdleShiftWeight	Male, shifting weight from one foot to another.
MaleIdleStretch	Male, stretching.
MaleLaugh	Male, laughing.
MaleSurprised	Male, surprised.
MaleYawn	Male, yawning.
Stand0	Gender-neutral, standing, variation 0.
Stand1	Gender-neutral, standing, variation 1.
Stand2	Gender-neutral, standing, variation 2.
Stand3	Gender-neutral, standing, variation 3.
Stand4	Gender-neutral, standing, variation 4.
Stand5	Gender-neutral, standing, variation 5.
Stand6	Gender-neutral, standing, variation 6.
Stand7	Gender-neutral, standing, variation 7.
Wave	Gender-neutral, waving.

AvatarBodyType

Defines the body type of the avatar.

Female	Female avatar.
Male	Male avatar.

AvatarBone

Defines a list of the useful bones of the avatar model.

AnkleLeft (11)	Left ankle.
AnkleRight (15)	Right ankle.
BackLower (1)	Lower back.
BackUpper (5)	Upper back.
CollarLeft (12)	Left collar.
CollarRight (16)	Right collar.
ElbowLeft (25)	Left elbow.
ElbowRight (28)	Right elbow.
FingerIndex2Left (51)	Left index finger, second joint.
FingerIndex2Right (56)	Right index finger, second joint.
FingerIndex3Left (61)	Left index finger, third joint.
FingerIndex3Right (66)	Right index finger, third joint.
FingerIndexLeft (37)	Left index finger, first joint.
FingerIndexRight (44)	Right index finger, first joint.
FingerMiddle2Left (52)	Left middle finger, second joint.
FingerMiddle2Right (57)	Right middle finger, second joint.
FingerMiddle3Left (62)	Left middle finger, third joint.
FingerMiddle3Right (67)	Right middle finger, third joint.
FingerMiddleLeft (38)	Left middle finger, first joint.
FingerMiddleRight (45)	Right middle finger, first joint.
FingerRing2Left (53)	Left ring finger, second joint.
FingerRing2Right (58)	Right ring finger, second joint.
FingerRing3Left (63)	Left ring finger, third joint.
FingerRing3Right (68)	Right ring finger, third joint.
FingerRingLeft (39)	Left ring finger, first joint.
FingerRingRight (46)	Right ring finger, first joint.
FingerSmall2Left (54)	Left pinky finger, second joint.
FingerSmall2Right (59)	Right pinky finger, second joint.
FingerSmall3Left (64)	Left pinky finger, third joint.
FingerSmall3Right (69)	Right pinky finger, third joint.
FingerSmallLeft (40)	Left pinky finger, first joint.
FingerSmallRight (47)	Right pinky finger, second joint.
FingerThumb2Left (55)	Left thumb, second joint.
FingerThumb2Right (60)	Right thumb, second joint.
FingerThumb3Left (65)	Left thumb, third joint.
FingerThumb3Right (70)	Right thumb, third joint.

FingerThumbLeft (43)	Left thumb, first joint.
FingerThumbRight (50)	Right thumb, first joint.
Head (19)	Head.
HipLeft (2)	Left hip.
HipRight (3)	Right hip.
KneeLeft (6)	Left knee.
KneeRight (8)	Right knee.
Neck (14)	Neck.
PropLeft (41)	A separate object held in the left hand.
PropRight (48)	A separate object held in the right hand.
Root (0)	Root bone of the avatar skeleton.
ShoulderLeft (20)	Left shoulder.
ShoulderRight (22)	Right shoulder.
SpecialLeft (42)	A special bone located near the left hand of the avatar model.
SpecialRight (49)	A special bone located near the right hand of the avatar model.
ToeLeft (21)	Left toe.
ToeRight (23)	Right toe.
WristLeft (33)	Left wrist.
WristRight (36)	Right wrist.

AvatarEye

Defines the standard animation textures for an avatar's eyes.

Angry	Angry eye position.
Blink	Blinking eye position.
Confused	Confused eye position.
Happy	Happy eye position.
Laughing	Laughing eye position.
LookDown	Looking down eye position.
LookLeft	Looking left position.
LookRight	Looking right eye position.
LookUp	Looking up eye position.
Neutral	Neutral eye position.
Sad	Sad eye position.
Shocked	Shocked eye position.
Sleeping	Sleeping eye position.
Yawning	Yawning eye position.

AvatarEyebrow

Defines the standard animation textures for an avatar's eyebrows.

Angry	Angry eyebrow position.
Confused	Confused eyebrow position.
Neutral	Neutral eyebrow position.
Raised	Raised eyebrow position.
Sad	Sad eyebrow position.

AvatarMouth

Defines the standard animation textures for an avatar's mouth.

Angry	Angry mouth position.
Confused	Confused mouth position.
Happy	Happy mouth position.
Laughing	Laughing mouth position.
Neutral	Neutral mouth position.
PhoneticAi	Phonetic "ai" mouth position (for lip sync).
PhoneticDth	Phonetic "dth" mouth position (for lip sync).
PhoneticEe	Phonetic "ee" mouth position (for lip sync).
PhoneticFv	Phonetic "fv" mouth position (for lip sync).
PhoneticL	Phonetic "l" mouth position (for lip sync).
PhoneticO	Phonetic "o" mouth position (for lip sync).
PhoneticW	Phonetic "w" mouth position (for lip sync).
Sad	Sad mouth position.
Shocked	Shocked mouth position.

AvatarRendererState

Indicates avatar state.

Loading (0)	The avatar is still loading required assets.
Ready (1)	Loading is complete.
Unavailable (2)	The avatar is unavailable.

ControllerSensitivity

Indicates how sensitive this gamer prefers controller input to be.

High	Highly sensitive controller input is preferred.
Low	Below-average sensitivity is preferred.
Medium	Average controller sensitivity is preferred.

GameDifficulty

Indicates how difficult this gamer likes things to be.

Easy	Below-average difficulty.
Hard	Above-average difficulty.
Normal	Average difficulty.

GamerPresenceMode

Settings defining the status string that will appear when you view a friend through the Xbox Live Guide or on Xbox.com. Use the PresenceMode property to set this option.

ArcadeMode	Displays the Arcade Mode status string.
AtMenu	Displays the At Menu status string.
BattlingBoss	Displays the Battling Boss status string.
CampaignMode	Displays the Campaign Mode status string.
ChallengeMode	Displays the Challenge Mode status string.
ConfiguringSettings	Displays the Configuring Settings status string.
CoOpLevel	Displays the Co-Op: Level status string. Includes a numeric value specified with PresenceValue.
CoOpStage	Displays the Co-Op: Stage status string. Includes a numeric value specified with PresenceValue.
CornflowerBlue	Displays the Cornflower Blue status string.
CustomizingPlayer	Displays the Customizing Player status string.
DifficultyEasy	Displays the Difficulty: Easy status string.
DifficultyExtreme	Displays the Difficulty: Extreme status string.
DifficultyHard	Displays the Difficulty: Hard status string.
DifficultyMedium	Displays the Difficulty: Medium status string.
EditingLevel	Displays the Editing Level status string.
ExplorationMode	Displays the Exploration Mode status string.
FoundSecret	Displays the Found Secret status string.

(Continued)

FreePlay	Displays the Free Play status string.
GameOver	Displays the Game Over status string.
InCombat	Displays the In Combat status string.
InGameStore	Displays the In Game Store status string.
Level	Displays the Level status string. Includes a numeric value specified with PresenceValue.
LocalCoOp	Displays the Local Co-Op status string.
LocalVersus	Displays the Local Versus status string.
LookingForGames	Displays the Looking For Games status string.
Losing	Displays the Losing status string.
Multiplayer	Displays the Multiplayer status string.
NearlyFinished	Displays the Nearly Finished status string.
None	Displays the No Presence String Displayed status string.
OnARoll	Displays the On a Roll status string.
OnlineCoOp	Displays the Online Co-Op status string.
OnlineVersus	Displays the Online Versus status string.
Outnumbered	Displays the Outnumbered status string.
Paused	Displays the Paused status string.
PlayingMinigame	Displays the Playing Minigame status string.
PlayingWithFriends	Displays the Playing With Friends status string.
PracticeMode	Displays the Practice Mode status string.
PuzzleMode	Displays the Puzzle Mode status string.
ScenarioMode	Displays the Scenario Mode status string.
Score	Displays the Score status string. Includes a numeric value specified with PresenceValue.
ScoreIsTied	Displays the Score is Tied status string.
SettingUpMatch	Displays the Setting Up Match status string.
SinglePlayer	Displays the Single Player status string.
Stage	Displays the Stage status string. Includes a numeric value specified with PresenceValue.
StartingGame	Displays the Starting Game status string.
StoryMode	Displays the Story Mode status string.
StuckOnAHardBit	Displays the Stuck on a Hard Bit status string.
SurvivalMode	Displays the Survival Mode status string.
TimeAttack	Displays the Time Attack status string.
TryingForRecord	Displays the Trying For Record status string.
TutorialMode	Displays the Tutorial Mode status string.
VersusComputer	Displays the Versus Computer status string.
VersusScore	Displays the Versus: Score status string. Includes a numeric value specified with PresenceValue.
WaitingForPlayers	Displays the Waiting For Players status string.

WaitingInLobby	Displays the Waiting In Lobby status string.
WastingTime	Displays the Wasting Time status string.
WatchingCredits	Displays the Watching Credits status string.
WatchingCutscene	Displays the Watching Cutscene status string.
Winning	Displays the Winning status string.
WonTheGame	Displays the Won the Game status string.

GamerPrivilegeSetting

Describes the conditions in which a privilege is available.

Blocked	This privilege is not available for the current gamer profile.
Everyone	This privilege is available for the current gamer profile.
FriendsOnly	This privilege is only available for friends of the current gamer profile. Use the IsFriend method to check which gamers are friends.

GamerZone

The style of social gaming preferred by this Xbox Live member.

Family	Family-friendly gameplay.
Pro	Competitive gameplay.
Recreation	Non-competitive gameplay.
Underground	Alternative approach to gameplay.
Unknown	Unknown.

LeaderboardKey

Values used with LeaderboardIdentity.Create to select which leaderboard to access.

BestScoreLifeTime	Best lifetime score for this player and his or her Xbox Live friends.
BestScoreRecent	Best recent scores for this player and his or her Xbox Live friends.
BestTimeLifeTime	Best lifetime times for this player and his or her Xbox Live friends.
BestTimeRecent	Best recent times for this player and his or her Xbox Live friends.

LeaderboardOutcome

Values used to provide an outcome for a player's leaderboard entry.

Loss	Player lost the match.
None	No result reported.
Tie	Match resulted in a tie; no player won.
Win	Player won the match.

MessageBoxIcon

Defines the different icons for a message box.

Alert	Displays the Alert icon.
Error	Displays the Error icon.
None	No icon is displayed.
Warning	Displays the Warning icon.

NotificationPosition

Determines where notifications appear on the screen.

BottomCenter	Positions the message box at the bottom of the screen and centered.
BottomLeft	Positions the message box at the bottom-left of the screen.
BottomRight	Positions the message box at the bottom-right of the screen.
Center	Positions the message box at the center of the screen.
CenterLeft	Positions the message box at the center of the screen and left-aligned.
CenterRight	Positions the message box at the center of the screen and right-aligned.
TopCenter	Positions the message box at the top of the screen and centered.
TopLeft	Positions the message box at the top-left of the screen.
TopRight	Positions the message box at the top-right of the screen.

RacingCameraAngle

Indicates which camera angle this gamer prefers to use in racing games.

Back	Traditional third-person camera view from behind the car.
Front	Camera view from in front of the car. The car itself is not visible.
Inside	Camera view from inside the car, looking through the windscreen.

GAMERPROFILE DEMO PROGRAM

To demonstrate the GamerServices namespace, I've prepared the following sample program, called GamerProfile Demo, to print some information on the screen about the currently logged-in profile. You will need to run this example on your Xbox 360, as it will not display anything under Windows (where no gamer profile exists). You do not need to have an active Xbox Live membership for this to work, but some of the information is only useful for an active account. Figure 6.1 shows the program running on an Xbox 360 with my gamer profile displayed.

The key to accessing the GamerServices class is to add a new GamerServices-Component to the public Components collection, usually in the constructor of the Game class:

```
Components.Add(new GamerServicesComponent(this));
```

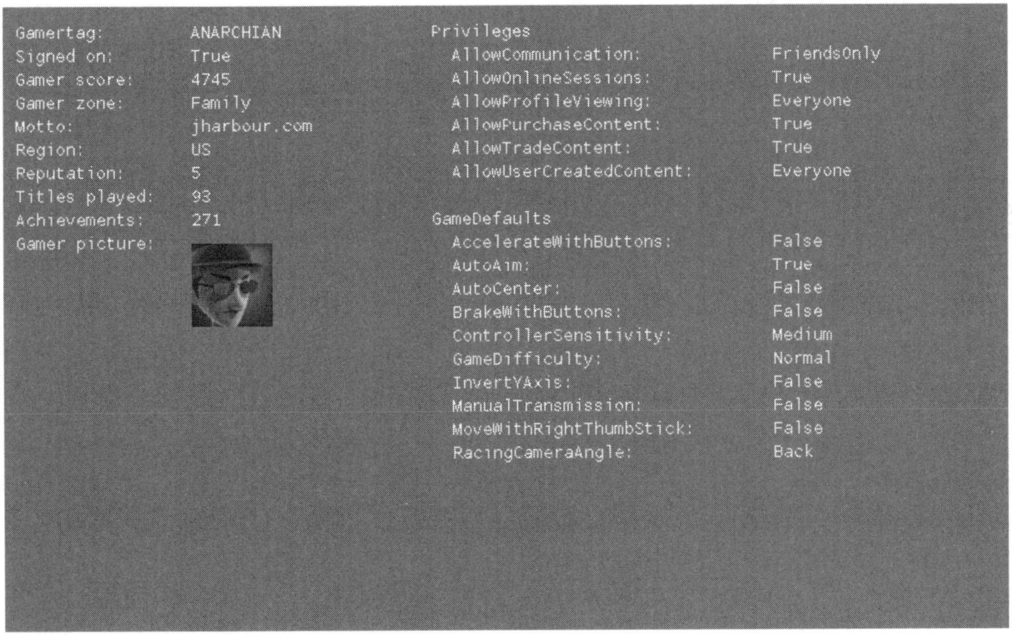

Figure 6.1
The GamerProfile Demo displays information about your Xbox Live gamer profile, but it only runs on an Xbox 360.

With the component added and running, you can access the currently signed-in gamer profiles—yes, that includes co-players currently using the Xbox. The following code iterates through the currently signed-in profiles to retrieve the name of each one. (Note: Normally, only one profile will be active at a time—your own profile.)

```
foreach (SignedInGamer gamer in SignedInGamer.SignedInGamers)
{
}
```

To grab just the default profile, you can just look at `PlayerIndex.One`:

```
if (Gamer.SignedInGamers[PlayerIndex.One] != null)
{
}
```

To keep the profile information up to date, we need to add this line to the `Update()` function:

```
GamerServicesDispatcher.Update();
```

Based on the reference information covered in this chapter and the `SignedInGamer` class, the code in Listing 6.1 should provide some pointers into the type of data available from the gamer profile.

Listing 6.1   Data in the Gamer Profile

```
using System;
using System.Collections.Generic;
using System.Linq;
using Microsoft.Xna.Framework;
using Microsoft.Xna.Framework.Audio;
using Microsoft.Xna.Framework.Content;
using Microsoft.Xna.Framework.GamerServices;
using Microsoft.Xna.Framework.Graphics;
using Microsoft.Xna.Framework.Input;
using Microsoft.Xna.Framework.Media;
using Microsoft.Xna.Framework.Net;
using Microsoft.Xna.Framework.Storage;

namespace GamerServices_Demo
{
public class Game1 : Microsoft.Xna.Framework.Game
```

```
{
    GraphicsDeviceManager graphics;
    SpriteBatch spriteBatch;
    SpriteFont font;
    GamerProfile profile;
    SignedInGamer gamer;
    string labels1 = "", labels2 = "";
    string values1 = "", values2 = "";
    Texture2D picture;

    public Game1()
    {
        graphics = new GraphicsDeviceManager(this);
        Content.RootDirectory = "Content";
        Components.Add(new GamerServicesComponent(this));
    }

    protected override void Initialize()
    {
        base.Initialize();
    }

    protected override void LoadContent()
    {
        spriteBatch = new SpriteBatch(GraphicsDevice);
        font = Content.Load<SpriteFont>("font1");
    }
    protected override void UnloadContent() { }

    protected override void Update(GameTime gameTime)
    {
        if (GamePad.GetState(PlayerIndex.One).Buttons.Back ==
            ButtonState.Pressed)
            this.Exit();
        if (gamer == null)
        {
            if (Gamer.SignedInGamers[PlayerIndex.One] != null)
            {
                gamer = Gamer.SignedInGamers[PlayerIndex.One];
                profile = gamer.GetProfile();
```

```
            }
        }
        if (gamer != null)
        {
            if (picture == null)
            {
                picture = Texture2D.FromStream(this.GraphicsDevice,
                    profile.GetGamerPicture());
            }
            labels1 = "Gamertag: \n" +
                "Signed on: \n" +
                "Gamer score: \n" +
                "Gamer zone: \n" +
                "Motto: \n" +
                "Region: \n" +
                "Reputation: \n" +
                "Titles played: \n" +
                "Achievements: \n" +
                "Gamer picture: ";
            values1 = gamer.Gamertag + "\n" +
                gamer.IsSignedInToLive.ToString() + "\n" +
                profile.GamerScore.ToString() + "\n" +
                profile.GamerZone.ToString() + "\n" +
                profile.Motto + "\n" +
                profile.Region.Name + "\n" +
                profile.Reputation.ToString() + "\n" +
                profile.TitlesPlayed.ToString() + "\n" +
                profile.TotalAchievements.ToString() + "\n";
            labels2 = "Privileges \n" +
                "   AllowCommunication: \n" +
                "   AllowOnlineSessions: \n" +
                "   AllowProfileViewing: \n" +
                "   AllowPurchaseContent: \n" +
                "   AllowTradeContent: \n" +
                "   AllowUserCreatedContent: \n\n" +
                "GameDefaults \n" +
                "   AccelerateWithButtons: \n" +
                "   AutoAim: \n" +
                "   AutoCenter: \n" +
                "   BrakeWithButtons: \n" +
```

```
              "  ControllerSensitivity: \n" +
              "  GameDifficulty: \n" +
              "  InvertYAxis: \n" +
              "  ManualTransmission: \n" +
              "  MoveWithRightThumbStick: \n" +
              "  RacingCameraAngle: ";
        values2 = "\n" +
        gamer.Privileges.AllowCommunication.ToString() + "\n" +
        gamer.Privileges.AllowOnlineSessions.ToString() + "\n" +
        gamer.Privileges.AllowProfileViewing.ToString() + "\n" +
        gamer.Privileges.AllowPurchaseContent.ToString() + "\n" +
        gamer.Privileges.AllowTradeContent.ToString() + "\n" +
        gamer.Privileges.AllowUserCreatedContent.ToString() + "\n" +
        "\n\n" +
        gamer.GameDefaults.AccelerateWithButtons.ToString() + "\n" +
        gamer.GameDefaults.AutoAim.ToString() + "\n" +
        gamer.GameDefaults.AutoCenter.ToString() + "\n" +
        gamer.GameDefaults.BrakeWithButtons.ToString() + "\n" +
        gamer.GameDefaults.ControllerSensitivity.ToString() + "\n" +
        gamer.GameDefaults.GameDifficulty.ToString() + "\n" +
        gamer.GameDefaults.InvertYAxis.ToString() + "\n" +
        gamer.GameDefaults.ManualTransmission.ToString() + "\n" +
        gamer.GameDefaults.MoveWithRightThumbStick.ToString() + "\n" +
        gamer.GameDefaults.RacingCameraAngle.ToString();
    }
    GamerServicesDispatcher.Update();
    base.Update(gameTime);
}


protected override void Draw(GameTime gameTime)
{
    GraphicsDevice.Clear(Color.CornflowerBlue);
    spriteBatch.Begin();

    if (Environment.OSVersion.Platform != PlatformID.Xbox)
    {
        labels1 = "This demo only runs on an Xbox 360";
        values1 = "";
        labels2 = "";
        values2 = "";
```

```
        }

        //print first column
        print(10, 10, labels1, Color.White);
        print(150, 10, values1, Color.White);

        //print second column
        print(340, 10, labels2, Color.White);
        print(610, 10, values2, Color.White);

        //draw gamer picture
        if (picture != null)
        {
            Vector2 size = font.MeasureString(labels1);
            Vector2 pos = new Vector2(150, size.Y);
            spriteBatch.Draw(picture, pos, Color.White);
        }

        spriteBatch.End();
        base.Draw(gameTime);
    }

    void print(int x, int y, string text, Color color)
    {
        spriteBatch.DrawString(font, text,
            new Vector2((float)x, (float)y), color);
    }
}
}
```

SUMMARY

The GamerServices namespace contains a lot of amazing information about the gamer profile, including the gamer picture, gamer tag, friends list, and even the 3D avatar animations. We only scratched the surface of what's available in GamerServices with the sample program, but it should give you an idea about how to use this information in your own projects.

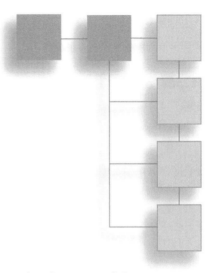

CHAPTER 7

GRAPHICS

This chapter provides a reference to and explores the features of the Graphics namespace, which is part of the XNA Framework. The Graphics namespace contains the low-level classes and methods for rendering 3D objects with hardware-accelerated video cards. We will study the Graphics namespace to learn the capabilities of XNA Game Studio with a special emphasis on 3D rendering on the Xbox 360.

Here's what this chapter will cover:

- Graphics classes
- Graphics interfaces
- Graphics structures
- Graphics enumerations

MICROSOFT.XNA.FRAMEWORK.GRAPHICS REFERENCE

The following pages provide a complete reference to the Graphics namespace, which is the largest of the namespaces in the XNA Framework. This is a great resource because it's easy to miss the many classes, structures, and events built in to the framework unless one sees a list of those features in a quick reference format, such as this one. As was the case in previous reference chapters, inherited items are omitted from the list of properties, methods, etc., for each item.

Classes

Following are the classes found within the `Graphics` namespace.

AlphaTestEffect

`public class AlphaTestEffect : Effect, IEffectMatrices, IEffectFog`

Contains a configurable effect that supports alpha testing.

Public Properties	
Alpha	Gets or sets the material alpha, which determines its transparency. Range is from 1 (fully opaque) to 0 (fully transparent).
AlphaFunction	Gets or sets the compare function for alpha test. The default value is Greater.
DiffuseColor	Gets or sets the diffuse color for a material. The range of color values is from 0 to 1.
FogColor	Gets or sets the fog color. The range of color values is from 0 to 1.
FogEnabled	Gets or sets the fog enable flag.
FogEnd	Gets or sets the maximum z value for fog, which ranges from 0 to 1.
FogStart	Gets or sets the minimum z value for fog, which ranges from 0 to 1.
Projection	Gets or sets the projection matrix.
ReferenceAlpha	Gets or sets the reference alpha value. The default value is 0.
Texture	Gets or sets the current texture.
VertexColorEnabled	Gets or sets whether vertex color is enabled.
View	Gets or sets the view matrix.
World	Gets or sets the world matrix.
Protected Methods	
OnApply	Computes derived parameter values immediately before applying the effect using a lazy architecture.

BasicEffect

`public class BasicEffect : Effect, IEffectMatrices, IEffectLights, IEffectFog`

Contains a basic rendering effect.

Public Properties	
Alpha	Gets or sets the material alpha, which determines its transparency. Range is from 1 (fully opaque) to 0 (fully transparent).
AmbientLightColor	Gets or sets the ambient color for a light. The range of color values is from 0 to 1.

DiffuseColor	Gets or sets the diffuse color for a material. The range of color values is from 0 to 1.
DirectionalLight0	Gets the first directional light for this effect.
DirectionalLight1	Gets the second directional light for this effect.
DirectionalLight2	Gets the third directional light for this effect.
EmissiveColor	Gets or sets the emissive color for a material. The range of color values is from 0 to 1.
FogColor	Gets or sets the fog color. The range of color values is from 0 to 1.
FogEnabled	Enables fog.
FogEnd	Gets or sets the maximum z value for fog, which ranges from 0 to 1.
FogStart	Gets or sets the minimum z value for fog, which ranges from 0 to 1.
LightingEnabled	Enables lighting for this effect.
PreferPerPixelLighting	Gets or sets a value indicating that per-pixel lighting should be used if it is available for the current adapter. Per-pixel lighting is available if a graphics adapter supports Pixel Shader Model 2.0.
Projection	Gets or sets the projection matrix.
SpecularColor	Gets or sets the specular color for a material. The range of color values is from 0 to 1.
SpecularPower	Gets or sets the specular power of this effect material.
Texture	Gets or sets a texture to be applied by this effect.
TextureEnabled	Enables textures for this effect.
VertexColorEnabled	Enables the use of vertex colors for this effect.
View	Gets or sets the view matrix.
World	Gets or sets the world matrix.

Public Methods

EnableDefaultLighting	Enables default lighting for this effect.

Protected Methods

OnApply	Computes derived parameter values immediately before applying the effect.

BlendState

`public class BlendState : GraphicsResource`

Contains the blend state for the device.

Public Fields

Additive	A built-in state object with settings for additive blend (that is, adding the destination data to the source data without using alpha).
AlphaBlend	A built-in state object with settings for alpha blend (that is, blending the source and destination data using alpha).

| NonPremultiplied | A built-in state object with settings for blending with non-premultipled alpha (that is, blending source and destination data using alpha while assuming the color data contains no alpha information). |
| Opaque | A built-in state object with settings for opaque blend (that is, overwriting the source with the destination data). |

Public Properties

AlphaBlendFunction	Gets or sets the arithmetic operation when blending alpha values. The default is `BlendFunction.Add`.
AlphaDestinationBlend	Gets or sets the blend factor for the destination alpha, which is the percentage of the destination alpha included in the blended result. The default is `Blend.One`.
AlphaSourceBlend	Gets or sets the alpha blend factor. The default is `Blend.One`.
BlendFactor	Gets or sets the four-component (RGBA) blend factor for alpha blending.
ColorBlendFunction	Gets or sets the arithmetic operation when blending color values. The default is `BlendFunction.Add`.
ColorDestinationBlend	Gets or sets the blend factor for the destination color. The default is `Blend.One`.
ColorSourceBlend	Gets or sets the blend factor for the source color. The default is `Blend.One`.
ColorWriteChannels	Gets or sets which color channels (RGBA) are enabled for writing during color blending. The default value is `ColorWriteChannels.None`.
ColorWriteChannels1	Gets or sets which color channels (RGBA) are enabled for writing during color blending. The default value is `ColorWriteChannels.None`.
ColorWriteChannels2	Gets or sets which color channels (RGBA) are enabled for writing during color blending. The default value is `ColorWriteChannels.None`.
ColorWriteChannels3	Gets or sets which color channels (RGBA) are enabled for writing during color blending. The default value is `ColorWriteChannels.None`.
MultiSampleMask	Gets or sets a bitmask, which defines which samples can be written during multisampling. The default is `0xffffffff`.

DepthStencilState

```
public class DepthStencilState : GraphicsResource
```

Contains the depth-stencil state for the device.

Public Fields

Default	A built-in state object with default settings for using a depth-stencil buffer.
DepthRead	A built-in state object with settings for enabling a read-only depth-stencil buffer.
None	A built-in state object with settings for not using a depth-stencil buffer.

Public Properties

CounterClockwiseStencil-DepthBufferFail	Gets or sets the stencil operation to perform if the stencil test passes and the depth-buffer test fails for a counterclockwise triangle. The default is StencilOperation.Keep.
CounterClockwise-StencilFail	Gets or sets the stencil operation to perform if the stencil test fails for a counterclockwise triangle. The default is StencilOperation.Keep.
CounterClockwise-StencilFunction	Gets or sets the comparison function to use for counterclockwise stencil tests. The default is CompareFunction.Always.
CounterClockwise-StencilPass	Gets or sets the stencil operation to perform if the stencil and depth tests pass for a counterclockwise triangle. The default is StencilOperation.Keep.
DepthBufferEnable	Enables or disables depth buffering. The default is true.
DepthBufferFunction	Gets or sets the comparison function for the depth-buffer test. The default is CompareFunction.LessEqual.
DepthBufferWriteEnable	Enables or disables writing to the depth buffer. The default is true.
ReferenceStencil	Specifies a reference value to use for the stencil test. The default is 0.
StencilDepthBufferFail	Gets or sets the stencil operation to perform if the stencil test passes and the depth test fails. The default is StencilOperation.Keep.
StencilEnable	Gets or sets stencil enabling. The default is false.
StencilFail	Gets or sets the stencil operation to perform if the stencil test fails. The default is StencilOperation.Keep.
StencilFunction	Gets or sets the comparison function for the stencil test. The default is CompareFunction.Always.
StencilMask	Gets or sets the mask applied to the reference value and each stencil-buffer entry to determine the significant bits for the stencil test. The default mask is Int32.MaxValue.
StencilPass	Gets or sets the stencil operation to perform if the stencil test passes. The default is StencilOperation.Keep.
StencilWriteMask	Gets or sets the write mask applied to values written into the stencil buffer. The default mask is Int32.MaxValue.
TwoSidedStencilMode	Enables or disables two-sided stenciling. The default is false.

DeviceLostException

public sealed class DeviceLostException : Exception

This exception is thrown when the device has been lost but cannot be reset at this time. Therefore, rendering is not possible.

DeviceNotResetException

public sealed class DeviceNotResetException : Exception

This exception is thrown when the device has been lost but can be reset at this time.

DirectionalLight

`public sealed class DirectionalLight`

Creates a `DirectionalLight` object.

Public Properties	
DiffuseColor	Gets or sets the diffuse color of the light.
Direction	Gets or sets the light direction. This value must be a unit vector.
Enabled	Gets or sets light enable flag.
SpecularColor	Gets or sets the specular color of the light.

DisplayMode

`public class DisplayMode`

Describes the display mode.

Public Properties	
AspectRatio	Gets the aspect ratio used by the graphics device.
Format	Gets a value indicating the surface format of the display mode.
Height	Gets a value indicating the screen height, in pixels.
TitleSafeArea	Returns the title safe area of the display.
Width	Gets a value indicating the screen width, in pixels.

DisplayModeCollection

`public class DisplayModeCollection : IEnumerable<DisplayMode>, IEnumerable`

Manipulates a collection of `DisplayMode` structures.

Public Properties	
Item	Retrieves the DisplayMode structure with the specified format.
Public Methods	
GetEnumerator	Gets an enumerator that can iterate through the DisplayModeCollection.

DualTextureEffect

`public class DualTextureEffect : Effect, IEffectMatrices, IEffectFog`

Contains a configurable effect that supports two-layer multitexturing.

Public Properties

Alpha	Gets or sets the material alpha, which determines its transparency. Range is from 1 (fully opaque) to 0 (fully transparent).
DiffuseColor	Gets or sets the diffuse color for a material. The range of color values is from 0 to 1.
FogColor	Gets or sets the fog color. The range of color values is from 0 to 1.
FogEnabled	Gets or sets the fog enable flag.
FogEnd	Gets or sets the maximum z value for fog, which ranges from 0 to 1.
FogStart	Gets or sets the minimum z value for fog, which ranges from 0 to 1.
Projection	Gets or sets the projection matrix.
Texture	Gets or sets the current base texture.
Texture2	Gets or sets the current overlay texture.
VertexColorEnabled	Gets or sets whether per-vertex color is enabled.
View	Gets or sets the view matrix.
World	Gets or sets the world matrix.

Protected Methods

OnApply	Computes derived parameter values immediately before applying the effect.

DynamicIndexBuffer

`public class DynamicIndexBuffer : IndexBuffer`

Describes the rendering order of the vertices in a vertex buffer.

Public Properties

IsContentLost	Determines whether the index buffer data has been lost due to a lost-device event.

Public Methods

SetData	Copies array data to the index buffer.

Public Events

ContentLost	Occurs when resources are lost due to a lost-device event.

DynamicVertexBuffer

`public class DynamicVertexBuffer : VertexBuffer`

Represents a list of 3D vertices to be streamed to the graphics device. In situations where your game frequently modifies a vertex buffer, it is recommended that the buffer be instantiated or derived from `DynamicVertexBuffer` instead of the `VertexBuffer` class. `DynamicVertexBuffer` is optimized for frequent vertex data modification. However, to fully maximize the benefits of this class, your data must be restored after any occurrence of a `ContentLost` event. This event occurs whenever the related graphics device is lost. After resetting the graphics device and restoring any static resources, the `ContentLost` event handler is then called. Calling `SetData` inside this handler restores any dynamic resource data.

Public Properties

IsContentLost	Determines whether the index buffer data has been lost due to a lost-device event.

Public Methods

SetData	Copies array data to the vertex buffer.

Public Events

ContentLost	Occurs when resources are lost due to a lost-device event.

Effect

`public class Effect : GraphicsResource`

Used to set and query effects, and to choose techniques.

Public Properties

CurrentTechnique	Gets or sets the active technique.
Parameters	Gets a collection of parameters used for this effect.
Techniques	Gets a collection of techniques that are defined for this effect.

Protected Methods

OnApply	Applies the effect state just prior to rendering the effect.

EffectAnnotation

`public sealed class EffectAnnotation`

Represents an annotation to an `EffectParameter`.

Public Properties

ColumnCount	Gets the number of columns in this effect annotation.
Name	Gets the name of the effect annotation.
ParameterClass	Gets the parameter class of this effect annotation.
ParameterType	Gets the parameter type of this effect annotation.

RowCount	Gets the row count of this effect annotation.
Semantic	Gets the semantic of this effect annotation.

Public Methods

GetValueBoolean	Gets the value of the EffectAnnotation as a Boolean.
GetValueInt32	Gets the value of the EffectAnnotation as an Int32.
GetValueMatrix	Gets the value of the EffectAnnotation as an Int32.
GetValueSingle	Gets the value of the EffectAnnotation as a Single.
GetValueString	Gets the value of the EffectAnnotation as a String.
GetValueVector2	Gets the value of the EffectAnnotation as a Vector2.
GetValueVector3	Gets the value of the EffectAnnotation as a Vector3.
GetValueVector4	Gets the value of the EffectAnnotation as a Vector4.

EffectAnnotationCollection

public sealed class EffectAnnotationCollection : IEnumerable<EffectAnnotation>

Manipulates a collection of EffectAnnotation objects.

Public Properties

Count	Gets the number of EffectAnnotation objects in this EffectAnnotationCollection.
Item	Gets an EffectAnnotation object.

Public Methods

GetEnumerator	Gets an enumerator that can iterate through the EffectAnnotationCollection.

Explicit Interface Implementations

System.Collections.IEnumerable.GetEnumerator	Gets an enumerator that can iterate through the EffectAnnotationCollection.
System.Collections.Generic.IEnumerable{T}.GetEnumerator	Gets an enumerator that can iterate through the EffectAnnotationCollection.

EffectMaterial

public class EffectMaterial : Effect

Contains an effect subclass that is used to load data for an EffectMaterialContent type. For most purposes, this type can be ignored, and treated exactly like a regular effect. When an EffectMaterial type is loaded from XNB format, its parameter values and textures are also loaded and automatically set on the effect, in addition to the HLSL shader code. Use this class to write a content pipeline extension to store materials inside a custom data type.

EffectParameter

`public sealed class EffectParameter`

Represents an `Effect` parameter. Creating and assigning an `EffectParameter` instance for each technique in your `Effect` is significantly faster than using the `Parameters` indexed property on `Effect`.

Public Properties

Annotations	Gets the collection of `EffectAnnotation` objects for this parameter.
ColumnCount	Gets the number of columns in the parameter description.
Elements	Gets the collection of effect parameters.
Name	Gets the name of the parameter.
ParameterClass	Gets the class of the parameter.
ParameterType	Gets the type of the parameter.
RowCount	Gets the number of rows in the parameter description.
Semantic	Gets the semantic meaning, or usage, of the parameter.
StructureMembers	Gets the collection of structure members.

Public Methods

GetValueBoolean	Gets the value of the `EffectParameter` as a Boolean.
GetValueBooleanArray	Gets the value of the `EffectParameter` as an array of Boolean.
GetValueInt32	Gets the value of the `EffectParameter` as an Int32.
GetValueInt32Array	Gets the value of the `EffectParameter` as an array of Int32.
GetValueMatrix	Gets the value of the `EffectParameter` as a Matrix.
GetValueMatrixArray	Gets the value of the `EffectParameter` as an array of Matrix.
GetValueMatrixTranspose	Gets the value of the `EffectParameter` as a Matrix transpose.
GetValueMatrixTranspose-Array	Gets the value of the `EffectParameter` as an array of Matrix transpose.
GetValueQuaternion	Gets the value of the `EffectParameter` as a Quaternion.
GetValueQuaternionArray	Gets the value of the `EffectParameter` as an array of Quaternion.
GetValueSingle	Gets the value of the `EffectParameter` as a Single.
GetValueSingleArray	Gets the value of the `EffectParameter` as an array of Single.
GetValueString	Gets the value of the `EffectParameter` as a String.
GetValueTexture2D	Gets the value of the `EffectParameter` as a Texture2D.
GetValueTexture3D	Gets the value of the `EffectParameter` as a Texture3D.
GetValueTextureCube	Gets the value of the `EffectParameter` as a TextureCube.
GetValueVector2	Gets the value of the `EffectParameter` as a Vector2.
GetValueVector2Array	Gets the value of the `EffectParameter` as an array of Vector2.
GetValueVector3	Gets the value of the `EffectParameter` as a Vector3.

GetValueVector3Array	Gets the value of the `EffectParameter` as an array of Vector3.
GetValueVector4	Gets the value of the `EffectParameter` as a Vector4.
GetValueVector4Array	Gets the value of the `EffectParameter` as an array of Vector4.
SetValue	Sets the value of the `EffectParameter`.
SetValueTranspose	Sets the value of the `EffectParameter`.

EffectParameterCollection

`public sealed class EffectParameter`

Manipulates a collection of `EffectParameter` objects. Creating and assigning an `EffectParameter` instance for each technique in your `Effect` is significantly faster than using the `Parameters` indexed property on `Effect`.

Public Properties	
Count	Gets the number of `EffectParameter` objects in this `EffectParameterCollection`.
Item	Gets an `EffectParameter` object.
Public Methods	
GetEnumerator	Gets an enumerator that can iterate through `EffectParameterCollection`.
GetParameterBySemantic	Gets an effect parameter from its semantic usage.
Explicit Interface Implementations	
System.Collections.IEnumerable.GetEnumerator	Gets an enumerator that can iterate through `EffectParameterCollection`.
System.Collections.Generic.IEnumerable{T}.GetEnumerator	Gets an enumerator that can iterate through `EffectParameterCollection`.

EffectPass

`public sealed class EffectPass`

Contains the rendering state for drawing with an effect; an effect can contain one or more passes.

Public Properties	
Annotations	Gets the set of `EffectAnnotation` objects for this `EffectPass`.
Name	Gets the name of this pass.
Public Methods	
Apply	Begins this pass.

EffectPassCollection

`public sealed class EffectPassCollection : IEnumerable<EffectPass>`

Manipulates a collection of `EffectPass` objects.

Public Properties	
Count	Gets the number of objects in the collection.
Item	Gets an element in the collection.
Public Methods	
GetEnumerator	Gets an enumerator that can iterate through the EffectPassCollection.
Explicit Interface Implementations	
System.Collections.IEnumerable .GetEnumerator	Gets an enumerator that can iterate through the EffectPassCollection.
System.Collections.Generic .IEnumerable{T}.GetEnumerator	Gets an enumerator that can iterate through the EffectPassCollection.

EffectTechnique

`public sealed class EffectTechnique`

Represents an effect technique. Creating and assigning an `EffectTechnique` instance for each technique in your `Effect` is significantly faster than using the `Techniques` indexed property on `Effect`.

Public Properties	
Annotations	Gets the `EffectAnnotation` objects associated with this technique.
Name	Gets the name of this technique.
Passes	Gets the collection of `EffectPass` objects this rendering technique requires.

EffectTechniqueCollection

`public sealed class EffectTechniqueCollection : IEnumerable<EffectTechnique>`

Manipulates a collection of `EffectTechnique` objects.

Public Properties	
Count	Gets the number of objects in the collection.
Item	Gets an element in the collection.

Public Methods

GetEnumerator	Gets an enumerator that can iterate through the EffectTechniqueCollection.

Explicit Interface Implementations

System.Collections.IEnumerable.GetEnumerator	Gets an enumerator that can iterate through the EffectTechniqueCollection.
System.Collections.Generic.IEnumerable{T}.GetEnumerator	Gets an enumerator that can iterate through the EffectTechniqueCollection.

EnvironmentMapEffect

public class EnvironmentMapEffect : Effect, IEffectMatrices, IEffectLights, IEffectFog

Contains a configurable effect that supports environment mapping.

Public Properties

Alpha	Gets or sets the material alpha, which determines its transparency. Range is between 1 (fully opaque) and 0 (fully transparent).
AmbientLightColor	Gets or sets the ambient color for a light. The range of color values is from 0 to 1.
DiffuseColor	Gets or sets the diffuse color for a material. The range of color values is from 0 to 1.
DirectionalLight0	Gets the first directional light.
DirectionalLight1	Gets the second directional light.
DirectionalLight2	Gets the third directional light.
EmissiveColor	Gets or sets the emissive color for a material. The range of color values is from 0 to 1.
EnvironmentMap	Gets or sets the current environment map texture.
EnvironmentMapAmount	Gets or sets the amount of the environment map color (RGB) that will be blended over the base texture. The value ranges from 0 to 1; the default value is 1.
EnvironmentMapSpecular	Gets or sets the amount of the environment map alpha value that will be added to the base texture. The value ranges from 0 to 1; the default value is 0.
FogColor	Gets or sets the fog color. The range of color values is from 0 to 1.
FogEnabled	Gets or sets the fog enable flag.
FogEnd	Gets or sets the maximum z value for fog, which ranges from 0 to 1.
FogStart	Gets or sets the minimum z value for fog, which ranges from 0 to 1.
FresnelFactor	Gets or sets the Fresnel factor used for the environment map blending.
Projection	Gets or sets the projection matrix.
Texture	Gets or sets the current texture.

View	Gets or sets the view matrix.
World	Gets or sets the world matrix.
Public Methods	
EnableDefaultLighting	Sets up standard key, fill, and back lighting for an EnvironmentMapEffect.
Protected Methods	
OnApply	Computes derived parameter values immediately before applying the effect.
Explicit Interface Implementations	
LightingEnabled Property	Enables lighting in an EnvironmentMapEffect.

GraphicsAdapter

public sealed class GraphicsAdapter

Provides methods to retrieve and manipulate graphics adapters.

Public Properties	
Adapters	Collection of available adapters on the system.
CurrentDisplayMode	Gets the current display mode.
DefaultAdapter	Gets the default adapter.
Description	Retrieves a string used for presentation to the user.
DeviceId	Retrieves a value that is used to help identify a particular chip set.
DeviceName	Retrieves a string that contains the device name for a Microsoft Windows Graphics Device Interface (GDI).
IsDefaultAdapter	Determines whether this instance of GraphicsAdapter is the default adapter.
IsWideScreen	Determines whether the graphics adapter is in widescreen mode.
MonitorHandle	Retrieves the handle of the monitor associated with the Microsoft Direct3D object.
Revision	Retrieves a value used to help identify the revision level of a particular chip set.
SubSystemId	Retrieves a value used to identify the subsystem.
SupportedDisplayModes	Returns a collection of supported display modes for the current adapter.
UseNullDevice	Gets or sets a null device.
UseReferenceDevice	Gets or sets a reference device.
VendorId	Retrieves a value used to identify the manufacturer.
Public Methods	
IsProfileSupported	Tests to see whether the adapter supports the requested profile.
QueryBackBufferFormat	Queries the adapter for support for the requested back-buffer format.
QueryRenderTargetFormat	Queries the adapter for support for the requested render target format.

GraphicsDevice

`public class GraphicsDevice : IDisposable`

Performs primitive-based rendering, creates resources, handles system-level variables, adjusts gamma ramp levels, and creates shaders.

Public Properties

`Adapter`	Gets the graphics adapter.
`BlendFactor`	Gets or sets the color used for a constant-blend factor during alpha blending. The default value is `Color.White`.
`BlendState`	Gets or sets a system-defined instance of a blend state object initialized for alpha blending. The default value is `BlendState.Opaque`.
`DepthStencilState`	Gets or sets a system-defined instance of a depth-stencil state object. The default value is `DepthStencilState.Default`.
`DisplayMode`	Retrieves the display mode's spatial resolution, color resolution, and refresh frequency.
`GraphicsDeviceStatus`	Retrieves the status of the device.
`GraphicsProfile`	Gets the graphics profile. The default value is `GraphicsProfile.Reach`.
`Indices`	Gets or sets index data. The default value is `null`.
`MultiSampleMask`	Gets or sets a bitmask controlling modification of the samples in a multisample render target. The default value is -1 (`0xffffffff`).
`PresentationParameters`	Gets the presentation parameters associated with this graphics device.
`RasterizerState`	Gets or sets rasterizer state. The default value is `RasterizerState.CullCounterClockwise`.
`ReferenceStencil`	Gets or sets a reference value for stencil testing. The default value is `0`.
`SamplerStates`	Retrieves a collection of `SamplerState` objects for the current `GraphicsDevice`.
`ScissorRectangle`	Gets or sets the rectangle used for scissor testing. By default, the size matches the render target size.
`Textures`	Returns the collection of textures that have been assigned to the texture stages of the device.
`VertexSamplerStates`	Gets the collection of vertex sampler states.
`VertexTextures`	Gets the collection of vertex textures that support texture lookup in the vertex shader using the `texldl` statement. The vertex engine contains four texture sampler stages.
`Viewport`	Gets or sets a viewport identifying the portion of the render target to receive draw calls.

Public Methods

`Clear`	Clears resource buffers.
`DrawIndexedPrimitives`	Renders the specified geometric primitive, based on indexing into an array of vertices.

DrawInstancedPrimitives	Draws a series of instanced models.
DrawPrimitives	Renders a sequence of non-indexed geometric primitives of the specified type from the current set of data-input streams.
DrawUserIndexedPrimitives	Renders geometric primitives with an index.
DrawUserPrimitives	Renders geometric primitives.
GetBackBufferData	Gets the contents of the back buffer.
GetRenderTargets	Gets a render target surface.
GetVertexBuffers	Gets the vertex buffers.
Present	Presents the display with the contents of the next buffer in the sequence of back buffers owned by the GraphicsDevice.
Reset	Resets the presentation parameters for the current GraphicsDevice.
SetRenderTarget	Sets a new color buffer for a GraphicsDevice.
SetRenderTargets	Sets an array of render targets.
SetVertexBuffer	Sets or binds a vertex buffer to a device.
SetVertexBuffers	Sets the vertex buffers.
Public Events	
DeviceLost	Occurs when a GraphicsDevice is about to be lost (for example, immediately before a reset).
DeviceReset	Occurs after a GraphicsDevice is reset, allowing an application to re-create all resources.
DeviceResetting	Occurs when a GraphicsDevice is resetting, allowing the application to cancel the default handling of the reset.
ResourceCreated	Occurs when a resource is created.
ResourceDestroyed	Occurs when a resource is destroyed.

GraphicsResource

public abstract class GraphicsResource : IDisposable

Queries and prepares resources.

Public Properties	
GraphicsDevice	Gets the GraphicsDevice associated with this GraphicsResource.
Name	Gets the name of the resource.
Tag	Gets the resource tags for this resource.

IndexBuffer

public class IndexBuffer : GraphicsResource

Describes the rendering order of the vertices in a vertex buffer. The vertex stream and index data of the graphics device must be set before any call to

`DrawIndexedPrimitives`. It associates a user-created vertex buffer of type `VertexPositionNormalTexture` with vertex stream 0 (zero) of the graphics device.

Public Properties	
BufferUsage	Gets the state of the related `BufferUsage` enumeration.
IndexCount	Gets the number of indices in this buffer.
IndexElementSize	Gets a value indicating the size of this index element.
Public Methods	
GetData	Gets the index buffer into an array.
SetData	Copies array data to the index buffer.

Model
`public sealed class Model`

Represents a 3D model composed of multiple `ModelMesh` objects, which may be moved independently.

Public Properties	
Bones	Gets a collection of `ModelBone` objects, which describe how each mesh in the `Meshes` collection for this model relates to its parent mesh.
Meshes	Gets a collection of `ModelMesh` objects, which compose the model. Each `ModelMesh` in a model may be moved independently and may be composed of multiple materials identified as `ModelMeshPart` objects.
Root	Gets the root bone for this model.
Tag	Gets or sets an object identifying this model.
Public Methods	
CopyAbsoluteBoneTransformsTo	Copies a transform of each bone in a model relative to all parent bones of the bone into a given array.
CopyBoneTransformsFrom	Copies an array of transforms into each bone in the model.
CopyBoneTransformsTo	Copies each bone transform relative only to the parent bone of the model to a given array.
Draw	Renders a model after applying the matrix transformations.

ModelBone
`public sealed class ModelBone`

Represents bone data for a model. A model bone is a matrix that represents the position of a mesh as it relates to other meshes in a 3D model. A complex computer-generated object, often called a model, is made up of many vertices and materials organized into a set of meshes. In the XNA Framework, a model is represented by the `Model` class. A model contains one or more meshes, each of which is represented by a `ModelMesh` class. Each mesh is associated with one bone represented by the `ModelBone` class.

Public Properties	
Children	Gets a collection of bones that are children of this bone.
Index	Gets the index of this bone in the `Bones` collection.
Name	Gets the name of this bone.
Parent	Gets the parent of this bone.
Transform	Gets or sets the matrix used to transform this bone relative to its parent bone.

ModelBoneCollection

`public sealed class ModelBoneCollection : ReadOnlyCollection<ModelBone>`

Represents a set of bones associated with a model.

Public Properties	
Item	Retrieves a `ModelBone` from the collection.
Public Methods	
GetEnumerator	Returns a `ModelBoneCollection.Enumerator` that can iterate through a `ModelBoneCollection`.
TryGetValue	Finds a bone with a given name if it exists in the collection.

ModelEffectCollection

`public sealed class ModelEffectCollection : ReadOnlyCollection<Effect>`

Represents a collection of effects associated with a model.

Public Methods	
GetEnumerator	Returns a `ModelEffectCollection.Enumerator` that can iterate through a `ModelEffectCollection`.

ModelMesh
`public sealed class ModelMesh`

Represents a mesh that is part of a Model.

Public Properties	
BoundingSphere	Gets the `BoundingSphere` that contains this mesh.
Effects	Gets a collection of effects associated with this mesh.
MeshParts	Gets the `ModelMeshPart` objects that make up this mesh. Each part of a mesh is composed of a set of primitives that share the same material.
Name	Gets the name of this mesh.
ParentBone	Gets the parent bone for this mesh. The parent bone of a mesh contains a transformation matrix that describes how the mesh is located relative to any parent meshes in a model.
Tag	Gets or sets an object identifying this mesh.
Public Methods	
Draw	Draws all the `ModelMeshPart` objects in this mesh, using their current `Effect` settings.

ModelMeshCollection
`public sealed class ModelMeshCollection : ReadOnlyCollection<ModelMesh>`

Represents a collection of `ModelMesh` objects.

Public Properties	
Item	Retrieves a `ModelMesh` from the collection.
Public Methods	
GetEnumerator	Returns a `ModelMeshCollection.Enumerator` that can iterate through a `ModelMeshCollection`.
TryGetValue	Finds a mesh with a given name if it exists in the collection.

ModelMeshPart
`class definition`

Represents a batch of geometry information to submit to the graphics device during rendering. Each `ModelMeshPart` is a subdivision of a `ModelMesh` object. The `ModelMesh` class is split into multiple `ModelMeshPart` objects, typically based on material information. It is not necessary to use this class directly. In advanced rendering scenarios, it is possible to draw using `ModelMeshPart` properties in combination with the vertex and index buffers on `ModelMesh`. However, in most cases, `ModelMesh.Draw` will be sufficient.

Public Properties	
Effect	Gets or sets the material Effect for this mesh part.
IndexBuffer	Gets the index buffer for this mesh part.
NumVertices	Gets the number of vertices used during a Draw call.
PrimitiveCount	Gets the number of primitives to render.
StartIndex	Gets the location in the index array at which to start reading vertices.
Tag	Gets or sets an object identifying this model mesh part.
VertexBuffer	Gets the vertex buffer for this mesh part.
VertexOffset	Gets the offset (in vertices) from the top of vertex buffer.

ModelMeshPartCollection

`public sealed class ModelMeshPartCollection : ReadOnlyCollection<ModelMeshPart>`

Represents a collection of `ModelMeshPart` objects.

Public Methods	
GetEnumerator	Returns a ModelMeshPartCollection.Enumerator that can iterate through a ModelMeshPartCollection.

NoSuitableGraphicsDeviceException

`public sealed class NoSuitableGraphicsDeviceException : Exception`

Thrown when no available graphics device fits the given device preferences.

OcclusionQuery

`public class OcclusionQuery : GraphicsResource`

Used to perform an occlusion query against the latest drawn objects. An occlusion query is a technique that determines how many pixels were actually drawn during a set of `Draw` calls. This is useful for certain rendering techniques and rendering optimizations. The number of non-occluded pixels (indicated by `PixelCount`) can differ based on the platform.

For Xbox 360 games, `PixelCount` represents the number of pixels modified by drawing. This includes `GraphicsDevice.Clear` calls and any drawing associated with sprite batches.

For Windows games, `PixelCount` represents the number of pixels that passed the depth and stencil tests. This does not include sprite-batch drawing (because the depth test is turned off) or calls to `GraphicsDevice.Clear`.

To achieve consistent results across all platforms, use occlusion queries only when the depth buffer is enabled. In addition, avoid calling `Clear` or changing the assigned render target inside an occlusion query begin/end block.

Public Properties	
IsComplete	Gets a value that indicates whether the occlusion query has completed.
PixelCount	Gets the number of visible pixels.
Public Methods	
Begin	Begins the application of the query.
End	Ends the application of the query.

PresentationParameters

`public class PresentationParameters`

Contains presentation parameters.

Public Properties	
BackBufferFormat	Gets or sets the format of the back buffer.
BackBufferHeight	Gets or sets a value indicating the height of the new swap chain's back buffer.
BackBufferWidth	Gets or sets a value indicating the width of the new swap chain's back buffer.
Bounds	Gets the size of this resource.
DepthStencilFormat	Gets or sets the depth-stencil data format.
DeviceWindowHandle	Gets or sets the handle to the device window.
DisplayOrientation	Gets or sets the orientation of the display. The default value is `DisplayOrientation.Default`, which means orientation is determined automatically from the `BackBufferWidth` and `BackBufferHeight`.
IsFullScreen	Gets or sets a value indicating whether the application is in full-screen mode.
MultiSampleCount	Gets or sets a value indicating the number of sample locations during multisampling.
PresentationInterval	Gets or sets the maximum rate at which the swap chain's back buffers can be presented to the front buffer.
RenderTargetUsage	Gets or sets render target usage flags.

RasterizerState

`public class RasterizerState : GraphicsResource`

Contains the rasterizer state, which determines how to convert vector data (shapes) into raster data (pixels).

Public Fields

CullClockwise	A built-in state object with settings for culling primitives with clockwise winding order.
CullCounterClockwise	A built-in state object with settings for culling primitives with counter-clockwise winding order.
CullNone	A built-in state object with settings for not culling any primitives.

Public Properties

CullMode	Specifies the conditions for culling or removing triangles. The default value is `CullMode.CounterClockwise`.
DepthBias	Sets or retrieves the depth bias for polygons, which is the amount of bias to apply to the depth of a primitive to alleviate depth-testing problems for primitives of similar depth. The default value is `0`.
FillMode	The fill mode, which defines how a triangle is filled during rendering. The default is `FillMode.Solid`.
MultiSampleAntiAlias	Enables or disables multisample anti-aliasing. The default is `true`.
ScissorTestEnable	Enables or disables scissor testing. The default is `false`.
SlopeScaleDepthBias	Gets or sets a bias value that takes into account the slope of a polygon. This bias value is applied to coplanar primitives to reduce aliasing and other rendering artifacts caused by z-fighting. The default is `0`.

RenderTarget2D

`public class RenderTarget2D : Texture2D`

Contains a 2D texture that can be used as a render target.

Public Properties

DepthStencilFormat	Gets the data format for the depth-stencil data.
IsContentLost	Determines whether the index-buffer data has been lost due to a lost-device event.
MultiSampleCount	Gets the number of sample locations during multisampling.
RenderTargetUsage	Gets or sets the render-target usage.

Public Events

ContentLost	Occurs when resources are lost due to a lost-device event.

RenderTargetCube

`public class RenderTargetCube : TextureCube`

Represents a cubic texture resource that will be written to at the end of a render pass.

Public Properties	
DepthStencilFormat	Gets the depth format of this render target.
IsContentLost	Determines whether the data has been lost due to a lost-device event.
MultiSampleCount	Gets the number of multisample locations.
RenderTargetUsage	Gets the usage mode of this render target.
Public Events	
ContentLost	Occurs when a resource is lost due to a device being lost.

ResourceCreatedEventArgs

`public sealed class ResourceCreatedEventArgs : EventArgs`

Contains event data.

Public Properties	
Resource	The object raising the event.

ResourceDestroyedEventArgs

`public sealed class ResourceDestroyedEventArgs : EventArgs`

Arguments for a `ResourceDestroyed` event.

Public Properties	
Name	Gets the name of the destroyed resource.
Tag	Gets the resource-manager tag of the destroyed resource.

SamplerState

`public class SamplerState : GraphicsResource`

Contains sampler state, which determines how to sample texture data.

Public Fields

AnisotropicClamp	Contains the default state for anisotropic filtering and texture-coordinate clamping.
AnisotropicWrap	Contains the default state for anisotropic filtering and texture-coordinate wrapping.
LinearClamp	Contains the default state for linear filtering and texture-coordinate clamping.
LinearWrap	Contains the default state for linear filtering and texture-coordinate wrapping.
PointClamp	Contains the default state for point filtering and texture-coordinate clamping.
PointWrap	Contains the default state for point filtering and texture-coordinate wrapping.

Public Properties

AddressU	Gets or sets the texture-address mode for the u-coordinate.
AddressV	Gets or sets the texture-address mode for the v-coordinate.
AddressW	Gets or sets the texture-address mode for the w-coordinate.
Filter	Gets or sets the type of filtering during sampling.
MaxAnisotropy	Gets or sets the maximum anisotropy. The default value is 0.
MaxMipLevel	Gets or sets the level-of-detail (LOD) index of the largest map to use.
MipMapLevelOfDetailBias	Gets or sets the mipmap LOD bias. The default value is 0.

SamplerStateCollection

`public sealed class SamplerStateCollection`

Collection of SamplerState objects.

Public Properties

Item	Gets a specific `SamplerState` object using an index value.

SkinnedEffect

`public class SkinnedEffect : Effect, IEffectMatrices, IEffectLights, IEffectFog`

Contains a configurable effect for rendering skinned character models.

Public Fields

MaxBones	The maximum number of bones.

Public Properties

Alpha	Gets or sets the material alpha, which determines its transparency. Range is between 1 (fully opaque) and 0 (fully transparent).

AmbientLightColor	Gets or sets the ambient color for a light. The range of color values is from 0 to 1.
DiffuseColor	Gets or sets the diffuse color for a material, the range of color values is from 0 to 1.
DirectionalLight0	Gets the first directional light.
DirectionalLight1	Gets the second directional light.
DirectionalLight2	Gets the third directional light.
EmissiveColor	Gets or sets the emissive color for a material. The range of color values is from 0 to 1.
FogColor	Gets or sets the fog color. The range of color values is from 0 to 1.
FogEnabled	Gets or sets the fog enable flag.
FogEnd	Gets or sets the maximum z value for fog, which ranges from 0 to 1.
FogStart	Gets or sets the minimum z value for fog, which ranges from 0 to 1.
PreferPerPixelLighting	Gets or sets the per-pixel prefer lighting flag.
Projection	Gets or sets the projection matrix.
SpecularColor	Gets or sets the specular color for a material. The range of color values is from 0 to 1.
SpecularPower	Gets or sets the material specular power.
Texture	Gets or sets the current texture.
View	Gets or sets the view matrix.
WeightsPerVertex	Gets or sets the number of per-vertex skinning weights to evaluate, which is either 1, 2, or 4.
World	Gets or sets the world matrix.

Public Methods

EnableDefaultLighting	Sets up standard key, fill, and back lighting for a SkinnedEffect.
GetBoneTransforms	Gets the bone-transform matrices for a SkinnedEffect.
SetBoneTransforms	Sets an array of bone transform matrices for a SkinnedEffect.

Protected Methods

OnApply	Computes derived parameter values immediately before applying the effect.

Explicit Interface Implementations

LightingEnabled	Enables lighting in a SkinnedEffect.

SpriteBatch

`public class SpriteBatch : GraphicsResource`

Enables a group of sprites to be drawn using the same settings.

Public Methods

Begin	Begins a sprite-batch operation.
Draw	Adds a sprite to a batch of sprites to be rendered.

| DrawString | Adds a string to a batch of sprites to be rendered. |
| End | Flushes the sprite batch and restores the device state to how it was before Begin was called. |

SpriteFont

`public sealed class SpriteFont`

Represents a font texture. To load a `SpriteFont`, click Sprite Font on the Add New Item dialog box. This adds an XML file to your project describing how to build a texture map for your font. At build time, XNA Game Studio creates a texture with the image of the characters of the font you specify, with the specified font point size. At run time, load the font using `ContentManager.Load()` and pass it to `SpriteBatch.DrawString()` when drawing text.

Public Properties

Characters	Gets a collection of all the characters that are included in the font.
DefaultCharacter	Gets or sets the default character for the font.
LineSpacing	Gets or sets the vertical distance (in pixels) between the base lines of two consecutive lines of text. Line spacing includes the blank space between lines as well as the height of the characters.
Spacing	Gets or sets the spacing of the font characters.

Public Methods

| MeasureString | Returns the width and height of a string. |

Texture

`public abstract class Texture : GraphicsResource`

Represents a texture resource.

Public Properties

| Format | Gets the format of the texture data. |
| LevelCount | Gets the number of texture levels in a multilevel texture. |

Texture2D

`public class Texture2D : Texture`

Represents a 2D grid of texels. A texel represents the smallest unit of a texture that can be read from or written to by the GPU. A texel is composed of one to four components. Specifically, a texel may be any one of the available texture formats represented in the SurfaceFormat enumeration. A Texture2D resource contains a 2D grid of texels. Each texel is addressable by a u, v vector. Because it is a texture resource, it may contain mipmap levels.

Public Properties	
Bounds	Gets the size of this resource.
Height	Gets the height of this texture resource, in pixels.
Width	Gets the width of this texture resource, in pixels.
Public Methods	
FromStream	Methods for loading an image.
GetData	Copies texture data into an array.
SaveAsJpeg	Saves texture data as a JPEG.
SaveAsPng	Saves texture data as a PNG.
SetData	Sets data to the texture.

Texture3D

public class Texture3D : Texture

Represents a 3D volume of texels. A texel represents the smallest unit of a texture that can be read from or written to by the GPU. A Texture3D resource (also known as a volume texture) contains a 3D volume of texels. Because it is a texture resource, it may contain mipmap levels.

Public Properties	
Depth	Gets the depth of this volume texture resource, in pixels.
Height	Gets the height of this texture resource, in pixels.
Width	Gets the width of this texture resource, in pixels.
Public Methods	
GetData	Gets a copy of the texture data.
SetData	Sets data.

TextureCollection

public sealed class TextureCollection

Represents a collection of Texture objects.

Public Properties

Item	Gets or sets the `Texture` at the specified sampler number.

TextureCube
`class definition`

Represents a set of six 2D textures, one for each face of a cube. A cube texture is a collection of six textures, one for each face of the cube. All faces must be present in the cube texture. Also, a cube map surface must be the same pixel size in all three dimensions (x, y, and z).

Public Properties

Size	Gets the width and height of this texture resource, in pixels.

Public Methods

GetData	Returns a copy of the texture data.
SetData	Sets texture data.

VertexBuffer
`public class VertexBuffer : GraphicsResource`

Represents a list of 3D vertices to be streamed to the graphics device.

Public Properties

BufferUsage	Gets the state of the related `BufferUsage` enumeration.
VertexCount	Gets the number of vertices.
VertexDeclaration	Defines per-vertex data in a buffer.

Public Methods

GetData	Returns a copy of the vertex-buffer data.
SetData	Sets the vertex-buffer data.

VertexDeclaration
`public class VertexDeclaration : GraphicsResource`

A vertex declaration, which defines per-vertex data.

Public Properties	
VertexStride	The number of bytes from one vertex to the next.
Public Methods	
GetVertexElements	Gets the vertex-shader declaration.

Interfaces

The following interfaces are found in the Graphics namespace.

IEffectFog

`public interface IEffectFog`

Gets or sets fog parameters for the current effect.

Public Properties	
FogColor	Gets or sets the fog color.
FogEnabled	Enables or disables fog.
FogEnd	Gets or sets the fog ending distance.
FogStart	Gets or sets the fog ending distance.

IEffectLights

`public interface IEffectLights`

Gets or sets lighting parameters for the current effect.

Public Properties	
AmbientLightColor	Gets or sets the ambient light color for the current effect.
DirectionalLight0	Gets the first directional light for the current effect.
DirectionalLight1	Gets the second directional light for the current effect.
DirectionalLight2	Gets the third directional light for the current effect.
LightingEnabled Property	Enables or disables lighting in an IEffectLights.
Public Methods	
EnableDefaultLighting	Enables default lighting for the current effect.

IEffectMatrices

`public interface IEffectMatrices`

Gets or sets transformation-matrix parameters for the current effect.

Public Properties	
Projection	Gets or sets the projection matrix in the current effect.
View	Gets or sets the view matrix in the current effect.
World	Gets or sets the world matrix in the current effect.

IGraphicsDeviceService

`public interface IGraphicsDeviceService`

Defines a mechanism for retrieving `GraphicsDevice` objects.

Public Properties	
GraphicsDevice	Retrieves a graphics device.
Public Events	
DeviceCreated	The event that occurs when a graphics device is created.
DeviceDisposing	The event that occurs when a graphics device is disposing.
DeviceReset	The event that occurs when a graphics device is reset.
DeviceResetting	The event that occurs when a graphics device is in the process of resetting.

IVertexType

`public interface IVertexType`

Vertex type interface, which is implemented by a custom vertex type structure.

Public Properties	
VertexDeclaration	Vertex declaration, which defines per-vertex data.

Structures

The following structures are found in the `Graphics` namespace.

ModelBoneCollection.Enumerator

```
public struct ModelBoneCollection.Enumerator :
    IEnumerator<ModelBone>, IDisposable, IEnumerator
```

Provides the ability to iterate through the bones in a `ModelBoneCollection`.

Public Properties	
Current	Gets the current element in the ModelBoneCollection.
Public Methods	
MoveNext	Advances the enumerator to the next element of the ModelBoneCollection.
Explicit Interface Implementations	
System.Collections.IEnumerator.Current	Gets the current element in the ModelBoneCollection as an Object.
System#Collections-#IEnumerator#Reset	Sets the enumerator to its initial position, which is before the first element in the ModelBoneCollection.

ModelEffectCollection.Enumerator

```
public struct ModelEffectCollection.Enumerator :
    IEnumerator<Effect>, IDisposable, IEnumerator
```

Provides the ability to iterate through the bones in a `ModelEffectCollection`.

Public Properties	
Current	Gets the current element in the ModelEffectCollection.
Public Methods	
MoveNext	Advances the enumerator to the next element of the ModelEffectCollection.
Explicit Interface Implementations	
System.Collections.IEnumerator.Current	Gets the current element in the ModelEffectCollection as an Object.
System#Collections-#IEnumerator#Reset	Sets the enumerator to its initial position, which is before the first element in the ModelEffectCollection.

ModelMeshCollection.Enumerator

```
public struct ModelMeshCollection.Enumerator : IEnumerator<ModelMesh>, IDisposable,
IEnumerator
```

Provides the ability to iterate through the bones in a `ModelMeshCollection`.

Public Properties

Current	Gets the current element in the ModelMeshCollection.

Public Methods

MoveNext	Advances the enumerator to the next element of the ModelMeshCollection.

Explicit Interface Implementations

System.Collections .IEnumerator.Current	Gets the current element in the ModelMeshCollection as an Object.
System#Collections- #IEnumerator#Reset	Sets the enumerator to its initial position, which is before the first element in the ModelMeshCollection.

ModelMeshPartCollection.Enumerator

public struct ModelMeshPartCollection.Enumerator : IEnumerator<ModelMeshPart>, IDisposable, IEnumerator

Provides the ability to iterate through the bones in a ModelMeshPartCollection.

Public Properties

Current	Gets the current element in the ModelMeshPartCollection.

Public Methods

MoveNext	Advances the enumerator to the next element of the ModelMeshPartCollection.

Explicit Interface Implementations

System.Collections .IEnumerator.Current	Gets the current element in the ModelMeshPartCollection as an Object.
System#Collections- #IEnumerator#Reset	Sets the enumerator to its initial position, which is before the first element in the ModelMeshPartCollection.

RenderTargetBinding

public struct RenderTargetBinding

Binds an array of render targets.

Public Properties

CubeMapFace	Gets one face of a cube map.
RenderTarget	Gets a 2D texture.

VertexBufferBinding
`public struct VertexBufferBinding`

Binding structure that specifies a vertex buffer and other per-vertex parameters (such as offset and instancing) for a graphics device.

Public Properties	
InstanceFrequency	Gets the instancing frequency.
VertexBuffer	Gets a vertex buffer.
VertexOffset	Gets the offset between the beginning of the buffer and the vertex data to use.

VertexElement
`public struct VertexElement`

Defines input vertex data to the pipeline.

Public Properties	
Offset	Retrieves or sets the offset (if any) from the beginning of the stream to the beginning of the vertex data.
UsageIndex	Modifies the usage data to allow the user to specify multiple usage types.
VertexElementFormat	Gets or sets the format of this vertex element.
VertexElementUsage	Gets or sets a value describing how the vertex element is to be used.

VertexPositionColor
`public struct VertexPositionColor : IVertexType`

Describes a custom vertex-format structure that contains position and color information.

Public Fields	
Color	The vertex color.
Position	The XYZ position.
VertexDeclaration	Vertex declaration, which defines per-vertex data.
Explicit Interface Implementations	
Microsoft.Xna.Framework .Graphics.IVertexType .VertexDeclaration	Gets a vertex declaration.

VertexPositionColorTexture

`public struct VertexPositionColorTexture : IVertexType`

Describes a custom vertex-format structure that contains position information, color information, and one set of texture coordinates.

Public Fields

Color	The vertex color.
Position	The XYZ position.
TextureCoordinate	UV texture coordinates.
VertexDeclaration	Vertex declaration, which defines per-vertex data.

Explicit Interface Implementations

Microsoft.Xna.Framework .Graphics.IVertexType .VertexDeclaration	Gets a vertex declaration.

VertexPositionNormalTexture

`public struct VertexPositionNormalTexture : IVertexType`

Describes a custom vertex-format structure that contains position, normal data, and one set of texture coordinates.

Public Fields

Normal	The XYZ surface normal.
Position	The XYZ position.
TextureCoordinate	UV texture coordinates.
VertexDeclaration	Vertex declaration, which defines per-vertex data.

Explicit Interface Implementations

Microsoft.Xna.Framework .Graphics.IVertexType .VertexDeclaration	Gets a vertex declaration.

VertexPositionTexture

`public struct VertexPositionTexture : IVertexType`

Describes a custom vertex-format structure that contains position information and one set of texture coordinates.

Public Fields

Position	The XYZ position.
TextureCoordinate	UV texture coordinates.
VertexDeclaration	Vertex declaration, which defines per-vertex data.

Explicit Interface Implementations

Microsoft.Xna.Framework .Graphics.IVertexType .VertexDeclaration	Gets a vertex declaration.

Viewport

`public struct Viewport`

Defines the window dimensions of a render-target surface onto which a 3D volume projects.

Public Properties

AspectRatio	Gets the aspect ratio used by the viewport.
Bounds	Gets the size of this resource.
Height	Gets or sets the height dimension of the viewport on the render-target surface, in pixels.
MaxDepth	Gets or sets the maximum depth of the clip volume.
MinDepth	Gets or sets the minimum depth of the clip volume.
TitleSafeArea	Returns the title-safe area of the current viewport.
Width	Gets or sets the width dimension of the viewport on the render-target surface, in pixels.
X	Gets or sets the X pixel coordinate value of the upper-left corner of the viewport on the render-target surface.
Y	Gets or sets the Y pixel coordinate value of the upper-left corner of the viewport on the render-target surface.

Public Methods

Project	Projects a 3D vector from object space into screen space.
Unproject	Converts a screen-space point into a corresponding point in world space.

Enumerations

Following are the enumerations in the `Graphics` namespace.

Blend

`public enum Blend`

Defines color-blending factors.

`Zero`	Each component of the color is multiplied by (0, 0, 0, 0).
`One`	Each component of the color is multiplied by (1, 1, 1, 1).
`SourceColor`	Each component of the color is multiplied by the source color. This can be represented as (Rs, Gs, Bs, As), where R, G, B, and A stand for the red, green, blue, and alpha source values, respectively.
`InverseSourceColor`	Each component of the color is multiplied by the inverse of the source color. This can be represented as (1 − Rs, 1 − Gs, 1 − Bs, 1 − As) where R, G, B, and A stand for the red, green, blue, and alpha destination values, respectively.
`SourceAlpha`	Each component of the color is multiplied by the alpha value of the source. This can be represented as (As, As, As, As), where As is the alpha source value.
`InverseSourceAlpha`	Each component of the color is multiplied by the inverse of the alpha value of the source. This can be represented as (1 − As, 1 − As, 1 − As, 1 − As), where As is the alpha destination value.
`DestinationAlpha`	Each component of the color is multiplied by the alpha value of the destination. This can be represented as (Ad, Ad, Ad, Ad), where Ad is the destination alpha value.
`InverseDestinationAlpha`	Each component of the color is multiplied by the inverse of the alpha value of the destination. This can be represented as (1 − Ad, 1 − Ad, 1 − Ad, 1 − Ad), where Ad is the alpha destination value.
`DestinationColor`	Each component color is multiplied by the destination color. This can be represented as (Rd, Gd, Bd, Ad), where R, G, B, and A stand for red, green, blue, and alpha destination values, respectively.
`InverseDestinationColor`	Each component of the color is multiplied by the inverse of the destination color. This can be represented as (1 − Rd, 1 − Gd, 1 − Bd, 1 − Ad), where Rd, Gd, Bd, and Ad stand for the red, green, blue, and alpha destination values, respectively.
`SourceAlphaSaturation`	Each component of the color is multiplied by either the alpha of the source color or the inverse of the alpha of the source color, whichever is greater. This can be represented as (f, f, f, 1), where f = min(A, 1 − Ad).
`BlendFactor`	Each component of the color is multiplied by a constant set in `BlendFactor`.
`InverseBlendFactor`	Each component of the color is multiplied by the inverse of a constant set in `BlendFactor`.

BlendFunction

public enum BlendFunction

Defines how to combine a source color with the destination color already on the render target for color blending.

Add	The result is the destination added to the source.
	Result = (Source Color * Source Blend) + (Destination Color * Destination Blend)
Max	The result is the maximum of the source and destination.
	Result = max((Source Color * Source Blend), (Destination Color * Destination Blend))
Min	The result is the minimum of the source and destination.
	Result = min((Source Color * Source Blend), (Destination Color * Destination Blend))
ReverseSubtract	The result is the source subtracted from the destination.
	Result = (Destination Color * Destination Blend) − (Source Color * Source Blend)
Subtract	The result is the destination subtracted from the source.
	Result = (Source Color * Source Blend) − (Destination Color * Destination Blend)

BufferUsage

public enum BufferUsage

Specifies special usage of the buffer contents.

None	None
WriteOnly	Indicates that the application only writes to the vertex buffer. If specified, the driver chooses the best memory location for efficient writing and rendering. Attempts to read from a write-only vertex buffer fail.

ClearOptions

public enum ClearOptions

Specifies the buffer to use when calling Clear.

DepthBuffer	A depth buffer.
Stencil	A stencil buffer.
Target	A render target.

ColorWriteChannels

`public enum ColorWriteChannels`

Defines the color channels that can be chosen for a per-channel write to a render-target color buffer.

All	All buffer channels.
Alpha	Alpha channel of a buffer.
Blue	Blue channel of a buffer.
Green	Green channel of a buffer.
None	No channel selected.
Red	Red channel of a buffer.

CompareFunction

`public enum CompareFunction`

Defines comparison functions that can be chosen for alpha, stencil, or depth-buffer tests.

Always	Always pass the test.
Equal	Accept the new pixel if its value is equal to the value of the current pixel.
Greater	Accept the new pixel if its value is greater than the value of the current pixel.
GreaterEqual	Accept the new pixel if its value is greater than or equal to the value of the current pixel.
Less	Accept the new pixel if its value is less than the value of the current pixel.
LessEqual	Accept the new pixel if its value is less than or equal to the value of the current pixel.
Never	Always fail the test.
NotEqual	Accept the new pixel if its value does not equal the value of the current pixel.

CubeMapFace

`public enum CubeMapFace`

Defines the faces of a cube map in the TextureCube class type.

NegativeX	Negative x-face of the cube map.
NegativeY	Negative y-face of the cube map.
NegativeZ	Negative z-face of the cube map.

PositiveX	Positive x-face of the cube map.
PositiveY	Positive y-face of the cube map.
PositiveZ	Positive z-face of the cube map.

CullMode

public enum CullMode

Defines winding orders that may be used to identify back faces for culling.

CullClockwiseFace	Cull back faces with clockwise vertices.
CullCounterClockwiseFace	Cull back faces with counterclockwise vertices.
None	Do not cull back faces.

DepthFormat

public enum DepthFormat

Defines the format of data in a depth-stencil buffer. A depth buffer contains depth data and possibly stencil data. Control a depth buffer using a state object.

Depth16	A buffer that contains 16 bits of depth data.
Depth24	A buffer that contains 24 bits of depth data.
Depth24Stencil8	A 32-bit buffer that contains 24 bits of depth data and 8 bits of stencil data.
None	Do not create a depth buffer.

EffectParameterClass

public enum EffectParameterClass

Defines classes that can be used for effect parameters or shader constants.

Matrix	The constant is a matrix.
Object	The constant is either a texture, a shader, or a string.
Scalar	The constant is a scalar.
Struct	The constant is a structure.
Vector	The constant is a vector.

EffectParameterType

public enum EffectParameterType

Defines types that can be used for effect parameters or shader constants.

Bool	Parameter is a Boolean. Any non-zero value passed in will be mapped to 1 (true) before being written into the constant table; otherwise, the value will be set to 0 in the constant table.
Int32	Parameter is an integer. Any floating-point values passed in will be rounded off (to zero decimal places) before being written into the constant table.
Single	Parameter is a floating-point number.
String	Parameter is a string.
Texture	Parameter is a texture.
Texture1D	Parameter is a 1D texture.
Texture2D	Parameter is a 2D texture.
Texture3D	Parameter is a 3D texture.
TextureCube	Parameter is a cube texture.
Void	Parameter is a void pointer.

FillMode

public enum FillMode

Describes options for filling the vertices and lines that define a primitive.

Solid	Draw solid faces for each primitive.
WireFrame	Draw lines connecting the vertices that define a primitive face.

GraphicsDeviceStatus

public enum GraphicsDeviceStatus

Describes the status of the device.

Lost	The device has been lost.
Normal	The device is normal.
NotReset	The device has not been reset.

GraphicsProfile

`public enum GraphicsProfile`

Identifies the set of supported devices for the game based on device capabilities.

HiDef	Use the largest available set of graphic features and capabilities to target devices, such as an Xbox 360 console and a Windows-based computer, that have more enhanced graphic capabilities.
Reach	Use a limited set of graphic features and capabilities, allowing the game to support the widest variety of devices, including all Windows-based computers and Windows Phones.

IndexElementSize

`public enum IndexElementSize`

Defines the size of an element of an index buffer.

SixteenBits	16 bits.
ThirtyTwoBits	32 bits.

PresentInterval

`public enum PresentInterval`

Defines flags that describe the relationship between the adapter refresh rate and the rate at which `Present` operations are completed.

Default	Equivalent to setting One.
One	The driver waits for the vertical retrace period. `Present` operations are not affected more frequently than the screen-refresh rate; the runtime completes one `Present` operation per adapter refresh period, at most. This option is always available for both windowed and full-screen swap chains.
Two	The driver waits for the vertical retrace period. `Present` operations are not affected more frequently than every second screen refresh.
Immediate	The runtime updates the window client area immediately, and might do so more than once during the adapter refresh period. `Present` operations might be affected immediately. This option is always available for both windowed and full-screen swap chains.

PrimitiveType

public enum PrimitiveType

Defines how vertex data is ordered.

TriangleList	The data is ordered as a sequence of triangles; each triangle is described by three new vertices. Back-face culling is affected by the current winding-order render state.
TriangleStrip	The data is ordered as a sequence of triangles; each triangle is described by two new vertices and one vertex from the previous triangle. The back-face culling flag is flipped automatically on even-numbered triangles.
LineList	The data is ordered as a sequence of line segments; each line segment is described by two new vertices. The count may be any positive integer.
LineStrip	The data is ordered as a sequence of line segments; each line segment is described by one new vertex and the last vertex from the previous line seqment. The count may be any positive integer.

RenderTargetUsage

public enum RenderTargetUsage

Determines how render target data is used once a new render target is set.

DiscardContents	Always clears the render target data.
PlatformContents	Either clears or keeps the data, depending on the current platform. On Xbox 360, the render target will discard contents. On a PC, the render target will discard if multisampling is enabled, and preserve the contents if not.
PreserveContents	Always keeps the render-target data.

SetDataOptions

public enum SetDataOptions

Describes whether existing vertex or index-buffer data will be overwritten or discarded during a SetData operation.

Discard	The SetData operation will discard the entire buffer. A pointer to a new memory area is returned so that the direct memory access (DMA) and rendering from the previous area do not stall.

| None | Portions of existing data in the buffer may be overwritten during this operation. |
| NoOverwrite | The SetData operation will not overwrite existing data in the vertex and index buffers. Specifying this option allows the driver to return immediately from a SetData operation and continue rendering. |

SpriteEffects

public enum SpriteEffects

Defines sprite-mirroring options.

FlipHorizontally	Rotate 180 degrees about the Y axis before rendering.
FlipVertically	Rotate 180 degrees about the X axis before rendering.
None	No rotations specified.

SpriteSortMode

public enum SpriteSortMode

Defines sprite sort-rendering options.

BackToFront	Same as Deferred mode, except sprites are sorted by depth in back-to-front order prior to drawing. This procedure is recommended when drawing transparent sprites of varying depths.
Deferred	Sprites are not drawn until End is called. End will apply graphics-device settings and draw all the sprites in one batch, in the same order calls to Draw were received. This mode allows Draw calls to two or more instances of SpriteBatch without introducing conflicting graphics-device settings. SpriteBatch defaults to Deferred mode.
FrontToBack	Same as Deferred mode, except sprites are sorted by depth in front-to-back order prior to drawing. This procedure is recommended when drawing opaque sprites of varying depths.
Immediate	Begin will apply new graphics-device settings, and sprites will be drawn within each Draw call. In Immediate mode, there can only be one active SpriteBatch instance without introducing conflicting device settings.
Texture	Same as Deferred mode, except sprites are sorted by texture prior to drawing. This can improve performance when drawing non-overlapping sprites of uniform depth.

StencilOperation

public enum StencilOperation

Defines stencil-buffer operations.

Decrement	Decrements the stencil-buffer entry, wrapping to the maximum value if the new value is less than 0.
DecrementSaturation	Decrements the stencil-buffer entry, clamping to 0.
Increment	Increments the stencil-buffer entry, wrapping to 0 if the new value exceeds the maximum value.
IncrementSaturation	Increments the stencil-buffer entry, clamping to the maximum value.
Invert	Inverts the bits in the stencil-buffer entry.
Keep	Does not update the stencil-buffer entry. This is the default value.
Replace	Replaces the stencil-buffer entry with a reference value.
Zero	Sets the stencil-buffer entry to 0.

SurfaceFormat

public enum SurfaceFormat

Defines various types of surface formats. Two-dimensional (2D) images are represented by a range of memory called a surface. Within a surface, each element holds a color value representing a small section of the image, called a pixel. An image's detail level is defined by the number of pixels needed to represent the image and the number of bits needed for the image's color spectrum. For example, an image that is 800 pixels wide by 600 pixels high with 32 bits of color for each pixel (written as $800 \times 600 \times 32$) is more detailed than an image that is 640 pixels wide by 480 pixels tall with 16 bits of color for each pixel (written as $640 \times 480 \times 16$). Likewise, the more-detailed image requires a larger surface to store the data. For an $800 \times 600 \times 32$ image, the surface's array dimensions are 800×600, and each element holds a 32-bit value to represent its color.

All formats are listed from left to right, most-significant bit to least-significant bit. For example, ARGB formats are ordered from the most-significant bit channel A (alpha) to the least-significant bit channel B (blue). When traversing surface data, the data is stored in memory from least-significant bit to most-significant bit, which means the channel order in memory is from least-significant bit (blue) to most-significant bit (alpha).

The default value for formats that contain undefined channels (Rg32, Alpha8, and so on) is 1. The only exception is the Alpha8 format, which is initialized to 000 for the three color channels.

Color	(Unsigned format) 32-bit ARGB pixel format with alpha, using 8 bits per channel.
Bgr565	(Unsigned format) 16-bit BGR pixel format with 5 bits for blue, 6 bits for green, and 5 bits for red.
Bgra5551	(Unsigned format) 16-bit BGRA pixel format where 5 bits are reserved for each color and 1 bit is reserved for alpha.
Bgra4444	(Unsigned format) 16-bit BGRA pixel format with 4 bits for each channel.
Dxt1	DXT1 compression texture format. The runtime will not allow an application to create a surface using a DXTn format unless the surface dimensions are multiples of 4. This applies to off-screen–plain surfaces, render targets, 2D textures, cube textures, and volume textures.
Dxt3	DXT3 compression texture format. The runtime will not allow an application to create a surface using a DXTn format unless the surface dimensions are multiples of 4. This applies to offscreen-plain surfaces, render targets, 2D textures, cube textures, and volume textures.
Dxt5	DXT5 compression texture format. The runtime will not allow an application to create a surface using a DXTn format unless the surface dimensions are multiples of 4. This applies to offscreen-plain surfaces, render targets, 2D textures, cube textures, and volume textures.
NormalizedByte2	(Signed format) 16-bit bump-map format using 8 bits each for U and V data.
NormalizedByte4	(Signed format) 32-bit bump-map format using 8 bits for each channel.
Rgba1010102	(Unsigned format) 32-bit RGBA pixel format using 10 bits for each color and 2 bits for alpha.
Rg32	(Unsigned format) 32-bit pixel format using 16 bits each for red and green.
Rgba64	(Unsigned format) 64-bit RGBA pixel format using 16 bits for each component.
Alpha8	(Unsigned format) 8-bit alpha only.
Single	(IEEE format) 32-bit float format using 32 bits for the red channel.
Vector2	(IEEE format) 64-bit float format using 32 bits for the red channel and 32 bits for the green channel.
Vector4	(IEEE format) 128-bit float format using 32 bits for each channel (alpha, blue, green, red).
HalfSingle	(Floating-point format) 16-bit float format using 16 bits for the red channel.
HalfVector2	(Floating-point format) 32-bit float format using 16 bits for the red channel and 16 bits for the green channel.
HalfVector4	(Floating-point format) 64-bit float format using 16 bits for each channel (alpha, blue, green, red).
HdrBlendable	(Floating-point format) For high dynamic range data.

TextureAddressMode

public enum TextureAddressMode

Defines modes for addressing texels using texture coordinates that are outside the typical range of 0.0 to 1.0.

Clamp	Texture coordinates outside the range [0.0, 1.0] are set to the texture color at 0.0 or 1.0, respectively.
Mirror	Similar to Wrap, except that the texture is flipped at every integer junction. For U values between 0 and 1, for example, the texture is addressed normally; between 1 and 2, the texture is flipped (mirrored); between 2 and 3, the texture is normal again, and so on.
Wrap	Tile the texture at every integer junction. For example, for U values between 0 and 3, the texture is repeated three times; no mirroring is performed.

TextureFilter

public enum TextureFilter

Defines filtering types during texture sampling. A texture coordinate determines where to sample a texture. When a texel does not map exactly to one pixel, filtering is necessary to magnify (enlarge) or minify (shrink) the texture.

Not all valid filtering modes for a device apply to volume maps. In general, Point and Linear magnification filters are supported for volume maps. Devices that support anisotropic filtering for 2D maps do not necessarily support it for volume maps. However, applications that enable anisotropic filtering, even if they do not support it, receive the best available filtering (probably linear).

Linear	Use linear filtering.
Point	Use point filtering.
Anisotropic	Use anisotropic filtering.
LinearMipPoint	Use linear filtering to shrink (minify) or expand (magnify), and point filtering between mipmap levels (mip).
PointMipLinear	Use point filtering to shrink (minify) or expand (magnify), and linear filtering between mipmap levels.
MinLinearMagPoint MipLinear	Use linear filtering to shrink (minify), point filtering to expand (magnify), and linear filtering between mipmap levels.
MinLinearMagPointMipPoint	Use linear filtering to shrink (minify), point filtering to expand (magnify), and point filtering between mipmap levels.

MinPointMagLinearMipLinear	Use point filtering to shrink (minify), linear filtering to expand (magnify), and linear filtering between mipmap levels.
MinPointMagLinearMipPoint	Use point filtering to shrink (minify), linear filtering to expand (magnify), and point filtering between mipmap levels.

VertexElementFormat

`public enum VertexElementFormat`

Defines vertex element formats.

Single	Single-component, 32-bit floating-point, expanded to (float, 0, 0, 1).
Vector2	Two-component, 32-bit floating-point, expanded to (float, Float32 value, 0, 1).
Vector3	Three-component, 32-bit floating point, expanded to (float, float, float, 1).
Vector4	Four-component, 32-bit floating point, expanded to (float, float, float, float).
HalfVector2	Two-component, 16-bit floating point expanded to (value, value, value, value). This type is valid for vertex shader version 2.0 or higher.
HalfVector4	Four-component, 16-bit floating-point expanded to (value, value, value, value). This type is valid for vertex shader version 2.0 or higher.
Color	Four-component, packed, unsigned byte, mapped to 0 to 1 range. Input is in Int32 format (ARGB) expanded to (R, G, B, A).
NormalizedShort2	Normalized, two-component, signed short, expanded to (first short/32767.0, second short/32767.0, 0, 1). This type is valid for vertex shader version 2.0 or higher.
NormalizedShort4	Normalized, four-component, signed short, expanded to (first short/32767.0, second short/32767.0, third short/32767.0, fourth short/32767.0). This type is valid for vertex shader version 2.0 or higher.
Short2	Two-component, signed short expanded to (value, value, 0, 1).
Short4	Four-component, signed short expanded to (value, value, value, value).
Byte4	Four-component, unsigned byte.

VertexElementUsage

`public enum VertexElementUsage`

Defines usage for vertex elements.

Binormal	Vertex binormal data.
BlendIndices	Blending indices data. (`BlendIndices` with `UsageIndex = 0`) specifies matrix indices for fixed-function vertex processing using indexed paletted skinning.
BlendWeight	Blending weight data. (`BlendWeight` with `UsageIndex = 0`) specifies the blend weights in fixed-function vertex processing.

Color	Vertex data contains diffuse or specular color. (`Color` with `UsageIndex` = 0) specifies the diffuse color in the fixed-function vertex shader and in pixel shaders prior to `ps_3_0`. (Color with UsageIndex = 1) specifies the specular color in the fixed-function vertex shader and in pixel shaders prior to `ps_3_0`.
Depth	Vertex data contains depth data.
Fog	Vertex data contains fog data. (`Fog` with `UsageIndex` = 0) specifies a fog blend value to use after pixel shading is finished. This flag applies to pixel shaders prior to version `ps_3_0`.
Normal	Vertex normal data. (`Normal` with `UsageIndex` = 0) specifies vertex normals for fixed-function vertex processing and the N-patch tessellator. (`Normal` with `UsageIndex` = 1) specifies vertex normals for fixed-function vertex processing for skinning.
PointSize	Point size data. (`PointSize` with `UsageIndex` = 0) specifies the point-size attribute used by the setup engine of the rasterizer to expand a point into a quad for the point-sprite functionality.
Position	Position data. (`Position` with `UsageIndex` = 0) specifies the non-transformed position in fixed-function vertex processing and the N-patch tessellator. (`Position` with `UsageIndex` = 1) specifies the non-transformed position in the fixed-function vertex shader for skinning.
Sample	Vertex data contains sampler data. (`Sample` with `UsageIndex` = 0) specifies the displacement value to look up.
Tangent	Vertex tangent data.
TessellateFactor	Single, positive floating-point value. (`TessellateFactor` with `UsageIndex` = 0) specifies a tessellation factor used in the tessellation unit to control the rate of tessellation.
TextureCoordinate	Texture-coordinate data. (`TextureCoordinate`, n) specifies texture coordinates in fixed-function vertex processing and in pixel shaders prior to `ps_3_0`. These coordinates can be used to pass user-defined data.

Hint

There is no `Graphics` demo project in this chapter because we cover rendering in the whole later in this book.

SUMMARY

This chapter was wholly devoted to the `Graphics` namespace, which is quite large and extensive, but only because it is jam packed with features. You may refer back to this chapter at any time when working on the rendering projects later in this book.

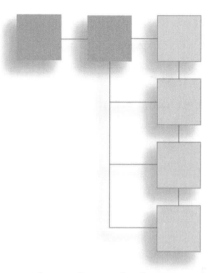

CHAPTER 8

Input

For most programmers and designers, user input often takes a back seat to rendering in the priority list. But user input is far more important to gameplay than many people realize. There's more to user input than just reading the keyboard, mouse, and controller, just as there is more to rendering than just a video card. Timing is of paramount importance, as is synchronization with game objects such as the player's character or vehicle, depending on the game. This chapter examines the entire Input namespace by looking at all the classes, interfaces, and so forth. It then looks at how to work with the input devices on both the Windows and Xbox 360 platforms. Because we aren't touching any other system, we won't be getting into touch controls.

Here's what you will learn about:

- Input classes
- Input structures
- Input enumerations
- Input Demo program

Microsoft.Xna.Framework.Input REFERENCE

The following pages provide a complete reference to the Input namespace. This is a great resource because it's easy to miss the many classes, structures, and events built in to the framework unless you see a list of those features in a quick-reference format, such as this one. As was the case in previous reference chapters, inherited items are omitted from the list of properties, methods, etc., for each item.

Classes

Following are the classes found within the Input namespace.

GamePad

public static class GamePad

Allows retrieval of user interaction with an Xbox 360 controller (or other input device such as a steering wheel) and setting of controller vibration motors.

Public Methods	
GetCapabilities	Retrieves the capabilities of an Xbox 360 controller.
GetState	Gets the current state of a gamepad controller. As an option, it specifies a dead-zone processing method for the analog sticks.
SetVibration	Sets the vibration motor speeds on an Xbox 360 controller.

Keyboard

public static class Keyboard

Allows retrieval of keystrokes from a keyboard input device, which can be a normal keyboard under Windows or a Chatpad on an Xbox 360 system.

Public Methods	
GetState	Returns the current keyboard or Chatpad state.

Mouse

public static class Mouse

Allows retrieval of position and button clicks from a mouse input device. Mouse functionality is not supported on the Xbox 360, but mouse-related code will compile and execute. Values returned by these calls are inaccurate.

Public Properties	
WindowHandle	Gets or sets the window used for mouse processing. Mouse coordinates returned by GetState are relative to the upper-left corner of this window.

Public Methods	
GetState	Gets the current state of the mouse, including mouse position and buttons pressed.
SetPosition	Sets the position of the mouse cursor relative to the upper-left corner of the window.

Structures

The following structures are found in the Input namespace.

GamePadButtons

public struct GamePadButtons

Indicates whether buttons on an Xbox 360 controller are pressed or released.

Public Properties	
A	Indicates whether the A button on the Xbox 360 controller is pressed.
B	Indicates whether the B button on the Xbox 360 controller is pressed.
Back	Indicates whether the Back button on the Xbox 360 controller is pressed.
BigButton	Indicates whether the BigButton button is pressed (on a unique controller).
LeftShoulder	Indicates whether the left shoulder (bumper) button on the Xbox 360 controller is pressed.
LeftStick	Indicates whether the left stick button on the Xbox 360 controller is pressed (the stick is clicked in).
RightShoulder	Indicates whether the right shoulder (bumper) button on the Xbox 360 controller is pressed.
RightStick	Indicates whether the right stick button on the Xbox 360 controller is pressed (the stick is clicked in).
Start	Indicates whether the Start button on the Xbox 360 controller is pressed.
X	Indicates whether the X button on the Xbox 360 controller is pressed.
Y	Indicates whether the Y button on the Xbox 360 controller is pressed.

GamePadCapabilities

public struct GamePadCapabilities

Describes the capabilities of an Xbox 360 controller input device, including controller type, and indicates whether the device supports voice chat.

Public Properties

GamePadType	Gets the type of controller.
HasAButton	Indicates whether the controller has an A button.
HasBackButton	Indicates whether the controller has a Back button.
HasBButton	Indicates whether the controller has a B button.
HasBigButton	Indicates whether the controller has a BigButton button.
HasDPadDownButton	Indicates whether the controller has a directional pad Down button.
HasDPadLeftButton	Indicates whether the controller has a directional pad Left button.
HasDPadRightButton	Indicates whether the controller has a directional pad Right button.
HasDPadUpButton	Indicates whether the controller has a directional pad Up button.
HasLeftShoulderButton	Indicates whether the controller has a left bumper button.
HasLeftStickButton	Indicates whether the controller has a digital button control on the left analog stick.
HasLeftTrigger	Indicates whether the controller has a left analog trigger.
HasLeftVibrationMotor	Indicates whether the controller has a low-frequency vibration motor.
HasLeftXThumbStick	Indicates whether the controller supports a left analog control with horizontal movement.
HasLeftYThumbStick	Indicates whether the controller supports a left analog control with vertical movement.
HasRightShoulderButton	Indicates whether the controller has a right bumper button.
HasRightStickButton	Indicates whether the controller has a digital button control on the right analog stick.
HasRightTrigger	Indicates whether the controller has a right analog trigger.
HasRightVibrationMotor	Indicates whether the controller has a high-frequency vibration motor.
HasRightXThumbStick	Indicates whether the controller supports a right analog control with horizontal movement.
HasRightYThumbStick	Indicates whether the controller supports a right analog control with vertical movement.
HasStartButton	Indicates whether the controller has a Start button.
HasVoiceSupport	Indicates whether the controller supports voice.
HasXButton	Indicates whether the controller has an X button.
HasYButton	Indicates whether the controller has a Y button.
IsConnected	Indicates whether the Xbox 360 controller is connected.

GamePadDPad

```
public struct GamePadDPad
```

Indicates which directions on the directional pad of an Xbox 360 controller are being pressed.

Public Properties

Down	Indicates whether the Down direction on the Xbox 360 controller directional pad is pressed.
Left	Indicates whether the Left direction on the Xbox 360 controller directional pad is pressed.
Right	Indicates whether the Right direction on the Xbox 360 controller directional pad is pressed.
Up	Indicates whether the Up direction on the Xbox 360 controller directional pad is pressed.

GamePadState

`public struct GamePadState`

Represents specific information about the state of an Xbox 360 controller, including the current state of buttons and sticks.

Public Properties

Buttons	Returns a structure that indicates what buttons on the Xbox 360 controller are pressed.
DPad	Returns a structure that indicates what directions of the directional pad on the Xbox 360 controller are pressed.
IsConnected	Indicates whether the Xbox 360 controller is connected.
PacketNumber	Gets the packet number associated with this state.
ThumbSticks	Returns a structure that indicates the position of the Xbox 360 controller sticks (thumbsticks).
Triggers	Returns a structure that indicates the position of triggers on the Xbox 360 controller.

Public Methods

IsButtonDown	Determines whether specified input device buttons are pressed in this GamePadState.
IsButtonUp	Determines whether specified input device buttons are up (not pressed) in this GamePadState.

GamePadThumbSticks

`public struct GamePadThumbSticks`

Structure that represents the position of left and right sticks (thumbsticks) on an Xbox 360 controller.

Public Properties

Left	Returns the position of the left Xbox 360 controller stick (thumbstick) as a 2D vector.
Right	Returns the position of the right Xbox 360 controller stick (thumbstick) as a 2D vector.

GamePadTriggers

`public struct GamePadTriggers`

Structure that defines the position of the left and right triggers on an Xbox 360 controller.

Public Properties

Left	Indicates the position of the left trigger on the Xbox 360 controller.
Right	Indicates the position of the right trigger on the Xbox 360 controller.

KeyboardState

`public struct KeyboardState`

Represents a state of keystrokes recorded by a keyboard input device.

Public Properties

Item	Returns the state of a particular key.

Public Methods

IsKeyDown	Returns whether a specified key is currently being pressed.
IsKeyUp	Returns whether a specified key is currently not being pressed.

MouseState

`public struct MouseState`

Represents the state of a mouse input device, including mouse-cursor position and buttons pressed.

Public Properties

LeftButton	Returns the state of the left mouse button.
MiddleButton	Returns the state of the middle mouse button.
RightButton	Returns the state of the right mouse button.
ScrollWheelValue	Gets the cumulative mouse scroll wheel value since the game was started.
X	Specifies the horizontal position of the mouse cursor.
XButton1	Returns the state of XButton1.
XButton2	Returns the state of XButton2.
Y	Specifies the vertical position of the mouse cursor.

Enumerations

Following are the enumerations in the Input namespace.

Buttons

public enum Buttons

Enumerates the input device buttons for a controller or other controller-type device such as a driving wheel or flight stick.

Members

A	A button.
B	B button.
Back	Back button.
BigButton	BigButton button.
DPadDown	Directional pad up.
DPadLeft	Directional pad left.
DPadRight	Directional pad right.
DPadUp	Directional pad down.
LeftShoulder	Left bumper (shoulder) button.
LeftStick	Left stick button (pressing the left stick).
LeftThumbstickDown	Left stick is toward down.
LeftThumbstickLeft	Left stick is toward the left.
LeftThumbstickRight	Left stick is toward the right.
LeftThumbstickUp	Left stick is toward up.
LeftTrigger	Left trigger.
RightShoulder	Right bumper (shoulder) button.

RightStick	Right stick button (pressing the right stick).
RightThumbstickDown	Right stick is toward down.
RightThumbstickLeft	Right stick is toward the left.
RightThumbstickRight	Right stick is toward the right.
RightThumbstickUp	Right stick is toward up.
RightTrigger	Right trigger.
Start	Start button.
X	X button.
Y	Y button.

ButtonState

public enum ButtonState

Indicates the state of a controller button.

Pressed	The button is pressed.
Released	The button is released.

GamePadDeadZone

public enum GamePadDeadZone

Specifies a type of dead-zone processing to apply to Xbox 360 controller analog sticks when calling GetState.

Circular	The combined X and Y position of each stick is compared to the dead zone. This provides better control than IndependentAxes when the stick is used as a two-dimensional control surface, such as when controlling a character's view in a first-person game.
IndependentAxes	The X and Y positions of each stick are compared against the dead zone independently. This setting is the default when calling GetState.
None	The values of each stick are not processed and are returned by GetState as raw values. This is best if you intend to implement your own dead-zone processing.

GamePadType

public enum GamePadType

Describes the type of a specified Xbox 360 controller.

AlternateGuitar	Controller is an alternate guitar (like the one included with some versions of *Guitar Hero*).
ArcadeStick	Controller is an Arcade stick (such as Capcom's *Street Fighter IV* controller).
BigButtonPad	Controller is a big button pad.
DancePad	Controller is a dance pad.
DrumKit	Controller is a drum kit.
FlightStick	Controller is a flight stick.
GamePad	Controller is the Xbox 360 controller.
Guitar	Controller is a guitar.
Unknown	Controller is an unknown type.
Wheel	Controller is a wheel.

Keys

`public enum Keys`

Indicates a particular key on a keyboard.

Xbox 360 Chatpad Keys

ChatPadGreen	Green Chatpad key.
ChatPadOrange	Orange Chatpad key.

Windows Keys

A	A key.
Add	Add key.
Apps	Applications key.
Attn	Attn key.
B	B key.
Back	Backspace key.
BrowserBack	Browser Back key.
BrowserFavorites	Browser Favorites key.
BrowserForward	Browser Forward key.
BrowserHome	Browser Start and Home key.
BrowserRefresh	Browser Refresh key.
BrowserSearch	Browser Search key.
BrowserStop	Browser Stop key.
C	C key.
CapsLock	Caps Lock key.
Crsel	CrSel key.
D	D key.

D0	Miscellaneous characters; varies by keyboard.
D1	Miscellaneous characters; varies by keyboard.
D2	Miscellaneous characters; varies by keyboard.
D3	Miscellaneous characters; varies by keyboard.
D4	Miscellaneous characters; varies by keyboard.
D5	Miscellaneous characters; varies by keyboard.
D6	Miscellaneous characters; varies by keyboard.
D7	Miscellaneous characters; varies by keyboard.
D8	Miscellaneous characters; varies by keyboard.
D9	Miscellaneous characters; varies by keyboard.
Decimal	Decimal key.
Delete	Del key.
Divide	Divide key.
Down	Down arrow key.
E	E key.
End	End key.
Enter	Enter key.
EraseEof	Erase EOF key.
Escape	Esc key.
Execute	Execute key.
Exsel	ExSel key.
F	F key.
F1	F1 key.
F10	F10 key.
F11	F11 key.
F12	F12 key.
F13	F13 key.
F14	F14 key.
F15	F15 key.
F16	F16 key.
F17	F17 key.
F18	F18 key.
F19	F19 key.
F2	F2 key.
F20	F20 key.
F21	F21 key.
F22	F22 key.
F23	F23 key.
F24	F24 key.
F3	F3 key.

F4	F4 key.
F5	F5 key.
F6	F6 key.
F7	F7 key.
F8	F8 key.
F9	F9 key.
G	G key.
H	H key.
Help	Help key.
Home	Home key.
I	I key.
ImeConvert	IME Convert key.
ImeNoConvert	IME NoConvert key.
Insert	Ins key.
J	J key.
K	K key.
Kana	Kana key on Japanese keyboards.
Kanji	Kanji key on Japanese keyboards.
L	L key.
LaunchApplication1	Start Application 1 key.
LaunchApplication2	Start Application 2 key.
LaunchMail	Start Mail key.
Left	Left arrow key.
LeftAlt	Left Alt key.
LeftControl	Left Ctrl key.
LeftShift	Left Shift key.
LeftWindows	Left Windows key.
M	M key.
MediaNextTrack	Next Track key.
MediaPlayPause	Play/Pause Media key.
MediaPreviousTrack	Previous Track key.
MediaStop	Stop Media key.
Multiply	Multiply key.
N	N key.
None	Reserved.
NumLock	Num Lock key.
NumPad0	Numeric keypad 0 key.
NumPad1	Numeric keypad 1 key.
NumPad2	Numeric keypad 2 key.
NumPad3	Numeric keypad 3 key.

NumPad4	Numeric keypad 4 key.
NumPad5	Numeric keypad 5 key.
NumPad6	Numeric keypad 6 key.
NumPad7	Numeric keypad 7 key.
NumPad8	Numeric keypad 8 key.
NumPad9	Numeric keypad 9 key.
O	O key.
Oem8	Miscellaneous characters; varies by keyboard.
OemAuto	OEM Auto key.
OemBackslash	OEM angle bracket or backslash (\) key.
OemClear	Clear key.
OemCloseBrackets	OEM close bracket (]) key.
OemComma	Comma (,) key.
OemCopy	OEM Copy key.
OemEnlW	OEM Enlarge Window key.
OemMinus	For any country/region, the minus (−) key.
OemOpenBrackets	OEM open bracket ([) key.
OemPeriod	Period (.) key.
OemPipe	OEM pipe (|) key.
OemPlus	For any country/region, the plus (+) key.
OemQuestion	OEM question mark (?) key.
OemQuotes	OEM single/double quote (') key.
OemSemicolon	OEM semicolon (;) key.
OemTilde	OEM tilde (~) key.
P	P key.
Pa1	PA1 key.
PageDown	Page Down key.
PageUp	Page Up key.
Pause	Pause key.
Play	Play key.
Print	Print key.
PrintScreen	Print Screen key.
ProcessKey	IME Process key.
Q	Q key.
R	R key.
Right	Right arrow key.
RightAlt	Right Alt key.
RightControl	Right Ctrl key.
RightShift	Right Shift key.
RightWindows	Right Windows key.

S	S key.
Scroll	Scroll Lock key.
Select	Select key.
SelectMedia	Select Media key.
Separator	Separator key.
Sleep	Computer Sleep key.
Space	Spacebar.
Subtract	Subtract key.
T	T key.
Tab	Tab key.
U	U key.
Up	Up arrow key.
V	V key.
VolumeDown	Volume Down key.
VolumeMute	Volume Mute key.
VolumeUp	Volume Up key.
W	W key.
X	X key.
Y	Y key.
Z	Z key.
Zoom	Zoom key.

KeyState

public enum KeyState

Indicates the state of a keyboard key.

Down	Key is pressed.
Up	Key is released.

Input Demo Program

The Input Demo program shows how to put the Keyboard, Mouse, and GamePad classes to work in a real project to read the state information about an installed keyboard, mouse, and one or more controllers. Figure 8.1 shows the output of the program running in Windows. Figure 8.2 shows the program running on an Xbox 360.

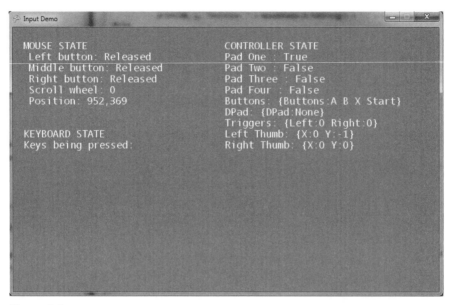

Figure 8.1
The Input Demo program reports the current state of the mouse, keyboard, and controllers.

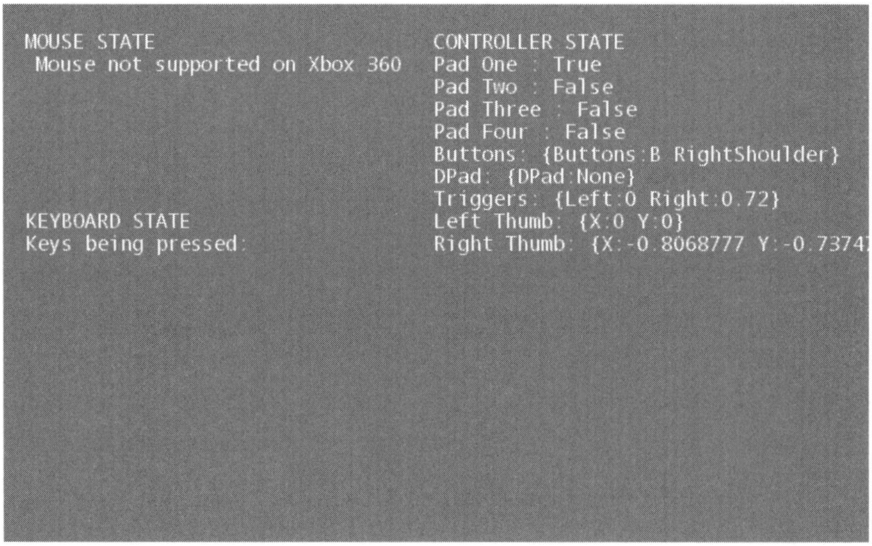

Figure 8.2
The mouse code is skipped when running on an Xbox 360.

Keyboard Input

You can detect individual key presses with `KeyboardState.IsKeyDown()` (for pressed) and `KeyboardState.IsKeyUp()` (for not pressed). To just retrieve a list of all currently pressed keys, `KeyboardState.GetPressedKeys()` will return an array of `Keys` containing all the keys currently being pressed. The keyboard state is read like this:

```
KeyboardState keyState;
keyState = Keyboard.GetState();
```

Normally, in a game project, you will need to know whether a specific key is being pressed in order to respond to that input event (for instance, using the right trigger to fire a weapon). For an individual key, such as Esc, use `keyState.IsKeyDown()`, like so:

```
if (keyState.IsKeyDown(Keys.Escape)) this.Exit();
```

Retrieving all the currently pressed keys might be a faster way to handle input events (instead of responding to them individually, one key at a time). To read all the currently pressed keys, use the following:

```
Keys[] keys;
keys = keyState.GetPressedKeys();
```

Mouse Input

Reading the mouse state is much simpler than reading the keyboard state because there is only one object with named properties for the mouse's hardware (such as the buttons and wheel). The `MouseState` class is used to retrieve the current state of the mouse:

```
MouseState mouseState;
mouseState = Mouse.GetState();
```

The `MouseState` variable will contain all the properties you need to use the mouse for input in a Windows game. You may refer to the `MouseState` structure definition earlier in the chapter for details about all the properties, but we'll go over the most common properties here. The three typical mouse buttons can be read as `LeftButton`, `MiddleButton`, and `RightButton`. The scroll wheel is called `ScrollWheel`. The mouse's position is returned with the X and Y properties.

Note

MouseState is also used to read a touch-screen device such as Windows Phone. Mouse input is not supported at all on the Xbox 360.

Controller Input

You can write code to support up to four controllers on Windows *and* Xbox 360 projects. It's important to perform a check on the controller states to verify that at least one controller is plugged in. This state is retrieved using the GamePadCapabilities structure and GamePad.GetCapabilities().

```
GamePadCapabilities caps;
caps = GamePad.GetCapabilities(PlayerIndex.One);
```

In the Input Demo project, all four controllers are polled for their state and the resulting state is printed on the screen. The capabilities reported here are dynamic, so it is possible to plug in a controller after the program has already started and then begin reading input from that controller.

An interesting property of GamePadCapabilities that we don't look at in the Input Demo project coming up is the *type* of controller device detected! The property is called GamePadCapabilities.GamePadType and is linked to the GamePadType enumeration (refer to "GamePadType" in the reference section).

- Unknown = 0
- GamePad = 1
- Wheel = 2
- ArcadeStick = 3
- FlightStick = 4
- DancePad = 5
- Guitar = 6
- AlternateGuitar = 7
- DrumKit = 8
- BigButtonPad = 768

N o t e

The GamePadState structure is used to hold data about a controller, and is retrieved with GamePad.GetState().

```
GamePadState padState;
padState = GamePad.GetState(PlayerIndex.One);
```

There are quite a few properties in GamePadState that report the essential data for controller input, including the following:

- Buttons
- Triggers
- ThumbSticks
- DPad (the old-school directional pad)

Input Demo Source

Listing 8.1 contains the source code for the Input Demo project.

Listing 8.1   Input Demo Project

```
using System;
using System.Collections.Generic;
using System.Linq;
using Microsoft.Xna.Framework;
using Microsoft.Xna.Framework.Audio;
using Microsoft.Xna.Framework.Content;
using Microsoft.Xna.Framework.GamerServices;
using Microsoft.Xna.Framework.Graphics;
using Microsoft.Xna.Framework.Input;
using Microsoft.Xna.Framework.Media;
using Microsoft.Xna.Framework.Net;
using Microsoft.Xna.Framework.Storage;

namespace Graphics_Demo
{
    public class Game1 : Microsoft.Xna.Framework.Game
    {
        GraphicsDeviceManager graphics;
        SpriteBatch spriteBatch;
```

```csharp
SpriteFont font;
KeyboardState keyState;
Keys[] keys;
MouseState mouseState;
GamePadState padState;

public Game1()
{
    graphics = new GraphicsDeviceManager(this);
    Content.RootDirectory = "Content";
}

protected override void Initialize()
{
    base.Initialize();
}

protected override void LoadContent()
{
    spriteBatch = new SpriteBatch(GraphicsDevice);
    font = Content.Load<SpriteFont>("font1");
}

protected override void UnloadContent() { }

protected override void Update(GameTime gameTime)
{
    //escape key exits
    keyState = Keyboard.GetState();
    if (keyState.IsKeyDown(Keys.Escape)) this.Exit();

    //controller button
    if (GamePad.GetState(PlayerIndex.One).Buttons.Back ==
        ButtonState.Pressed) this.Exit();

    base.Update(gameTime);
}

protected override void Draw(GameTime gameTime)
{
```

```
        GraphicsDevice.Clear(Color.CornflowerBlue);
        spriteBatch.Begin();
        UpdateKeyboard();
        UpdateMouse();
        UpdatePad();
        spriteBatch.End();
        base.Draw(gameTime);
    }

    void UpdateKeyboard()
    {
        //update keyboard
        keys = keyState.GetPressedKeys();
        int y = 180;
        print(20, y, "KEYBOARD STATE"); y += 20;
        print(20, y, "Keys being pressed:"); y += 20;
        foreach (Keys key in keys)
        {
            print(30, y, key.ToString());   y += 20;
        }
    }

    void UpdateMouse()
    {
        int y = 20;
        print(20, y, "MOUSE STATE"); y += 20;
#if WINDOWS
        mouseState = Mouse.GetState();
        print(30, y, "Left button: " + mouseState.LeftButton.
            ToString()); y += 20;
        print(30, y, "Middle button: " + mouseState.MiddleButton.
            ToString()); y += 20;
        print(30, y, "Right button: " + mouseState.RightButton.
            ToString()); y += 20;
        print(30, y, "Scroll wheel: " + mouseState.ScrollWheelValue.
            ToString()); y += 20;
        print(30, y, "Position: " + mouseState.X.ToString() + "," +
            mouseState.Y.ToString()); y += 20;
#else
        print(30, y, "Mouse not supported on Xbox 360");
```

```
#endif
    }

    void UpdatePad()
    {
        int x = 400, y = 20;
        print(x, y, "CONTROLLER STATE"); y += 20;
        GamePadCapabilities caps;
        for (PlayerIndex n=PlayerIndex.One; n<=PlayerIndex.Four; n++)
        {
            caps = GamePad.GetCapabilities(n);
            print(x, y, "Pad " + n.ToString() +" : " + caps.
                IsConnected.ToString());   y += 20;
        }

        padState = GamePad.GetState(PlayerIndex.One);
        print(x, y, "Buttons: " + padState.Buttons.ToString());
        y += 20;
        print(x, y, "DPad: " + padState.DPad.ToString()); y += 20;
        print(x, y, "Triggers: " + padState.Triggers.ToString());
        y += 20;
        print(x, y, "Left Thumb: " + padState.ThumbSticks.Left.
            ToString()); y += 20;
        print(x, y, "Right Thumb: " + padState.ThumbSticks.Right.
            ToString()); y += 20;
    }

    void print(int x, int y, string text)
    {
        spriteBatch.DrawString(font, text, new Vector2((float)x,
            (float)y), Color.White);
    }
    void print(int x, int y, string text, Color color)
    {
        spriteBatch.DrawString(font, text, new Vector2((float)x,
            (float)y), color);
    }
    }
}
```

Summary

Device input is remarkably easy to program in XNA Game Studio, thanks to the way in which the devices have been abstracted. Let this chapter be a reference for the three primary input devices and check back here for details should you wish to support an alternate device such as a large-button arcade fighting joystick, driving wheel, or flight stick.

CHAPTER 9

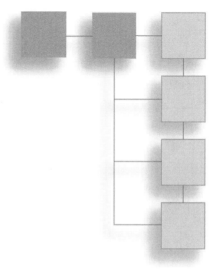

MEDIA

The Media namespace is filled with a rich collection of classes and supporting enumerations for working with audio and video files that have been added to a device by the user.

Here's what this chapter covers:

- Media classes
- Media enumerations
- Media Demo program

MICROSOFT.XNA.FRAMEWORK.MEDIA REFERENCE

The following pages provide a complete reference to the Media namespace, which gives us access to the custom music file playback capability of XNA Game Studio. This chapter includes a quick reference to the Media namespace as well as an example of a media player with a simple visualization. As was the case in previous reference chapters, inherited items are omitted from the list of properties, methods, etc., for each item.

Classes

Following are the classes found within the Media namespace.

Album

`public sealed class Album : IEquatable<Album>, IDisposable`

Provides access to an album in the media library. The `Album` class provides information about an album, including the album's Name, Artist, and Songs. You can obtain an `Album` object through the `AlbumCollection.Item` indexer and the `Song.Album` property.

Public Properties

Artist	Gets the artist of the album.
Duration	Gets the duration of the album.
Genre	Gets the genre of the album.
HasArt	Gets a value indicating whether the album has associated album art.
Name	Gets the name of the album.
Songs	Gets a `SongCollection` that contains the songs on the album.

Public Methods

GetAlbumArt	Returns the stream that contains the album art image data.
GetThumbnail	Returns the stream that contains the album thumbnail image data.

AlbumCollection

`public sealed class AlbumCollection : IEnumerable<Album>, IEnumerable, IDisposable`

A collection of albums in the media library. The `AlbumCollection` class provides access to albums in the device's media library.

Use the `MediaLibrary.Albums` property to obtain a collection of all albums in the media library, the `Artist.Albums` property to obtain a collection of albums associated with a particular artist, and the `Genre.Albums` property to obtain a collection of albums associated with a particular genre.

`AlbumCollection` does not immediately instantiate instances of all albums in the collection. Instead, individual `Album` objects are created each time an album is accessed through the collection's `Item` indexer. See the "Remarks" section of `Item` for the resource implications of maintaining references to multiple `Album` objects.

Public Properties	
Count	Gets the number of `Album` objects in the `AlbumCollection`.
Item	Gets the `Album` object at the specified index in the `AlbumCollection`.
Public Methods	
GetEnumerator	Returns an enumerator that iterates through the `AlbumCollection`.

Artist

```
public sealed class Artist : IEquatable<Artist>, IDisposable
```

Provides access to artist information in the media library. The `Artist` class provides information about an artist, including the artist's Name, Albums, and Songs. You can obtain an `Artist` object through the `ArtistCollection.Item` indexer and the `Album.Artist` and `Song.Artist` properties.

Public Properties	
Albums	Gets the `AlbumCollection` for the Artist.
Name	Gets the name of the Artist.
Songs	Gets the `SongCollection` for the Artist.

ArtistCollection

```
public sealed class ArtistCollection : IEnumerable<Artist>, IEnumerable, IDisposable
```

The collection of all artists in the media library. The `ArtistCollection` class provides access to all artists in the device's media library.

Use the `MediaLibrary.Artists` property to obtain the artist collection.

`ArtistCollection` does not immediately instantiate instances of all artists in the collection. Instead, individual `Artist` objects are created each time an artist is accessed through the collection's `Item` indexer.

Public Properties	
Count	Gets the number of `Artist` objects in the `ArtistCollection`.
Item	Gets the Artist at the specified index in the `ArtistCollection`.
Public Methods	
GetEnumerator	Returns an enumerator that iterates through the `ArtistCollection`.

Genre

`public sealed class Genre : IEquatable<Genre>, IDisposable`

Provides access to genre information in the media library. The `Genre` class provides information about a genre, including the genre's Name, and the Albums and Songs in that genre that are on the device.

You can obtain a `Genre` object through the `GenreCollection.Item` indexer and the `Album.Genre` and `Song.Genre` properties.

Public Properties	
Albums	Gets the `AlbumCollection` for the Genre.
Name	Gets the name of the Genre.
Songs	Gets the `SongCollection` for the Genre.

GenreCollection

`public sealed class GenreCollection : IEnumerable<Genre>, IEnumerable, IDisposable`

The collection of all genres in the media library. The `GenreCollection` class provides access to all genres in the device's media library.

Use the `MediaLibrary.Genres` property to obtain the genre collection.

The `GenreCollection` does not immediately instantiate instances of all genres in the collection. Instead, individual `Genre` objects are created each time a genre is accessed through the collection's `Item` indexer.

Public Properties	
Count	Gets the number of `Genre` objects in the `GenreCollection`.
Item	Gets the Genre at the specified index in the `GenreCollection`.
Public Methods	
GetEnumerator	Returns an enumerator that iterates through the `GenreCollection`.

MediaLibrary

`public sealed class MediaLibrary : IDisposable`

Provides access to songs, playlists, and pictures in the device's media library. `MediaLibrary` provides the following properties that return media collections: `Albums`, `Artists`, `Genres`, `Pictures`, `Playlists`, and `Songs`. Each property returns a collection that can be enumerated and indexed. The collection represents all media of that type in the device's media library.

The media collections do not retrieve or instantiate all media objects immediately. Instead, you can use the collections when needed to retrieve individual media objects such as Song and Artist objects.

On Windows, MediaLibrary can find songs only if the Windows Media Player previously found songs on the system. This means that Windows Media Player first must search the system for music before any songs can be accessed through MediaLibrary.

Public Properties	
Albums	Gets the AlbumCollection that contains all albums in the media library.
Artists	Gets the ArtistCollection that contains all artists in the media library.
Genres	Gets the GenreCollection that contains all genres in the media library.
MediaSource	Gets the MediaSource with which this media library was constructed.
Pictures	Gets the PictureCollection that contains all pictures in the media library.
Playlists	Gets the PlaylistCollection that contains all playlists in the media library.
RootPictureAlbum	Gets the root PictureAlbum for all pictures in the media library.
SavedPictures	Returns the collection of all saved pictures in the device's media library.
Songs	Gets the SongCollection that contains all songs in the media library.
Public Methods	
GetPictureFromToken	Retrieves a picture from the device's media library based on a picture token.
SavePicture	Saves the image to the media library.

MediaPlayer

public static class MediaPlayer

Provides methods and properties to play, pause, resume, and stop songs. MediaPlayer also exposes shuffle, repeat, volume, play position, and visualization capabilities. MediaPlayer provides methods and properties for playing songs in the media library.

To control song playback, use the Play, Pause, Stop, and Resume methods. The MoveNext and MovePrevious methods move to the next or previous song in the queue. They operate as if the queue was circular. That is, MoveNext, when the last song is playing, moves to the first song. MovePrevious, when the first song is playing, moves to the last song.

To get and set playback options, use the IsMuted, IsRepeating, IsShuffled, PlayPosition, and Volume properties.

To obtain visualization data for the currently playing song, call GetVisualizationData.

MediaPlayer is a static class, so you do not have to use new to instantiate an instance of the class. Instead, call methods and properties directly on the class.

Public Properties

GameHasControl	Determines whether the game has control of the background music.
IsMuted	Gets or set the muted setting for the media player.
IsRepeating	Gets or sets the repeat setting for the media player.
IsShuffled	Gets or sets the shuffle setting for the media player.
IsVisualizationEnabled	Gets or sets the visualization enabled setting for the media player.
PlayPosition	Gets the play position within the currently playing song.
Queue	Gets the media playback queue, MediaQueue.
State	Gets the media playback state, MediaState.
Volume	Gets or sets the media player volume.

Public Methods

GetVisualizationData	Retrieves visualization (frequency and sample) data for the currently playing song.
MoveNext	Moves to the next song in the queue of playing songs.
MovePrevious	Moves to the previous song in the queue of playing songs.
Pause	Pauses the currently playing song.
Play	Overloaded. Plays a song or collection of songs.
Resume	Resumes a paused song.
Stop	Stops playing a song.

Public Events

ActiveSongChanged	Raised when the active song changes due to active playback or due to explicit calls to the MoveNext or MovePrevious methods.
MediaStateChanged	Raised when the media player play state changes.

MediaQueue

public sealed class MediaQueue

Provides methods and properties to access and control the queue of playing songs. MediaQueue provides properties and methods that query and control the queue of playing songs. The `ActiveSong` property returns the currently playing Song. `ActiveSongIndex` gets or set the queue index of the currently playing song. `Count` returns the number of songs in the queue. The `Item` indexer returns the Song at the specified index in the queue.

`MediaQueue` is a read-only queue of songs. With `MediaQueue`, you can control which song is playing in the queue, but you cannot add or remove songs from the queue. Either `MediaPlayer.Play` or the songs already queued up when the game starts determine the songs that are in the queue of playing songs.

Public Properties

ActiveSong	Gets the current Song in the queue of playing songs.
ActiveSongIndex	Gets or sets the index of the current (active) song in the queue of playing songs.
Count	Gets the count of songs in the MediaQueue.
Item	Gets the Song at the specified index in the MediaQueue.

MediaSource

`public sealed class MediaSource`

Provides methods and properties to access the source or sources from which the media will be read. `MediaSource` provides access to the source or sources from which the media will be read. A source can be either the local device or a device connected through Windows Media Connect. On Windows and Zune, the only available `MediaSource` is the local device. On Xbox 360, a `MediaSource` can be either the local device or a device connected through Windows Media Connect. Windows Media Connect is software that lets you connect your Xbox 360 console to a computer running Microsoft Windows. Connecting this way enables you to view media on the connected computer in the Xbox 360 dashboard.

Public Properties

MediaSourceType	Gets the MediaSourceType of this media source.
Name	Gets the name of this media source.

Public Methods

GetAvailableMediaSources	Gets the available media sources.

Picture

```
public sealed class Picture : IEquatable<Picture>, IDisposable
```

Provides access to a picture in the media library. The `Picture` class provides information about a picture, including its Name, Date, Height, and Width.

You can obtain a `Picture` object through the `PictureCollection.Item` indexer.

Public Properties	
Album	Gets the picture album that contains the picture.
Date	Gets the picture's date.
Height	Gets the picture's height.
Name	Gets the name of the picture.
Width	Gets the picture's width.
Public Methods	
GetImage	Returns the stream that contains the image data.
GetThumbnail	Returns the stream that contains the picture's thumbnail image data.

PictureAlbum

```
public sealed class PictureAlbum : IEquatable<PictureAlbum>, IDisposable
```

Provides access to a picture album in the media library. The `PictureAlbum` class provides information about a picture album, including the picture album's Name, Pictures, and Parent.

A `PictureAlbum` can contain both pictures and other picture albums.

You obtain `PictureAlbum` objects through the `PictureAlbumCollection.Item` indexer.

Public Properties	
Albums	Gets the collection of picture albums that are contained within the picture album (that is, picture albums that are children of the picture album).
Name	Gets the name of the `PictureAlbum`.
Parent	Gets the parent picture album.
Pictures	Gets the collection of pictures in this picture album.

PictureAlbumCollection

```
public sealed class PictureAlbumCollection : IEnumerable<PictureAlbum>,
IEnumerable, IDisposable
```

A collection of picture albums in the media library. The `PictureAlbumCollection` class provides access to picture albums in the device's media library.

Use the `PictureAlbum.Albums` property to obtain a collection of picture albums that are contained within (that is, children of) a particular picture album. Use the `MediaLibrary.RootPictureAlbum` property to obtain the root (top-most) picture album, which contains both pictures and other picture albums.

`PictureAlbumCollection` does not immediately instantiate instances of all picture albums in the collection. Instead, individual `PictureAlbum` objects are created each time a picture album is accessed through the collection's `Item` indexer.

Public Properties	
Count	Gets the number of `PictureAlbum` objects in the `PictureAlbumCollection`.
Item	Gets the `PictureAlbum` at the specified index in the `PictureAlbumCollection`.
Public Methods	
GetEnumerator	Returns an enumerator that iterates through the `PictureAlbumCollection`.
Explicit Interface Implementations	
System.Collections.IEnumerable.GetEnumerator	Returns an enumerator that iterates through the collection.

PictureCollection

```
public sealed class PictureCollection : IEnumerable<Picture>, IEnumerable,
IDisposable
```

A collection of pictures in the media library. The `PictureCollection` class provides access to pictures in the device's media library.

Use the `MediaLibrary.Pictures` property to obtain a collection of all pictures in the media library, and use the `PictureAlbum.Pictures` property to obtain a collection of pictures in a particular picture album.

`PictureCollection` does not immediately instantiate instances of all pictures in the collection. Instead, individual `Picture` objects are created each time a picture is accessed through the collection's `Item` indexer. See the "Remarks" section of `Item` for the resource implications of maintaining references to multiple `Picture` objects.

Public Properties

Count	Gets the number of `Picture` objects in the `PictureCollection`.
Item	Gets the icture at the specified index in the `PictureCollection`.

Public Methods

GetEnumerator	Returns an enumerator that iterates through the `PictureCollection`.

Explicit Interface Implementations

System.Collections.IEnumerable.GetEnumerator	Returns an enumerator that iterates through the collection.

Playlist

`public sealed class Playlist : IEquatable<Playlist>, IDisposable`

Provides access to a playlist in the media library. The `Playlist` class provides information about a playlist, including the playlist's Name, Duration, and Songs.

Obtain `Playlist` objects through the `PlaylistCollection.Item` indexer.

Public Properties

Duration	Gets the duration of the playlist.
Name	Gets the name of the playlist.
Songs	Gets a `SongCollection` that contains the songs in the playlist.

PlaylistCollection

```
public sealed class PlaylistCollection : IEnumerable<Playlist>,
    IEnumerable, IDisposable
```

A collection of playlists in the media library. The `PlaylistCollection` class provides access to playlists in the device's media library.

Use the `MediaLibrary.Playlists` property to obtain a collection of all playlists in the media library.

The `PlaylistCollection` does not immediately instantiate instances of all playlists in the collection. Instead, individual `Playlist` objects are created each time a playlist is accessed through the collection's `Item` indexer.

Public Properties

Count	Gets the number of `Playlist` objects in the `PlaylistCollection`.
Item	Gets the Playlist at the specified index in the `PlaylistCollection`.

Public Methods

GetEnumerator	Returns an enumerator that iterates through the `PlaylistCollection`.

Explicit Interface Implementations

System.Collections.IEnumerable.GetEnumerator	Returns an enumerator that iterates through the collection.

Song

```
public sealed class Song : IEquatable<Song>, IDisposable
```

Provides access to a song in the song library. The `Song` class provides information about a song, including the song's Name, Artist, and Album.

You can obtain a `Song` object through the `SongCollection.Item` indexer and the `MediaQueue.ActiveSong` property.

Public Properties

Album	Gets the album on which the song appears.
Artist	Gets the artist of the song.
Duration	Gets the duration of the song.
Genre	Gets the genre of the song.
IsProtected	Gets a value that indicates whether the song is DRM-protected content.
IsRated	Gets a value that indicates whether the song has been rated by the user.

Name	Gets the name of the song.
PlayCount	Gets the song play count.
Rating	Gets the user's rating for the song.
TrackNumber	Gets the track number of the song on the song's album.
Public Methods	
FromUri	Constructs a new Song object based on the specified URI.

SongCollection

`public sealed class SongCollection : IEnumerable<Song>, IEnumerable, IDisposable`

A collection of songs in the song library. The SongCollection class provides access to songs in the device's song library.

Use the MediaLibrary.Songs property to obtain the following collections:

- All songs in the media library

- Songs on a particular album

- Songs associated with a particular artist

- Songs associated with a particular genre

SongCollection does not immediately instantiate instances of all songs in the collection. Instead, individual Song objects are created each time a user accesses a song through the collection's Item indexer. See the "Remarks" section of Item for the resource implications of maintaining references to multiple Song objects.

Public Properties	
Count	Gets the number of Song objects in the SongCollection.
Item	Gets the song at the specified index in the SongCollection.
Public Methods	
GetEnumerator	Returns an enumerator that iterates through the SongCollection.
Explicit Interface Implementations	
System.Collections.IEnumerable.GetEnumerator	Returns an enumerator that iterates through the collection.

Video

`public sealed class Video`

Represents a video.

Public Properties	
Duration	Gets the duration of the video.
FramesPerSecond	Gets the frame rate of this video.
Height	Gets the height of this video, in pixels.
VideoSoundtrackType	Gets the VideoSoundtrackType for this video.
Width	Gets the width of this video, in pixels.

VideoPlayer

`public sealed class VideoPlayer : IDisposable`

Provides methods and properties to play back, pause, resume, and stop video. VideoPlayer also exposes repeat, volume, and play position information.

Public Properties	
IsLooped	Gets a value that indicates whether the player is playing video in a loop.
IsMuted	Gets or sets the muted setting for the video player.
PlayPosition	Gets the play position within the currently playing video.
State	Gets the media playback state, MediaState.
Video	Gets the video that is currently playing.
Volume	Gets or sets the video player volume.
Public Methods	
GetTexture	Retrieves a Texture2D containing the current frame of video being played.
Pause	Pauses the currently playing video.
Play	Plays a video.
Resume	Resumes a paused video.
Stop	Stops playing a video.

VisualizationData

`public class VisualizationData`

Encapsulates visualization (frequency and sample) data for the currently playing song. (Note: Visualization data is not available on the Windows Phone 7 platform.)

Public Properties

Frequencies	Returns a collection of floats that contain frequency data.
Samples	Returns a collection of floats that contain sample data.

Enumerations

Following are the enumerations in the Media namespace.

MediaSourceType

public enum MediaSourceType

Indicates the type of the current media source. The type can be a local device or a device connected through Windows Media Connect. On Windows and Zune, the only available media source type is the local device. On Xbox 360, a media source can be either the local device or a device connected through Windows Media Connect.

The MediaSource.MediaSourceType property returns a MediaSourceType value.

LocalDevice	A local device.
WindowsMediaConnect	A Windows Media Connect device.

MediaState

public enum MediaState

Media playback state (playing, paused, or stopped). The MediaPlayer.State property returns a MediaState value.

Paused	Media playback is paused.
Playing	Media is currently playing.
Stopped	Media playback is stopped.

VideoSoundtrackType

public enum VideoSoundtrackType

The types of sounds in a video. A video that contains only music will be muted on playback if MediaPlayer is playing back music. Note: These settings have no effect on the Windows platform because there is no dashboard. The settings apply only on an Xbox 360.

Dialog	This video contains only dialog.
Music	This video contains only music.
MusicAndDialog	This video contains music and dialog.

Media Demo Program

The Media Demo program is shown in Figure 9.1. This example shows how to retrieve information about the media files detected on the system. When running under Windows, the program will retrieve information from Windows Media Player. It includes collections of the songs, albums, and artists, which can be easily parsed like an array. The code is the same for the Xbox 360 build, but the music files will have to be installed on the hard drive of your Xbox 360 for it to work because it doesn't parse media files plugged into a portable drive or

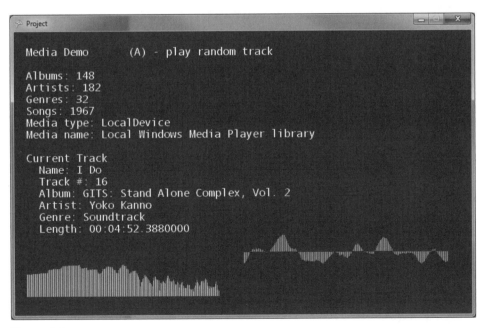

Figure 9.1
The Media Demo program plays a random audio file from the installed media files.

memory device (such as a Zune or iPod). You can *play* media files stored on those devices manually using the Xbox 360 dashboard or Media Center, but you won't be able to parse them with this code unless the music files have been physically installed on the hard drive.

All the resources you need to tap into the Media Player database are found in the MediaLibrary class, which is instantiated when the program starts up. From there, you can search for songs by name, album, artist, or any other criteria and then play the song using MediaLibrary.Play(). The sample program in Listing 9.1 displays information about the currently playing track, and also uses VisualizationData to display the frequency data and the sample data of the current track while it's playing in real time! This could be the start of your own little media player, or perhaps a game based on the visualization data, so that the gameplay is affected by the frequency of the current audio file. *That* would definitely be interesting!

Listing 9.1 Media Demo Program

```
using System;
using System.Collections.Generic;
using System.Linq;
using Microsoft.Xna.Framework;
using Microsoft.Xna.Framework.Audio;
using Microsoft.Xna.Framework.Content;
using Microsoft.Xna.Framework.GamerServices;
using Microsoft.Xna.Framework.Graphics;
using Microsoft.Xna.Framework.Input;
using Microsoft.Xna.Framework.Media;
using Microsoft.Xna.Framework.Net;
using Microsoft.Xna.Framework.Storage;

namespace Graphics_Demo
{
    public class Game1 : Microsoft.Xna.Framework.Game
    {
        GraphicsDeviceManager graphics;
        SpriteBatch spriteBatch;
        SpriteFont font;
        KeyboardState keyState;
```

```csharp
GamePadState padState;
MediaLibrary media;
Song song;
Random rand;
int albums, artists, genres, songs;
string mediaType, mediaName;
VisualizationData viz;
Texture2D texture;

public Game1()
{
    graphics = new GraphicsDeviceManager(this);
    Content.RootDirectory = "Content";
}

protected override void Initialize()
{
    base.Initialize();
    media = new MediaLibrary();
    viz = new VisualizationData();
    MediaPlayer.IsVisualizationEnabled = true;
    rand = new Random();
    albums = media.Albums.Count;
    artists = media.Artists.Count;
    genres = media.Genres.Count;
    songs = media.Songs.Count;
    mediaType = media.MediaSource.MediaSourceType.ToString();
    mediaName = media.MediaSource.Name;
}

protected override void LoadContent()
{
    spriteBatch = new SpriteBatch(GraphicsDevice);
    font = Content.Load<SpriteFont>("font1");
    texture = Content.Load<Texture2D>("dot");
}

protected override void UnloadContent() { }

protected override void Update(GameTime gameTime)
```

```
    {
        //escape key
        keyState = Keyboard.GetState();
        if (keyState.IsKeyDown(Keys.Escape)) this.Exit();

        //back button
        padState = GamePad.GetState(PlayerIndex.One);
        if (padState.Buttons.Back == ButtonState.Pressed) this.Exit();

        //A button plays
        if (padState.Buttons.A == ButtonState.Pressed
            || keyState.IsKeyDown(Keys.A))
        {
            if (songs > 0)
            {
                MediaPlayer.Stop();
                int i = rand.Next(0, songs - 1);
                song = media.Songs[i];
                MediaPlayer.Play(song);
            }
        }
        //update visualization data
        MediaPlayer.GetVisualizationData(viz);

        base.Update(gameTime);
    }

    protected override void Draw(GameTime gameTime)
    {
        GraphicsDevice.Clear(Color.DarkSlateBlue);
        spriteBatch.Begin();

        int y = 20;
        print(20, y, "Media Demo");
        print(200, y, "(A) - play random track"); y += 40;
        print(20, y, "Albums: " + albums.ToString()); y += 20;
        print(20, y, "Artists: " + artists.ToString()); y += 20;
        print(20, y, "Genres: " + genres.ToString()); y += 20;
        print(20, y, "Songs: " + songs.ToString()); y += 20;
        print(20, y, "Media type: " + mediaType); y += 20;
        print(20, y, "Media name: " + mediaName); y += 40;
```

```
    if (songs > 0 && song != null)
    {
        print(20, y, "Current Track"); y += 20;
        print(20, y, "  Name: " + song.Name); y += 20;
        print(20, y, "  Track #: " + song.TrackNumber.ToString());
        y += 20;
        print(20, y, "  Album: " + song.Album.Name); y += 20;
        print(20, y, "  Artist: " + song.Artist.Name); y += 20;
        print(20, y, "  Genre: " + song.Genre.Name); y += 20;
        print(20, y, "  Length: " + song.Duration.ToString());
        y += 40;
        doVisualization();
    }
    spriteBatch.End();
    base.Draw(gameTime);
}

void doVisualization()
{
    int x, y, height;

    //draw freq bars
    for (int f = 0; f < viz.Frequencies.Count; f++)
    {
        x = 20 + 180 * (f*2) / viz.Frequencies.Count;
        y = 350 + (int)(100 - viz.Frequencies[f] * 100);
        height = (int)(viz.Frequencies[f] * 100);
        spriteBatch.Draw(texture, new Rectangle(x, y, 1, height),
            Color.Orange);
    }

    //draw sample bars
    for (int s = 0; s < viz.Samples.Count; s++)
    {
        x = 400 + 180 * (s*2) / viz.Samples.Count;
        if (viz.Samples[s] > 0.0f)
        {
            y = 300 + (int)(80 - viz.Samples[s] * 100);
            height = (int)(viz.Samples[s] * 100);
        }
```

```
        else
        {
            y = 380;
            height = (int)(-1.0f * viz.Samples[s] * 100);
        }
        spriteBatch.Draw(texture, new Rectangle(x, y, 1, height),
            Color.Coral);
    }
}

void print(int x, int y, string text)
{
    print(x, y, text, Color.White);
}
void print(int x, int y, string text, Color color)
{
    spriteBatch.DrawString(font, text, new Vector2((float)x,
        (float)y), color);
}
    }
}
```

SUMMARY

The Media namespace contains several very useful classes for working with media files, especially the MediaLibrary class, which seems to do most of the hard work for us. The Media namespace also provides services for parsing photo albums and video files as well using code similar to the music player presented here.

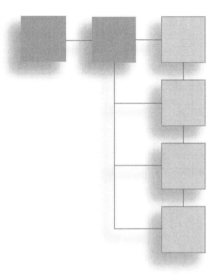

CHAPTER 10

NET

The Net namespace is one of the more interesting components of XNA Game Studio because it allows you to create networked, multiplayer games for use over system link or Xbox Live against other human players. The short gist of it is, yes, you can create a multiplayer game with a single Creators Club/App Hub account by writing and testing networking code on multiple PCs running the project in XNA Game Studio, with or without a connected Xbox 360. By developing with a mix of Windows and Xbox 360 machines, you can build a multiplayer game for the Creators Club/App Hub market without any extra licenses. This chapter focuses on covering the Net namespace as a quick reference. I will forego an example in this chapter because the subject is covered in more detail in Chapter 14, "Multiplayer Networking."

This chapter covers these topics:

- Net classes
- Net Enumerations

MICROSOFT.XNA.FRAMEWORK.NET REFERENCE

The following pages provide a complete reference to the Net namespace. As was the case in previous reference chapters, inherited items are omitted from the list of properties, methods, etc., for each item.

Classes

Following are the classes found within the Net namespace.

AvailableNetworkSession

`public sealed class AvailableNetworkSession`

Describes a multiplayer session that can be joined. Use the NetworkSession class to get a list of AvailableNetworkSession instances. Typically, the results populate some type of user interface, displayed by the game. The user then chooses a session, and the game adds the player to the chosen session with a call to Join.

Public Properties	
CurrentGamerCount	Gets the number of gamers in the session.
HostGamertag	Gets the gamertag of the session host.
OpenPrivateGamerSlots	Gets the number of private player slots.
OpenPublicGamerSlots	Gets the number of public player slots.
QualityOfService	Gets an estimate of the quality of network service between this local machine and the remote session.
SessionProperties	Gets any custom properties that have been attached to the session.

AvailableNetworkSessionCollection

`public sealed class AvailableNetworkSessionCollection : ReadOnlyCollection<AvailableNetworkSession>, IDisposable`

Represents a collection of sessions available for joining.

GameEndedEventArgs

`public class GameEndedEventArgs : EventArgs`

Represents the arguments passed to a GameEnded event.

GamerJoinedEventArgs

`public class GamerJoinedEventArgs : EventArgs`

Represents the arguments passed to a GamerJoined event.

Public Properties	
Gamer	Gets the gamer who just joined the session.

GamerLeftEventArgs

`public class GamerLeftEventArgs : EventArgs`

Represents the arguments passed to a `GamerLeft` event.

Public Properties	
Gamer	Gets the gamer who just left the session.

GameStartedEventArgs

`public class GameStartedEventArgs : EventArgs`

Represents the arguments passed to a `GameStarted` event.

HostChangedEventArgs

`public class HostChangedEventArgs : EventArgs`

Represents the arguments passed to a `HostChanged` event.

Public Properties	
NewHost	Gets the new host of the session.
OldHost	Gets the player who was the previous session host.

LocalNetworkGamer

`public sealed class LocalNetworkGamer : NetworkGamer`

Represents a local player in a network session.

Public Properties	
IsDataAvailable	Determines whether there is incoming packet data for this player.
SignedInGamer	Gets the SignedInGamer instance for this SignedInGamer object.
Public Methods	
EnableSendVoice	Specifies whether voice data should be sent to or received from the specified remote gamer.
ReceiveData	Reads the next incoming packet.
SendData	Sends data to a specified set of gamers in a network session.
SendPartyInvites	Sends game invitations to all party members who are not in the current game session.

NetworkGamer

`public class NetworkGamer : Gamer`

Represents a player in a network session. The `NetworkSession` class maintains a list of players in a network session. Some of the players may also be local players, who are represented in `LocalNetworkGamer`.

Public Properties	
HasLeftSession	Indicates whether this gamer has left the session.
HasVoice	Determines whether the player has a voice headset.
Id	Gets a unique identifier that can be used to refer to this gamer in network packets.
IsGuest	Determines whether this gamer is logged in as a guest profile.
IsHost	Determines whether the player is the host of the multiplayer session.
IsLocal	Determines whether the player is playing on a local machine.
IsMutedByLocalUser	Determines whether the player is muted by one or more local users.
IsPrivateSlot	Determines whether the player occupies a reserved private session slot.
IsReady	Determines whether the gamer is ready to leave the lobby screen and begin gameplay.
IsTalking	Determines whether the gamer is currently sending voice data.
Machine	Gets an object representing the physical gaming machine this `NetworkGamer` is playing on.
RoundtripTime	Gets an estimate of the network latency involved in sending a packet round trip from the local machine to this gamer and back again.
Session	Gets the multiplayer session of the gamer.

NetworkMachine

`public sealed class NetworkMachine`

Represents a physical machine (such as single Xbox 360 console or a Windows-based computer) that is participating in a multiplayer session. It can be used to detect when more than one `NetworkGamer` is playing on the same actual machine.

Public Properties	
Gamers	Gets a collection of all the gamers who are playing on this machine.
Public Methods	
RemoveFromSession	Forcibly removes this machine from the session.

NetworkSession

`public sealed class NetworkSession : IDisposable`

Represents a multiplayer game session. An XNA Framework game can initiate only a single multiplayer session at a time. To start a multiplayer session, make a call to `Create` or use `Find` or `BeginFind` to search for and join an existing network session.

Public Fields

MaxPreviousGamers	Represents the maximum number of gamers that can be held in the `PreviousGamers` property.
MaxSupportedGamers	Maximum number of gamers supported in a session.

Public Properties

AllGamers	Gets the collection of gamers currently in the session.
AllowHostMigration	Gets or sets whether host migration is allowed. This can be read by any machine in the session, but can only be changed by the host. The default value is `false`, indicating that host migration is disabled.
AllowJoinInProgress	Gets or sets whether join-in-progress is allowed. If the host enables this setting, new machines will be able to join at any time. The default value is `false`, indicating that join-in-progress is disabled. `AllowJoinInProgress` can be read by any machine in the session, but can only be changed by the host.
BytesPerSecondReceived	Gets a performance counter recording the amount of data being received from the network.
BytesPerSecondSent	Gets a performance counter recording the amount of data being sent over the network.
Host	Gets the current host of the multiplayer session.
IsEveryoneReady	Determines whether all gamers are ready to enter the session.
IsHost	Determines whether this machine is the session host.
LocalGamers	Get the collection of local gamers for a multiplayer session.
MaxGamers	Gets or sets the maximum number of players able to join this multiplayer session.
PreviousGamers	A collection of previous gamers in the network session.
PrivateGamerSlots	Gets or sets the number of private slots reserved for gamers who join using an invitation.
RemoteGamers	Gets the collection of remote gamers for a multiplayer session.
SessionProperties	Gets any custom properties that have been attached to the session.
SessionState	Gets the current state of a multiplayer session.
SessionType	Gets the current multiplayer session type.
SimulatedLatency	Gets or sets the amount of simulated network latency.
SimulatedPacketLoss	Gets or sets the amount of simulated packet loss.

(Continued)

Public Methods

AddLocalGamer	Adds the specified local gamer profile to the network session.
BeginCreate	Starts hosting a new multiplayer session.
BeginFind	Starts a matchmaking query to search for available multiplayer sessions.
BeginJoin	Starts a join operation for the specified multiplayer session.
BeginJoinInvited	Starts joining an existing network session in response to an InviteAccepted notification event. Call EndJoinInvited to access the asynchronous method results.
Create	Hosts a new multiplayer session.
EndCreate	Gets the result from a BeginCreate asynchronous call.
EndFind	Gets the result from a BeginFind asynchronous call.
EndGame	Changes the session state from NetworkSessionState.Playing to NetworkSessionState.Lobby.
EndJoin	Gets the result from a BeginJoin asynchronous call.
EndJoinInvited	Gets the result from a BeginJoinInvited asynchronous call.
Find	Issues a matchmaking query, searching for available multiplayer sessions.
FindGamerById	Looks up the network gamer with the specified ID.
Join	Joins an existing multiplayer session.
JoinInvited	Joins the specified local gamers, along with the local machine, to an existing network session in response to an InviteAccepted notification event from a non-local session.
ResetReady	Resets the IsReady property of all session gamers.
StartGame	Changes the session state from NetworkSessionState.Lobby to NetworkSessionState.Playing.
Update	Updates the state of the multiplayer session.

Public Events

GameEnded	Occurs when the game moves from gameplay to the lobby.
GamerJoined	Occurs when a new player joins a multiplayer session.
GamerLeft	Occurs when a player leaves the multiplayer session.
GameStarted	Occurs when the game moves from the lobby into actual gameplay.
HostChanged	Occurs when the session host has changed.
InviteAccepted	Occurs when a user has accepted an invitation to join a network session.
SessionEnded	Occurs when the multiplayer session ends.

NetworkSessionEndedEventArgs

public class NetworkSessionEndedEventArgs : EventArgs

Represents the arguments passed to a SessionEnded event. These arguments are passed to event handlers when a session ends.

Public Properties

EndReason	Gets the reason for ending a session.

NetworkSessionJoinException

`public class NetworkSessionJoinException : NetworkException`

Thrown if an error was encountered while joining a session.

Public Properties

JoinError	Gets or sets a more detailed description of the session join failure.

Public Methods

GetObjectData	When overridden in a derived class, returns information about the exception.

NetworkSessionProperties

`public class NetworkSessionProperties : IList<Nullable<int>>,`
`ICollection <Nullable<int>>, IEnumerable<Nullable<int>>, IEnumerable`

Describes custom, game-specific information about a `NetworkSession` object. Examples of custom properties include specifying the current game mode or the current level selection. Use these properties to filter the results from a search using the `Find` or `BeginFind` methods.

Public Properties

Count	Gets the number of custom session properties.
Item	Gets or sets a custom session property value at the specified index.

Public Methods

GetEnumerator	Gets an enumerator for iterating over the custom property values.

Explicit Interface Implementations

System.Collections.Generic.ICollection{T}. IsReadOnly	Gets a value indicating whether the collection is read-only.

(Continued)

`System.Collections.Generic.ICollection{T}.Add`	This interface method is not supported by `NetworkSessionProperties`.
`System.Collections.Generic.ICollection{T}.Clear`	This interface method is not supported by `NetworkSessionProperties`.
`System.Collections.Generic.ICollection{T}.Contains`	Checks whether the collection contains the specified value.
`System.Collections.Generic.ICollection{T}.CopyTo`	Copies the contents of the collection to an array.
`System.Collections.IEnumerable.GetEnumerator`	Gets an enumerator for iterating over the custom property values.
`System.Collections.Generic.IList{T}.IndexOf`	Gets the index of the specified value.
`System.Collections.Generic.IList{T}.Insert`	This interface method is not supported by `NetworkSessionProperties`.
`System.Collections.Generic.IList{T}.RemoveAt`	This interface method is not supported by `NetworkSessionProperties`.
`System.Collections.Generic.ICollection{T}.Remove`	This interface method is not supported by `NetworkSessionProperties`.

PacketReader

`public class PacketReader : BinaryReader`

Provides common functionality for efficiently reading incoming network packets. Commonly, a multiplayer game should create a single `PacketReader` instance at startup and then reuse it whenever a packet needs to be read. To read the packet, you pass the `PacketReader` instance to `ReceiveData` and then use various `Read` methods to extract the data.

Public Properties

`Length`	Gets the length of the packet being read.
`Position`	Gets or sets the current packet read position.

Public Methods

`ReadColor`	Reads a `Color` value.
`ReadDouble`	Reads an 8-byte floating-point value.
`ReadMatrix`	Reads a `Matrix` value.
`ReadQuaternion`	Reads a `Quaternion` value.

ReadSingle	Reads a 4-byte floating-point value.
ReadVector2	Reads a `Vector2` value.
ReadVector3	Reads a `Vector3` value.
ReadVector4	Reads a `Vector3` value.

PacketWriter

`public class PacketWriter : BinaryWriter`

Provides common functionality for efficiently formatting outgoing network packets.

Public Properties	
Length	Gets the length of the packet being written.
Position	Gets or sets the current packet write position.
Public Methods	
Write	Writes a value to an outgoing network packet.

QualityOfService

`public sealed class QualityOfService`

Describes the quality of the network connection between this machine and the host of a multiplayer session that was discovered with a matchmaking query.

Public Properties	
AverageRoundtripTime	Gets the average (median) round-trip time of all the network packets that were sent during the quality-of-service measurement process.
BytesPerSecondDownstream	Gets an estimate of the available downstream network bandwidth from the session host to this machine, measured in bytes per second.
BytesPerSecondUpstream	Gets an estimate of the available upstream network bandwidth from this machine to the session host, measured in bytes per second.
IsAvailable	Checks whether this quality-of-service operation has completed.
MinimumRoundtripTime	Gets the minimum round-trip time of any network packet that was sent during the quality-of-service measurement process.

WriteLeaderboardsEventArgs

`public sealed class WriteLeaderboardsEventArgs : EventArgs`

Represents the arguments passed to a `WriteArbitratedLeaderboard`, `WriteUnarbitratedLeaderboard`, or `WriteTrueSkill` event.

Public Properties	
`Gamer`	Gets the gamer whose statistics need to be written to the leaderboard.
`IsLeaving`	Indicates whether the player is leaving the session early.

Enumerations

Following are the enumerations in the `Net` namespace.

NetworkSessionEndReason

`public enum NetworkSessionEndReason`

Defines the reason a session ended.

`ClientSignedOut`	This client player has signed out of session.
`HostEndedSession`	The host left the session, removing all active players.
`RemovedByHost`	The host removed this client player from the session.
`Disconnected`	Network connectivity problems ended the session.

NetworkSessionJoinError

`public enum NetworkSessionJoinError`

Contains additional data about a `NetworkSessionJoinException`.

`SessionNotFound`	The session could not be found. Occurs if the session has ended after the matchmaking query but before the client joined, of if there is no network connectivity between the client and session host machines.
`SessionNotJoinable`	The session exists but is not joinable. Occurs if the session is in progress but does not allow gamers to join a session in progress.
`SessionFull`	The session exists but does not have any open slots for local signed-in gamers.

NetworkSessionState

`public enum NetworkSessionState`

Defines the different states of a multiplayer session.

Lobby	The local machine joins the session, waiting in the pregame lobby. The `GameStarted` event is raised when gameplay begins.
Playing	The local machine joins the session, currently in the middle of gameplay. The `GameEnded` event is raised when the session returns to the lobby.
Ended	The local machine has left the current session or the session has ended. The `SessionEnded` event is raised at this time. The event's arguments describe the reason for the session ending.

NetworkSessionType

`public enum NetworkSessionType`

Defines the different types of multiplayer sessions.

Local	Does not involve any networking traffic, but can be used for split-screen gaming on a single Xbox 360 console. Creating a local network session may also make it easier to share code between local and online game modes.
LocalWithLeaderboards	Creates a local session with access to write to leaderboards on the Xbox Live servers. This local session type allows guests or other Xbox Live player profiles to join the session.
SystemLink	Connects multiple Xbox 360 consoles or computers over a local subnet. These machines do not require a connection to Xbox Live or any Xbox Live accounts. However, connection to machines on different subnets is not allowed. If you are a Creators Club developer testing your game, you can use this type to connect an Xbox 360 console to a computer. However, cross-platform networking is not supported in games distributed to non–Creators Club community players.
PlayerMatch	Uses the Xbox Live servers. This enables connection to other machines over the Internet. It requires an Xbox Live Silver Membership for Windows-based games or an Xbox Live Gold membership for Xbox 360 games. Games in development will also require an XNA Creators Club premium membership. While in trial mode, indie games downloaded from Xbox Live Marketplace will not have access to Xbox Live matchmaking.
Ranked	All session matches are ranked. This option is available only for commercial games that have passed Xbox Live certification. Due to the competitive nature of the gameplay, this session type does not support join-in-progress.

SendDataOptions

`public enum SendDataOptions`

Defines options for network packet transmission.

None	Sends the data with no guarantees. Packets of this type may be delivered in any order, with occasional packet loss. This is the most efficient option in terms of network bandwidth and machine resource usage. However, it is recommended only in situations where your game can recover from occasional packet loss.
Reliable	Sends the data with reliable delivery, but no special ordering. Packets of this type are re-sent until arrival at the destination. They may arrive out of order.
InOrder	Sends the data with guaranteed ordering, but without reliable delivery. Occasionally, packets of this type are not delivered. However, any delivered packets always arrive in the order in which they are sent. Use this option in situations where the transmitted value changes constantly. Old versions never arrive after a more recent version.
ReliableInOrder	Sends the data with reliability and arrival in the order originally sent. Packets of this type are re-sent until arrival and ordered internally. This means they arrive in the same order in which they were sent. In terms of network-bandwidth usage, this is the strongest and most expensive option. Use this only when arrival and ordering are essential. Commonly, a game uses this option for a small percentage of packets. The majority of gameplay data is sent using None or Reliable.
Chat	Indicates that this packet contains chat data, such as a player-to-player message string entered using the keyboard. To comply with international regulations, you must send such data without packet encryption. Therefore, you must use this flag to mark it. To maintain security, other game data should not use this flag. It is acceptable and efficient to mix encrypted and unencrypted data. If you send packets both with and without this flag within a single frame, both the encrypted and unencrypted data streams will be merged into a single wire packet. This option can be combined with either or both of the Reliable and InOrder flags. When you request in-order delivery for chat packets, they will be ordered relative to other chat packets, but they may arrive out of order with respect to other non-chat data.

SUMMARY

The core networking and multiplayer features of XNA Game Studio are summarized in the Net namespace, reviewed in this chapter. We will spend quite a bit of time on this awesome subject in Chapter 14, where you will start small and build up to a fully playable networked game over system link and Xbox Live in the final chapter, using nothing more than an App Hub membership! In the meantime, refer to this chapter any time you need to look up details about the Net classes or enumerations.

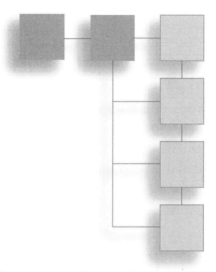

CHAPTER 11

STORAGE

The XNA Framework makes it possible to read and write files in the local file system using the classes in the Storage namespace. A storage medium might be a memory card, the hard drive of an Xbox 360, the file system of a Windows system, or more exotic memory when dealing with a mobile device. This chapter focuses on exploring just the file systems of Windows and Xbox 360. The Storage namespace is one of the most difficult things to work with in XNA, due to all of the potential problems that may occur with the user's Xbox 360, such as removal of a storage device during a read or write operation. You will learn in this chapter how to deal with such issues.

Here's the content:

- File input/output access
- Storage classes
- Storage Demo program

MICROSOFT.XNA.FRAMEWORK.STORAGE REFERENCE

Storage in XNA is any memory device that the system supports, such as an attached portable hard drive (formatted for the Xbox 360), a thumb drive, the built-in hard drive in most Xbox 360s, and various storage devices on a Windows PC—although normally, that will just be the hard drive. Although custom data files can be imported into the project, as we learned about back in Chapter 5, "Content," when a custom content reader was demonstrated, the most common use for the file system will be for saved games.

There are two storage areas that we can use for our games in XNA: Title storage space and User storage space. Title storage is where the game's runtime files are located. This is where updates are applied when they become available. (I'm sure you have tried to run a game while logged onto Xbox Live and had the "Update Required" message come up.) User storage, on the other hand, is used for player game data, and can be isolated on a per-profile basis or used for all player profiles. This is where user-created Forge levels are saved in *Halo 3*, for instance.

File Input/Output Access

As we learned in Chapter 5, any type of game asset can be imported into the Content Manager through existing or user-created content importers. This is the preferred way to read game data that does not change. For data that might change, such as generated data files, user-created game levels, or saved games, we can access the file system to stream data to our game. Any arbitrary data file can be opened and written to or read from using the classes in the Storage namespace, which we will learn about here.

Note

Any file added to the root of the XNA Game Studio project is added to the Title Storage area of the game.

Classes

The following pages provide a complete reference to the Storage namespace. As was the case in previous reference chapters, inherited items are omitted from the list of properties, methods, etc., for each item. Following are the classes found within the Storage namespace.

StorageContainer

```
public class StorageContainer : IDisposable
```

Represents a logical collection of storage files.

Public Properties

`DisplayName`	Gets the name of the title.
`StorageDevice`	Gets the `StorageDevice` that holds the files in this container.

Public Methods

`CreateDirectory`	Creates a new directory in the `StorageContainer` scope.
`CreateFile`	Creates a file at a specified path in the `StorageContainer`.
`DeleteDirectory`	Deletes a directory in the `StorageContainer` scope.
`DeleteFile`	Deletes a file in the `StorageContainer`.
`DirectoryExists`	Determines whether the specified path refers to an existing directory in the `StorageContainer`.
`FileExists`	Determines whether the specified path refers to an existing file in the `StorageContainer`.
`GetDirectoryNames`	Enumerates the directories in the root of a `StorageContainer`.
`GetFileNames`	Enumerates files in a `StorageContainer`.
`OpenFile`	Opens a file at a specified path in the `StorageContainer`.

StorageDevice

`public sealed class StorageDevice`

Represents a storage device for user data, such as a memory unit or hard drive.

Public Properties

`FreeSpace`	Gets the amount of free space on the device.
`IsConnected`	Gets whether the device is connected.
`TotalSpace`	Gets the total amount of space on the device.

Public Methods

`BeginOpenContainer`	Begins the process for opening a `StorageContainer` containing any files for the specified title.
`BeginShowSelector`	Overloaded. Overloaded methods for showing the storage device selector asynchronously.
`DeleteContainer`	Deletes a `StorageContainer` without opening it.
`EndOpenContainer`	Ends the process for opening a `StorageContainer`.
`EndShowSelector`	Ends the display of the storage selector user interface.

Public Events

`DeviceChanged`	Occurs when a device is removed or inserted.

StorageDeviceNotConnectedException

`public class StorageDeviceNotConnectedException : ExternalException`

The exception that is thrown when the requested `StorageDevice` is not connected.

Storage Demo Program

Since loading a saved game is the most common use for the file system of a game, the chapter example will explore this subject. First, the program will save data to a savegame file using XML serialization (which makes it a one-line affair), and then read it back and display the information. To verify that the example is working, we will want to run the program, save the data, then close the program and reopen it to make sure the data is still there. So, the example should read and write the data only when the user chooses to, not automatically. The example should run equally well on Windows or an Xbox 360 to be truly useful.

Saving Data

Figure 11.1 shows the Guide that pops up on the Xbox 360 when a storage device is requested. If no extra device is installed, the default (hard drive) is used

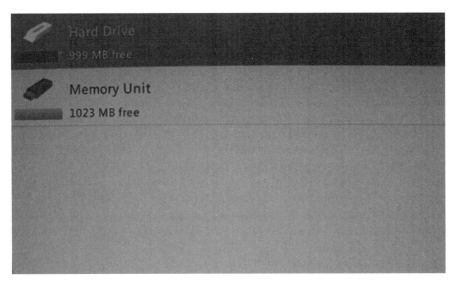

Figure 11.1
The Guide pops up if the Xbox 360 detects more than one storage device.

automatically. This will come up if you plug in a memory device such as a USB thumb drive.

Note

> If your Xbox 360 has only one storage device (the built-in hard drive), and you have not plugged in any other device such as a flash drive, then the storage selector will *not* pop up. The hard drive will be used by default.

The Storage Demo program uses XML serialization (via the System.Xml.Serialization namespace) to write data out to an XML file, which is then read back in using a deserializer. Both processes require only a single line of code to actually read from or write to the file. The real challenge is getting the storage device! If only one storage device is installed on the system (i.e., the hard drive), you can acquire the default device for the hard drive and no user input is required. But if more than one device is installed, then the Guide will pop up to ask the user to select a storage device for the file—for both saving data and loading data. There are several steps to acquiring the device:

1. Prepare to select the storage device

2. Select the storage device

3. Prepare to open a named storage container

4. Open the storage container

When the storage container is finally opened, you can perform file operations on the container, including reading and/or writing any type of data, whether it's formatted (such as Xml), raw text, or basic binary data. It's up to you to perform the file input/output operations once you have access to the file.

Note

> To save data written to a storage container, the device *must* be disposed! This requires a manual call to the Dispose() method for the storage device before the save will take effect.

Here are the contents of the file that the sample program will save and then reload:

```
<?xml version="1.0"?>
<SaveGameData xmlns:xsi="http://www.w3.org/2001/XMLSchema-instance"
```

```
xmlns:xsd="http://www.w3.org/2001/XMLSchema">
<PlayerName>Player</PlayerName>
<Position>
  <X>100</X>
  <Y>50</Y>
</Position>
<Level>2</Level>
<Score>400</Score>
</SaveGameData>
```

Storage Demo Program

Figure 11.2 shows the output from the `Storage` Demo program in Listing 11.1 after the data has been written and then read back again.

Note

The namespace `System.Xml.Serialization` *must* be manually added to the Xbox 360 project's references, even if you created the Windows project first and copied it to make the Xbox 360 project. This namespace reference is not added automatically, so you must add it manually. `System.Xml.Serialization` is found in the list of .NET components. (There are only a few under the Xbox 360 project; it is usually on the bottom of the list.)

```
STORAGE DEMO

Press A to save game data
Press B to load game data

State: NotSaving

    PlayerName: Player
    Position: {X:100 Y:50}
    Level: 2
    Score: 400
```

Figure 11.2
The saved game data is read back in and printed on the screen.

Listing 11.1   Storage Demo Program

```
using System;
using System.Collections.Generic;
using System.Diagnostics;
using System.IO;
using System.Xml;
using System.Xml.Serialization;
using Microsoft.Xna.Framework;
using Microsoft.Xna.Framework.GamerServices;
using Microsoft.Xna.Framework.Graphics;
using Microsoft.Xna.Framework.Input;
using Microsoft.Xna.Framework.Storage;

namespace Project
{
    public class SaveGameData
    {
        public string PlayerName { get; set; }
        public Vector2 Position { get; set; }
        public int Level { get; set; }
        public int Score { get; set; }
    }

    public class Game1 : Microsoft.Xna.Framework.Game
    {
        enum StorageState
        {
            NotSaving,
            SelectStorageDevice,
            SelectingStorageDevice,
            OpenStorageContainer,
            OpeningStorageContainer,
            ReadyToUse
        }

        enum SaveLoadMode
        {
            None, Load, Save
        }
```

```
            GraphicsDeviceManager graphics;
            SpriteBatch spriteBatch;
            SpriteFont font;
            KeyboardState keyState;
            GamePadState padState;
            StorageDevice storageDevice;
            StorageState storageState = StorageState.NotSaving;
            IAsyncResult asyncResult;
            PlayerIndex playerIndex = PlayerIndex.One;
            StorageContainer storageContainer;
            string filename = "savegame.dat";
            SaveLoadMode mode = SaveLoadMode.None;
            SaveGameData saveData;
            SaveGameData loadedData;

            public Game1()
            {
                graphics = new GraphicsDeviceManager(this);
                Content.RootDirectory = "Content";
#if XBOX
                this.Components.Add(new GamerServicesComponent(this));
#endif
            }

            protected override void Initialize()
            {
                base.Initialize();
                saveData = new SaveGameData();
                saveData.PlayerName = "Player";
                saveData.Position = new Vector2(100, 50);
                saveData.Score = 400;
                saveData.Level = 2;
                loadedData = null;
            }

            protected override void LoadContent()
            {
                spriteBatch = new SpriteBatch(GraphicsDevice);
                font = Content.Load<SpriteFont>("font1");
            }
```

```csharp
protected override void UnloadContent() { }

protected override void Update(GameTime gameTime)
{
    //update input states
    keyState = Keyboard.GetState();
    padState = GamePad.GetState(PlayerIndex.One);

    //exit program
    if (keyState.IsKeyDown(Keys.Escape)) this.Exit();
    if (padState.Buttons.Back == ButtonState.Pressed) this.Exit();

    //A saves data
    if (padState.Buttons.A == ButtonState.Pressed ||
        keyState.IsKeyDown(Keys.A))
    {
        mode = SaveLoadMode.Save;
        loadedData = null;
    }

    //B loads data
    if (padState.Buttons.B == ButtonState.Pressed ||
        keyState.IsKeyDown(Keys.B))
    {
        mode = SaveLoadMode.Load;
    }

    switch (mode)
    {
        case SaveLoadMode.Save:
            switch(storageState)
            {
                case StorageState.NotSaving:
                    storageState = StorageState.
                        OpenStorageContainer;
                    break;
                case StorageState.ReadyToUse:
                    SaveData();
                    mode = SaveLoadMode.None;
                    break;
```

```
                            default:
                                UpdateStorage();
                                break;
                        }
                        break;
                case SaveLoadMode.Load:
                    switch(storageState)
                    {
                        case StorageState.NotSaving:
                            storageState = StorageState.
                                OpenStorageContainer;
                            break;
                        case StorageState.ReadyToUse:
                            LoadData();
                            mode = SaveLoadMode.None;
                            break;
                        default:
                            UpdateStorage();
                            break;
                    }
                    break;
            }
            base.Update(gameTime);
        }

        private void UpdateStorage()
        {
            switch (storageState)
            {
                case StorageState.SelectStorageDevice:
#if XBOX
                    if (!Guide.IsVisible)
#endif
                    {
                        asyncResult = StorageDevice.BeginShowSelector(
                            playerIndex, null, null);
                        storageState = StorageState.SelectingStorageDevice;
                    }
                    break;
```

```
            case StorageState.SelectingStorageDevice:
                if (asyncResult.IsCompleted)
                {
                    storageDevice = StorageDevice.EndShowSelector(
                        asyncResult);
                    storageState = StorageState.OpenStorageContainer;
                }
                break;

            case StorageState.OpenStorageContainer:
                if (storageDevice == null || !storageDevice.IsConnected)
                {
                    storageState = StorageState.SelectStorageDevice;
                }
                else
                {
                    asyncResult = storageDevice.BeginOpenContainer(
                        "Chapter11_StorageContainer", null, null);
                    storageState = StorageState.OpeningStorageContainer;
                }
                break;

            case StorageState.OpeningStorageContainer:
                if (asyncResult.IsCompleted)
                {
                    storageContainer = storageDevice.
                        EndOpenContainer(asyncResult);
                    storageState = StorageState.ReadyToUse;
                }
                break;
        }
    }

    private void SaveData()
    {
        if (storageContainer == null)
        {
            storageState = StorageState.OpenStorageContainer;
        }
        else
```

```
        {
            try
            {
                //delete any existing file
                if (storageContainer.FileExists(filename))
                {
                    storageContainer.DeleteFile(filename);
                }
                //save new file
                using (Stream stream = storageContainer.
                    CreateFile(filename))
                {
                    XmlSerializer serializer = new XmlSerializer(
                        typeof(SaveGameData));
                    serializer.Serialize(stream, saveData);
                }
            }
            catch (IOException e)
            {
                //notify user of error saving
                Debug.WriteLine(e.Message);
            }
            finally
            {
                //write and close the file
                storageContainer.Dispose();
                storageContainer = null;
                storageState = StorageState.NotSaving;
            }
        }
    }

    private void LoadData()
    {
        if (storageContainer == null)
        {
            storageState = StorageState.OpenStorageContainer;
        }
        else
        {
```

```
        try
        {
            //attempt to read file
            using (Stream stream = storageContainer.OpenFile(
                filename, FileMode.Open, FileAccess.Read))
            {
                XmlSerializer serializer = new XmlSerializer(
                    typeof(SaveGameData));
                loadedData = (SaveGameData)serializer.
                    Deserialize(stream);
            }
        }
        catch (IOException e)
        {
            //notify user of error saving
            Debug.WriteLine(e.Message);
        }
        finally
        {
            //close the file
            storageContainer.Dispose();
            storageContainer = null;
            storageState = StorageState.NotSaving;
        }
    }
}

protected override void Draw(GameTime gameTime)
{
    GraphicsDevice.Clear(Color.DarkSlateBlue);
    spriteBatch.Begin();
    print(20, 20, "STORAGE DEMO");
    print(20, 80, "Press A to save game data");
    print(20, 100, "Press B to load game data");
    print(20, 140, "State: " + storageState.ToString());
    if (loadedData != null)
    {
        print(50, 200, "PlayerName: " + loadedData.PlayerName);
        print(50, 220, "Position: " + loadedData.Position.
            ToString());
```

```
                print(50, 240, "Level: " + loadedData.Level.ToString());
                print(50, 260, "Score: " + loadedData.Score.ToString());
            }
            spriteBatch.End();
            base.Draw(gameTime);
        }

        void print(int x, int y, string text)
        {
            print(x, y, text, Color.White);
        }

        void print(int x, int y, string text, Color color)
        {
            try {
                spriteBatch.DrawString(font, text, new Vector2(
                    (float)x, (float)y), color);
            }
            catch (Exception e) { Console.WriteLine(e.Message); }
        }
    }
}
```

Summary

The Storage namespace is one of the most challenging to break into for the first time. That said, it rewards your efforts with some remarkably useful features for saving and loading game data of any kind, whether it's save game data or generated content (such as textures or terrain) or any other file that needs to be loaded outside the Content Manager. Saving the player's progress in a game is a great way for your game to ingratiate itself with its players; something as simple as "remembering" the player's last position in the game and restoring to that point automatically can have a dramatic effect on the player's impression of your game.

Part III

Xbox Live

Xbox Live is Microsoft's online network for Xbox 360 gamers, providing online multiplayer game connectivity, online profile storage and management, game progress tracking, publicly visible achievements, support for chatting and texting with friends, support for inviting friends to play a game, and much more. This third and final part of the book explores the Xbox Live features that are available with a normal Xbox Live Gold account and a premiere App Hub developer account. Some features are still available with a no-cost Xbox Live Silver account, but the App Hub membership is required for developing games for Xbox 360. Here are the chapters in this part:

- Chapter 12: "Avatars"
- Chapter 13: "Guide"
- Chapter 14: "Multiplayer Networking"
- Chapter 15: "Meshes"
- Chapter 16: "Sprites"
- Chapter 17: "Multiplayer Game Engine"

CHAPTER 12

AVATARS

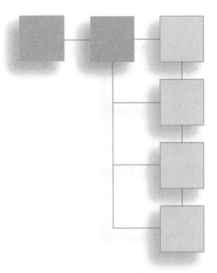

An avatar is a 3D model that serves as a gamer's virtual representation online in Xbox Live, and can be customized to the gamer's preferences with different body types, gender, hair style, clothing, and so forth. In this chapter, you will learn how to use an avatar in a game. In addition to retrieving and rendering the gamer's custom-designed avatar in your own code, you can also generate *random* avatars for use as non-player characters (NPCs) for computer-controlled AI players or for scenery.

Here are topics of import in this chapter:

- Retrieving a gamer avatar
- Creating a random avatar
- Rendering a gamer avatar
- Avatar Demo project
- Custom avatar animations

Note

Unfortunately, this feature is not available for a Windows game, so this chapter is necessarily specific only to the Xbox 360. The code will run under Windows but no avatars will render.

GAMER PROFILE AVATARS

There is a 3D model of the profile avatar available for use in our own games for the Xbox 360. It really adds a lot of fun to a game when the player can see his or her own avatar in the game! There are a couple of drawbacks, though. First, the avatar model is not available for Windows projects, only for Xbox 360 projects. Second, you must be signed on to your gamer profile on Xbox Live to retrieve your official gamer avatar model in order to render it.

Wouldn't it be great if we could just request the avatar mesh from Xbox Live without being officially signed on—like through an HTTP connection or by some other means? Alas, that is not possible. You simply must be signed on to retrieve it. There *is* an interesting workaround, though. In the `AvatarDescription` class is a property called `Description`. Despite its name, `Description` does not contain a string description of the avatar at all. Rather, it's a byte buffer with properties that describe the avatar, from the body type to the height to the clothes and so on. This `Description` property is used to synchronize the gamer profile avatars of multiple players in a multiplayer game. The buffer is only 1,021 bytes (in XNA 4.0), so this roughly 1KB of data can be transmitted to the other players in a game so they can render the avatar. One way to render an avatar offline would be to save this `Description` property to a file and then read it for rendering as if it had been transmitted over the network.

Retrieving a Gamer Avatar

The official avatar for a valid Xbox Live gamer profile can be retrieved and used as a character in an XNA game. Although you can render the avatar, you cannot save it as a mesh to local storage because no access to the mesh data is provided. You can, however, save the `Description` data for any avatar to a file and retrieve it later, even if Internet access is disrupted (due to a loss of wireless connection or an unplugged cable)! As mentioned, the `Description` property of `AvatarDescription` is a 1,021-byte buffer that describes the properties of an avatar. This is used to show everyone in a multiplayer game what their friends (or opponents) look like! To that end, the `Description` buffer is transmitted to each player in a multiplayer game so everyone sees the same avatars being rendered in their local game.

The first step to retrieving the avatar is to get a valid `Gamer` object initialized. This can be done a couple of ways, but the way I'll describe here is using the `Gamer.SignedInGamers[]` collection. Hard-coding `PlayerIndex.One` is the easiest way to pull the default gamer profile, but of course, multiple local player profiles can be retrieved by using the four player indexes in `SignedInGamers`. Once a gamer is accessed on the local system, the profile data can be retrieved by using `SignedInGamer.GetProfile()`. Here is a quick example:

```
SignedInGamer gamer = Gamer.SignedInGamers[PlayerIndex.One];
GamerProfile profile = gamer.GetProfile();
```

The profile object is actually not needed here, but it's common to retrieve this object with the gamer profile object at the same time. Using the gamer object, we can use an asynchronous function to retrieve the gamer avatar—an object containing properties and methods for rendering the avatar—without giving up any details or raw data. In other words, it's an object we can *use* but can't really modify in any meaningful way. The skeletal bone structure is available to you, however, so we can manipulate and transform it like any biped character, even with a physics system if desired.

```
IAsyncResult result =
    AvatarDescription.BeginGetFromGamer(gamer, null, null);
```

Once `BeginGetFromGamer()` is called, it will run in a background thread and update the `IAsyncResult` variable when the data has been fully received. We can look at `IAsyncResult.IsCompleted` to determine when it is finished. At that point, we need to call `AvatarDescription.EndGetFromGamer()` to retrieve the actual description data.

```
AvatarDescription avatarDesc =
    AvatarDescription.EndGetFromGamer(result);
```

Note

Refer to Chapter 6, "GamerServices," for quick-reference information about the `GamerServices` namespace and for a refresher on retrieving information for a gamer profile.

Figure 12.1 shows an example of a gamer avatar retrieved from Xbox Live and rendered using the example at the end of this chapter. This was my avatar, wearing an achievement item (the *Halo 3* ODST helmet).

Figure 12.1
A gamer profile avatar retrieved from Xbox Live.

Creating a Random Avatar

The `AvatarDescription` class has a method called `CreateRandom()` that will generate an avatar with randomized attributes for the body type, height, hair style, and so on. This can be used to create random characters for use in a game like so:

```
AvatarDescription avatarDesc = AvatarDescription.CreateRandom();
```

Figure 12.2 shows an example of a gamer avatar that was generated randomly and rendered using the program at the end of this chapter.

Rendering a Gamer Avatar

Once we obtain an avatar, either by retrieving one from the gamer's profile or by generating a random one, then we can render it using the usual shader-based rendering techniques. The primary rendering class is `AvatarRenderer`, which is used to render any and all avatars in the game. The `AvatarRenderer.Draw()` method accepts two parameters: the `BoneTransforms` property from a loaded `AvatarAnimation` object and the predefined `AvatarAnimation.Expression`.

Figure 12.2
Random gamer avatars can be quite diverse in appearance.

```
AvatarRenderer avatarRenderer;
AvatarAnimation avatarAnimation;
AvatarAnimationPreset animationIndex;
```

As of XNA 4.0, there are 31 animation sets defined in the AvatarAnimation-Preset enumeration. You can use these existing animations or tap into the BoneTransforms in order to manipulate an avatar with your own animation data (or physics system, for instance).

- Stand0 = 0

- Stand1 = 1

- Stand2 = 2

- Stand3 = 3

- Stand4 = 4

- Stand5 = 5

- Stand6 = 6

- Stand7 = 7
- Clap = 8
- Wave = 9
- Celebrate = 10
- FemaleIdleCheckNails = 11
- FemaleIdleLookAround = 12
- FemaleIdleShiftWeight = 13
- FemaleIdleFixShoe = 14
- FemaleAngry = 15
- FemaleConfused = 16
- FemaleLaugh = 17
- FemaleCry = 18
- FemaleShocked = 19
- FemaleYawn = 20
- MaleIdleLookAround = 21
- MaleIdleStretch = 22
- MaleIdleShiftWeight = 23
- MaleIdleCheckHand = 24
- MaleAngry = 25
- MaleConfused = 26
- MaleLaugh = 27
- MaleCry = 28
- MaleSurprised = 29
- MaleYawn = 30

Here is sample code to create the renderer object and establish the desired animation set:

```
avatarRenderer = new AvatarRenderer(avatarDesc, true);
animationIndex = (AvatarAnimationPreset) 0;
```

```
avatarAnimation = new AvatarAnimation(animationIndex);
```

Any existing camera code will work for the actual rendering of the scene. All that matters is that you have a properly set up projection matrix and view matrix to create a camera. The `AvatarRenderer` class has both `Matrix` properties built in, so you just set them to your existing camera properties or manually create a camera like so:

```
avatarRenderer.Projection = Matrix.CreatePerspectiveFieldOfView(
    MathHelper.ToRadians(45.0f), GraphicsDevice.Viewport.
    AspectRatio, .01f, 1000.0f);
Vector3 cameraPos = new Vector3(0, 2.0f, 1.5f);
Vector3 cameraLook = new Vector3(0, 1.5f, 0);
avatarRenderer.View = Matrix.CreateLookAt(cameraPos, cameraLook, Vector3.Up);
```

Finally, we can draw the avatar:

```
avatarRenderer.Draw( avatarAnimation.BoneTransforms,
    avatarAnimation.Expression);
```

Note

Note that the camera is usually handled elsewhere in the game code, and that this camera code is only included for the sake of demonstrating a simple working example.

Avatar Demo Project

Listing 12.1 contains the source code for the Avatar Demo project:

Listing 12.1   Avatar Demo Project

```
using System;
using System.Collections.Generic;
using System.Diagnostics;
using System.IO;
using System.Xml;
using System.Xml.Serialization;
using Microsoft.Xna.Framework;
using Microsoft.Xna.Framework.Audio;
using Microsoft.Xna.Framework.GamerServices;
using Microsoft.Xna.Framework.Graphics;
using Microsoft.Xna.Framework.Input;
using Microsoft.Xna.Framework.Net;
using Microsoft.Xna.Framework.Storage;
```

```
namespace Project
{
    public class Game1 : Microsoft.Xna.Framework.Game
    {
        GraphicsDeviceManager graphics;
        SpriteBatch spriteBatch;
        SpriteFont font;
        GamePadState padState;
        Random rand;
        IAsyncResult result;
        GamerProfile profile = null;
        SignedInGamer gamer = null;
        AvatarDescription avatarDesc;
        AvatarRenderer avatarRenderer;
        AvatarAnimation avatarAnimation;
        AvatarAnimationPreset animationIndex;
        Matrix rotate;
        Vector3 cameraPos, cameraLook;

        public Game1()
        {
            graphics = new GraphicsDeviceManager(this);
            Content.RootDirectory = "Content";
            Components.Add(new GamerServicesComponent(this));
        }

        protected override void Initialize()
        {
            base.Initialize();
            rand = new Random();
            cameraPos = new Vector3(0, 2.0f, 1.5f);
            cameraLook = new Vector3(0, 1.5f, 0);
            RandomizeAvatar();
        }

        protected override void LoadContent()
        {
            spriteBatch = new SpriteBatch(GraphicsDevice);
            font = Content.Load<SpriteFont>("font1");
        }
```

```
protected override void UnloadContent() { }

protected override void Update(GameTime gameTime)
{
    //update input states
    GamePadState oldState = padState;
    padState = GamePad.GetState(PlayerIndex.One);

    //back button
    if (padState.Buttons.Back == ButtonState.Pressed) this.Exit();

    //A - next animation
    if (padState.Buttons.A == ButtonState.Released &&
        oldState.Buttons.A == ButtonState.Pressed)
    {
        animationIndex += 1;
        if (animationIndex > (AvatarAnimationPreset)30)
            animationIndex = (AvatarAnimationPreset)0;
        avatarAnimation = new AvatarAnimation(animationIndex);
    }

    //B - prev animation
    if (padState.Buttons.B == ButtonState.Released &&
        oldState.Buttons.B == ButtonState.Pressed)
    {
        animationIndex -= 1;
        if (animationIndex < (AvatarAnimationPreset)0)
            animationIndex = (AvatarAnimationPreset)30;
        avatarAnimation = new AvatarAnimation(animationIndex);
    }

    //X - random avatar
    if (padState.Buttons.X == ButtonState.Released &&
        oldState.Buttons.X == ButtonState.Pressed)
    {
        RandomizeAvatar();
    }

    //Y - gamer avatar
    if (padState.Buttons.Y == ButtonState.Released &&
```

```
            oldState.Buttons.Y == ButtonState.Pressed)
    {
        GetGamerAvatar();
    }

    //update avatar animation
    avatarAnimation.Update(gameTime.ElapsedGameTime, true);

    GamerServicesDispatcher.Update();
    base.Update(gameTime);
}

protected override void Draw(GameTime gameTime)
{
    GraphicsDevice.Clear(Color.DarkSlateBlue);

    avatarRenderer.View = Matrix.CreateLookAt(cameraPos,
        cameraLook, Vector3.Up);

    for (float y = 0; y < 20.0f; y += 1.0f)
    {
        for (float x = 0; x < 20.0f; x += 1.0f)
        {
            avatarRenderer.World = rotate * Matrix.
                CreateTranslation(-10.5f + x, 0, -20.0f + y);
            avatarRenderer.Draw(avatarAnimation.BoneTransforms,
                avatarAnimation.Expression);
        }
    }

    spriteBatch.Begin();
    print(20, 20, "AVATAR DEMO");
    print(20, 50, "A - next animation");
    print(20, 65, "B - prev animation");
    print(20, 80, "X - randomize avatar");
    print(20, 95, "Y - get gamer avatar");
    print(400, 20, "Animation: " +
        ((AvatarAnimationPreset)animationIndex).ToString()
        + " (" + ((int)animationIndex).ToString() + ")");
    print(400, 35, "Position: " + avatarAnimation.CurrentPosition.
        ToString());
```

```
        print(400, 50, "Length: " + avatarAnimation.Length.ToString());
        print(400, 65, "BodyType: " + avatarDesc.BodyType.ToString());
        print(400, 80, "Height: " + avatarDesc.Height.ToString());
        print(400, 95, "Buffer size: " + avatarDesc.Description.
            Length.ToString());

        spriteBatch.End();
        base.Draw(gameTime);
    }

    void print(int x, int y, string text)
    {
        print(x, y, text, Color.White);
    }

    void print(int x, int y, string text, Color color)
    {
        try {
            spriteBatch.DrawString(font, text, new Vector2(
                (float)x, (float)y), color);
        }
        catch (Exception e) { Console.WriteLine(e.Message); }
    }

    void RandomizeAvatar()
    {
        avatarDesc = AvatarDescription.CreateRandom();
        avatarRenderer = new AvatarRenderer(avatarDesc, true);
        animationIndex = (AvatarAnimationPreset)rand.Next(30);
        avatarAnimation = new AvatarAnimation(animationIndex);
        rotate = Matrix.CreateRotationY(MathHelper.ToRadians(180.0f));
        avatarRenderer.Projection = Matrix.CreatePerspectiveFieldOfView(
            MathHelper.ToRadians(45.0f), GraphicsDevice.Viewport.
            AspectRatio, .01f, 1000.0f);
    }

    void GetGamerAvatar()
    {
        if (gamer == null)
```

```
    {
        if (Gamer.SignedInGamers[PlayerIndex.One] != null)
        {
            gamer = Gamer.SignedInGamers[PlayerIndex.One];
            profile = gamer.GetProfile();
        }
    }

    //request avatar from Xbox Live
    result = AvatarDescription.BeginGetFromGamer(gamer, null, null);

    //this locks up the program!
    while (!result.IsCompleted) { }
    if (result.IsCompleted)
    {
        avatarDesc = AvatarDescription.EndGetFromGamer(result);
        avatarRenderer = new AvatarRenderer(avatarDesc, true);
        animationIndex = (AvatarAnimationPreset)rand.Next(30);
        avatarAnimation = new AvatarAnimation(animationIndex);
        rotate = Matrix.CreateRotationY(
            MathHelper.ToRadians(180.0f));
        avatarRenderer.Projection =
            Matrix.CreatePerspectiveFieldOfView(
            MathHelper.ToRadians(45.0f),
            GraphicsDevice.Viewport.AspectRatio, .01f, 1000.0f);
    }
}
}
}
```

Custom Avatar Animations

The Microsoft XNA team has released an expanded collection of avatar animations
that you can download and use in your own games called the Avatar
Animation Pack. The pack can be downloaded from the following Web site:
http://create.msdn.com/en-US/education/catalog/utility/avatar_animation_pack.
(Because Web links often change, be aware that you may have to perform a
search for "XNA Avatar Animation Pack" if this URL expires.) Here is the list of
new animations that come with the pack:

Climb	Punch	Swim Freestyle
Crawl	Push	Swim Underwater
Faint	Run	Swing Bat
Jump	Sit Idle	Swing Club
Kick	Steer	Swing Hammer
Pick Up	Strafe Left	Throw
Pull	Strafe Right	Walk

After downloading the Avatar Animation Pack, you must add the animations to your XNA projects manually, one at a time (as needed). The animations are each stored in the Autodesk FBX format. The Maya format is also available for anyone who wants to open the avatar animation files to see how they are structured. To see these new animations in action, you can use one of the educational resources on the XNA App Hub Web site that demonstrates it. You can find them here: http://create.msdn.com/en-US/education/catalog/sample/custom_avatar_animation.

Summary

This short chapter explained how to use gamer avatars in an XNA game. Although this feature is available only on Xbox 360 builds of a game, it is compelling enough to warrant releasing a game only on that one platform, even though users of other platforms (Windows, etc.) will miss out on your game.

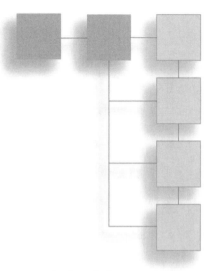

Chapter 13

Guide

The Guide is an Xbox 360 user-interface component with the ability to perform limited user input in the form of a message box and a virtual keyboard. The Guide makes many services available, including a virtual keyboard, displaying messages, getting user input, managing friends, reading and sending messages, inviting friends to a game, creating and joining parties with friends, and viewing profile information. The processes for bringing up all these options are fairly similar, so we will just look at the two most common: displaying a message box (and detecting which button was chosen) and using the virtual keyboard. For more detailed reference information on the Guide, refer to Chapter 6, which covers `GamerServices`.

Here's the deal:

- Using the Guide
- Displaying a message box
- Using the virtual keyboard

Using the Guide

The Guide makes available a lot of interesting features that will come in handy for a multiplayer game, such a the ability to create or join a party, invite friends to a game, send and read messages, display a message box (and know which button was pushed), and get user input from a virtual keyboard. We will focus

Figure 13.1
The Games for Windows Live start screen in an XNA Windows app.

on the latter two features of the Guide because they are the most commonly used features. For example, you might use the virtual keyboard to let the user enter his or her initials for a high-score list (if you don't want to use that user's gamertag), or let the player give custom names to game objects such as units in a war game.

When you start up an Xbox 360 program, the controller jewel button brings up the Gamer Profile window over the top of any currently running game or app. On a Windows build of an XNA program, the jewel brings up the Games for Windows Live screen shown in Figure 13.1.

The Games for Windows Live system has a separate login from Xbox Live, although you may use the same gamertag for both services. The reason you would want to create a Windows Live account is for testing networking code for a multiplayer game, using your Windows development PC and your Xbox 360 to test a two-player game. The alternative is to purchase another Xbox 360, subscribe to another fee-based Creator's Club/App Hub account, and then build and run the project on two target Xbox 360 systems from your one development

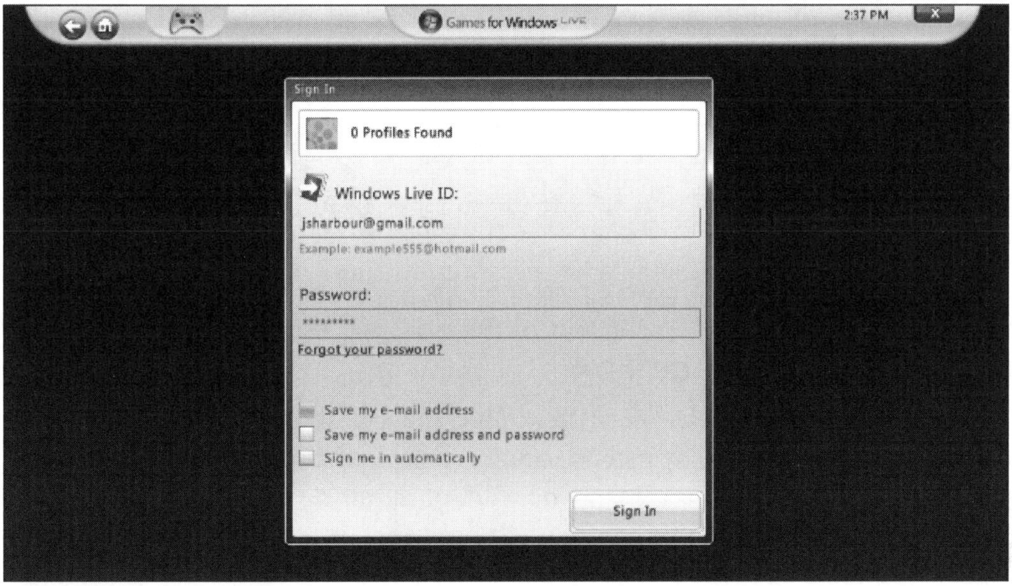

Figure 13.2
Signing in to Windows Live requires a separate account from Xbox Live.

PC (with two separate Xbox 360 systems configured in the Device Manager). It's a lot of work to set up, and maybe you would prefer to have two actual Xbox 360s for this type of multiplayer development and testing, but it doesn't hurt to throw a Windows build into the mix for additional players while testing networking code. The sign-in screen is shown in Figure 13.2.

Note

Fast-forward to Chapter 17, "Multiplayer Game Engine," for a complete sample networked game that is developed from the ground up with multiplayer gameplay.

Signing in to Windows Live brings many of the familiar Xbox Live features to the screen, but the user interface is different because it is designed to function with either a controller or a mouse. You can bring up your gamer profile, see your list of friends, send and receive messages, and basically take part in many common features found on the Xbox 360, including playing games with Xbox 360 users (for games that support it). See Figure 13.3.

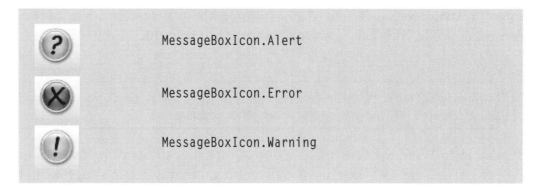

Figure 13.3
The Windows Live login syncs up with your Xbox Live gamertag.

Displaying a Message Box

The Guide makes available a customizable message box that you can use to display messages to the player. The message box is part of the Guide, which will pop up over the top of a running game without requiring any extra code on your part. The message box can be configured to use one, two, or three buttons, which you can define as a list:

```
List<string> buttons = new List<string>();
buttons.Add("Abort");
buttons.Add("Retry");
buttons.Add("Ignore");
```

We can also define which of the four possible icons to display on the message box (three plus "None" as the fourth). The following are the icon options you can use:

MessageBoxIcon.Alert

MessageBoxIcon.Error

MessageBoxIcon.Warning

To display a message box, you must use the asynchronous approach in a very similar manner to the process followed in the previous chapter on retrieving the gamer avatar. First, call `Guide.BeginShowMessageBox()` with the desired parameters. This method returns an `IAsyncResult`, which you can then use to

Figure 13.4
The `MessageBox` Demo shows how to display a message box pop-up window.

determine when the user has chosen one of the message box's buttons. When `IAsyncResult.IsCompleted` becomes true, you can get the button by calling `Guide.EndShowMessageBox()`. Figure 13.4 shows the message box being rendered in the Windows build of the example, while Figure 13.5 shows the same message box rendered on the Xbox 360 (with a more controller-friendly form of input). After choosing one of the buttons, the program then displays the choice, as shown in Figure 13.6.

Listing 13.1 contains the source code for the Guide `MessageBox` Demo program.

Listing 13.1 `MessageBox` Demo Program

```
using System;
using System.Collections.Generic;
using Microsoft.Xna.Framework;
using Microsoft.Xna.Framework.GamerServices;
using Microsoft.Xna.Framework.Graphics;
using Microsoft.Xna.Framework.Input;

namespace Project
{
    public class Game1 : Microsoft.Xna.Framework.Game
```

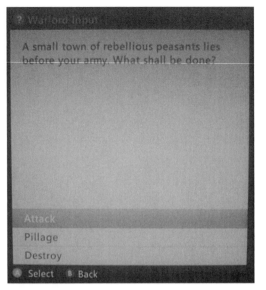

Figure 13.5
The same message box rendered on the Xbox 360 looks quite different.

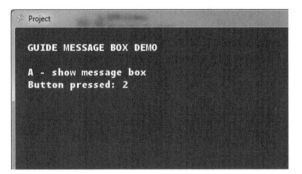

Figure 13.6
When one of the three buttons is selected, the button number is returned.

```
    {
        GraphicsDeviceManager graphics;
        SpriteBatch spriteBatch;
        SpriteFont font;
        GamePadState padState;
        int asyncState = 0;
        IAsyncResult result;
        int? button;
```

```
public Game1()
{
    graphics = new GraphicsDeviceManager(this);
    Content.RootDirectory = "Content";
    Components.Add(new GamerServicesComponent(this));
}

protected override void Initialize()
{
    base.Initialize();
}

protected override void LoadContent()
{
    spriteBatch = new SpriteBatch(GraphicsDevice);
    font = Content.Load<SpriteFont>("font1");
}
protected override void UnloadContent() { }

protected override void Update(GameTime gameTime)
{
    //update input states
    GamePadState oldState = padState;
    padState = GamePad.GetState(PlayerIndex.One);

    //back button
    if (padState.Buttons.Back == ButtonState.Pressed) this.Exit();

    if (padState.Buttons.A == ButtonState.Released &&
        oldState.Buttons.A == ButtonState.Pressed)
    {
        if (asyncState == 0) asyncState = 1;
    }

    switch(asyncState)
    {
    case 1:
        List<string> buttons = new List<string>();
        buttons.Add("Attack");
        buttons.Add("Pillage");
```

```
            buttons.Add("Destroy");
            result = Guide.BeginShowMessageBox(
                "Warlord Input",
                "A small town of rebellious peasants lies before "
                + "your army. What shall be done?",
                buttons, 0, MessageBoxIcon.Warning, null, null);
            asyncState = 2;
            break;
        case 2:
            if (result.IsCompleted)
            {
                button = Guide.EndShowMessageBox(result);
                asyncState = 0;
            }
            break;
    }
    GamerServicesDispatcher.Update();
    base.Update(gameTime);
}

protected override void Draw(GameTime gameTime)
{
    GraphicsDevice.Clear(Color.DarkSlateBlue);
    spriteBatch.Begin();
    print(20, 20, "GUIDE MESSAGE BOX DEMO");
    print(20, 60, "A - show message box");
    print(20, 80, "Button pressed: " + button.ToString());
    spriteBatch.End();
    base.Draw(gameTime);
}

void print(int x, int y, string text)
{
    print(x, y, text, Color.White);
}

void print(int x, int y, string text, Color color)
{
    try {
        spriteBatch.DrawString(font, text, new Vector2(
            (float)x, (float)y), color);
```

```
        }
        catch (Exception e) { Console.WriteLine(e.Message); }
    }
  }
}
```

Using the Virtual Keyboard

The Guide also makes available a software input panel, or SIP (a.k.a. virtual keyboard), that can be used to type in text without a keyboard. This is the primary means of getting user input on the Xbox 360, but you can use it in a Windows program as well (*with* hardware keyboard support) for any user input that is needed. The virtual keyboard is also programmed asynchronously. First, you bring up the keyboard with a call to Guide.BeginShowKeyboardInput() with the desired options. As usual, you observe an IAsyncState.IsComplete property, and then call Guide.EndShowKeyboardInput() to retrieve the entered text as a string.

Figure 13.7 shows the keyboard input panel in the Windows build. Because a keyboard is available in the Windows build, there is no software keyboard

Figure 13.7
Virtual keyboard input in the Windows build.

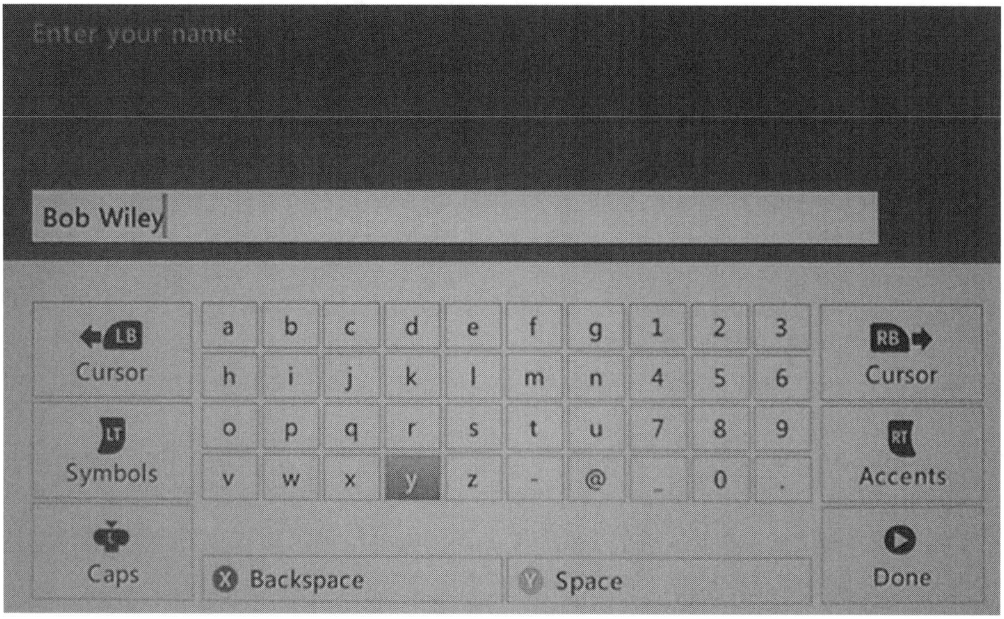

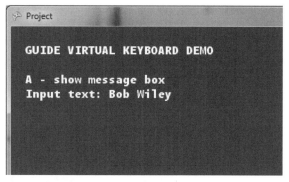

Figure 13.8
Virtual keyboard input in the Xbox 360 build.

Figure 13.9
Displaying the text that was entered by the virtual keyboard.

displayed like there is in the Xbox 360 build (shown in Figure 13.8). After getting input from the user, the system returns the input as a string that can be used for any purpose you wish to put it to, as shown in Figure 13.9.

Listing 13.2 contains the source code for the Guide Virtual Keyboard Demo.

Listing 13.2   Guide Virtual Keyboard Demo

```
using System;
using System.Collections.Generic;
using Microsoft.Xna.Framework;
using Microsoft.Xna.Framework.GamerServices;
using Microsoft.Xna.Framework.Graphics;
using Microsoft.Xna.Framework.Input;

namespace Project
{
    public class Game1 : Microsoft.Xna.Framework.Game
    {
        GraphicsDeviceManager graphics;
        SpriteBatch spriteBatch;
        SpriteFont font;
        GamePadState padState;
        int asyncState = 0;
        IAsyncResult result;
        string input;

        public Game1()
        {
            graphics = new GraphicsDeviceManager(this);
            Content.RootDirectory = "Content";
            Components.Add(new GamerServicesComponent(this));
        }

        protected override void Initialize()
        {
            base.Initialize();
        }

        protected override void LoadContent()
        {
            spriteBatch = new SpriteBatch(GraphicsDevice);
            font = Content.Load<SpriteFont>("font1");
        }
        protected override void UnloadContent() { }

        protected override void Update(GameTime gameTime)
```

```
    {
        //update input states
        GamePadState oldState = padState;
        padState = GamePad.GetState(PlayerIndex.One);

        //back button
        if (padState.Buttons.Back == ButtonState.Pressed) this.Exit();

        if (padState.Buttons.A == ButtonState.Released &&
            oldState.Buttons.A == ButtonState.Pressed)
        {
            if (asyncState == 0) asyncState = 1;
        }

        switch(asyncState)
        {
        case 1:
            result = Guide.BeginShowKeyboardInput( PlayerIndex.One,
                "Name", "Enter your name:", "", null, null);
            asyncState = 2;
            break;
        case 2:
            if (result.IsCompleted)
            {
                input = Guide.EndShowKeyboardInput(result);
                asyncState = 0;
            }
            break;
        }

        GamerServicesDispatcher.Update();
        base.Update(gameTime);
    }

    protected override void Draw(GameTime gameTime)
    {
        GraphicsDevice.Clear(Color.DarkSlateBlue);
        spriteBatch.Begin();
        print(20, 20, "GUIDE VIRTUAL KEYBOARD DEMO");
        print(20, 60, "A - show message box");
```

```
            print(20, 80, "Input text: " + input);
            spriteBatch.End();
            base.Draw(gameTime);
        }

        void print(int x, int y, string text)
        {
            print(x, y, text, Color.White);
        }

        void print(int x, int y, string text, Color color)
        {
            try {
                spriteBatch.DrawString(font, text, new Vector2(
                    (float)x, (float)y), color);
            }
            catch (Exception e) { Console.WriteLine(e.Message); }
        }
    }
}
```

SUMMARY

The Guide is a very useful component that's built into every XNA project. It brings access to the gamer profile and user input facilities. You should take advantage of the features made available through the Guide whenever you need to ask the user a question with multiple choice answers (via message box) or requiring text input from a virtual keyboard.

CHAPTER 14

MULTIPLAYER NETWORKING

This chapter covers the topic of network programming with XNA Game Studio 4.0, with a focus on system link networking. We will learn how to create a multiplayer game session, how to join existing sessions, and how to send and receive packets between players in a networked game environment. Most games today involve multiple players as part of the basic gameplay, without which the game simply would not work (or the experience would be less visceral). In the case of games like *Halo 3*, the single-player/co-op campaign or story part of the game can be completed in an afternoon; what keeps the *Halo 3* disc in millions of Xbox 360s around the world is the game's multiplayer capabilities, which go far beyond the campaign gameplay. As indie developers aspiring to publish a game on Xbox Live, we may or may not need multiplayer modes for our own game projects, but it certainly helps improve a game's odds of selling well if it does.

Here's the plan of attack:

- Network sessions
- Multiple accounts
- Creating a game session
- Joining a game session
- Sending data (outgoing packets)
- Receiving data (incoming packets)

- Disconnecting from a session
- Network Session Demo source code

NETWORK SESSIONS

All multiplayer networking takes place through session objects. A network session represents a *host* that acts as a server for a multiplayer game. As long as the server player remains online, the session will continue. A client gamer also creates a network session in order to connect to a host. So, everything is treated as a session, whether a gamer is hosting or joining a game.

Three types of sessions can be created for a multiplayer game:

- Local co-op or split-screen game
- System link game over local area network (LAN)
- Xbox Live online game

The network source code for working with these three session types is *the same*! That's good news; we don't need to write any different code for a local co-op/split-screen game or a system link game or an online Xbox Live game! All networking takes place through a NetworkSession object:

```
NetworkSession session;
```

A gamer connecting to a host will be looking for a game to join on the network with an object called AvailableNetworkSessionCollection:

```
AvailableNetworkSessionCollection games;
```

As usual, we'll also use a SignedInGamer object to manage the information for a local player's state:

```
SignedInGamer gamer;
```

As we have seen in prior chapters, when working with the Guide or networking, we have to use GamerServices. This requires that a new GamerServicesComponent be added to the list of components. Then, regularly, the component must be given a chance to run by having its Update() function called. First, initialize GamerServices in the constructor:

```
Components.Add(new GamerServicesComponent(this));
```

Then, in the `Update()` function, add the following:

```
GamerServicesDispatcher.Update();
```

Let's learn about creating additional gamer accounts in order to start developing and testing multiplayer code.

Multiple Accounts

The good news is you can develop and test a multiplayer game for Xbox 360 with just one App Hub membership account. For best results, it is probably a good idea to have two Xbox 360s set up so you can test the multiplayer features of your game on two actual systems, but that is cost-prohibitive for most indie/hobby developers. For this reason, Microsoft has made it possible to develop a multiplayer game using a network connection between one or more Windows development PCs and one Xbox 360 with just *one* App Hub account. Each of the Windows systems can be used as host or client and can run the same code as the Xbox 360. If you have an extra laptop available or another PC (such as an older system), you might be able to set up enough systems to test several players. What you *cannot* do, unfortunately, is run multiple instances of the program on the Windows PC as if each one is a separate connection. Unfortunately, XNA treats the whole Windows PC as a gamer connection, not each *program* running on the PC. This isn't too bad of a restriction considering the low cost of developing XNA games in the first place, but does require additional hardware for a serious networked game.

Hint

You do not need two Xbox 360s to develop and test multiplayer code on Xbox Live because one or more Windows PCs can be used for that purpose. However, if you want to really see how the game functions online, you may want to recruit a friend with an App Hub account to help you test the game.

Xbox Live

The ideal situation is to have two App Hub accounts and two Xbox 360s on your desk, with two LCD TVs. I say this is the ideal setup, not the most practical one for developers. Personally, I have a 22-inch 1080p TV on my desk that functions as a second LCD for my development computer (via its VGA input), and it doubles as an Xbox 360 display via HDMI input. I actually purchased a second

Xbox 360 with the intention of creating a second App Hub account for Xbox 360–to–Xbox 360 network programming, but once I started writing code, I realized this was complete overkill and unnecessary!

Windows Live

The networking code functions exactly the same on the Windows PC as it does on the Xbox 360, so there's really no requirement to have two accounts just for development if you are an indie developer. If you have a friend with a membership, then you could send that person your binary executable or the sources and ask him or her to help you test your multiplayer game on Xbox Live. Likewise, if you are a studio with more than one employee or partner, then each person can participate in the multiplayer development and testing.

To develop a multiplayer game, you will need to create a second Windows Live account on your Windows development PC. Odds are, if you've been working with XNA Game Studio, you created a Windows Live account that is linked to your Xbox Live account. It's convenient to do that, because you can manage your list of friends, send and receive messages with the convenience of a full PC keyboard, among other benefits. A full Windows Live account is not needed to use your Windows PC for multiplayer development with your Xbox 360. All you need is a gamer profile, as shown in Figure 14.1.

Note

The Windows build will often take a few seconds to start up while it tries to perform a network update during initialization.

Creating a Game Session

To host or join a game, you have to be signed in with a gamer profile, either locally or on Xbox Live. I like to automatically check whether the program already has my gamer profile signed in and bring up the sign-in system if not.

```
if (Gamer.SignedInGamers[PlayerIndex.One] == null)
    Guide.ShowSignIn(1, false);
```

Then, once signed in, we can get the current signed-in gamer:

```
SignedInGamer gamer = Gamer.SignedInGamers[PlayerIndex.One];
```

Figure 14.1
Creating a Windows Live account is not necessary! All you need is a local gamer profile.

Once that is taken care of, we can attempt to create a new network session to host a game (which will make it possible for other gamers to connect to our "game server"). That is done with the NetworkSession.Create() method. The first parameter will be the type of network to use, which is one of these options:

- NetworkSessionType.Local
- NetworkSessionType.LocalWithLeaderboards
- NetworkSessionType.PlayerMatch
- NetworkSessionType.Ranked
- NetworkSessionType.SystemLink

We're going to use the SystemLink option for development on a LAN. Although Xbox Live is required just to run anything on the Xbox 360, we won't be using any Xbox Live networking features. To do so would require one or more additional App Hub accounts.

```
NetworkSession session = NetworkSession.Create(
    NetworkSessionType.SystemLink, maxLocalGamers, maxGamers);
```

The second parameter defines the number of local gamer profiles that should be allowed. It will normally be four. The third parameter defines the total number of gamers allowed to play in the game. Unless you aspire to create the next great *Halo*-style slayer/death-match game, your players most likely will only be limited to a range of two to four or thereabouts.

When we have a valid session object, it is helpful to create event handlers to notify the program when players join or leave the game and when other things happen in the session. This is done with one of the following five session events:

- `GamerJoined`
- `GamerLeft`
- `GameStarted`
- `GameEnded`
- `SessionEnded`

The format for creating these event handlers will be like this:

```
session.GamerJoined += new EventHandler<GamerJoinedEventArgs>(func);
```

The `func` parameter should be the name of an event function. For instance, here is a method that will handle the `GamerJoined` event:

```
void session_GamerJoined(object sender, GamerJoinedEventArgs e)
{
    //new gamer joined the game
}
```

The first parameter will always be `object sender`, while the second will differ based on the type of event being handled. See the complete source code listing at the end of this chapter for examples of all the event handlers. In the sample project coming up, Network Session Demo, the player can either host a game or search for a game and attempt to join it. Figure 14.2 shows the program running with the gamer hosting a new game. "WindowsPC" is a local gamer profile.

Figure 14.2
Hosting a game session allows other players to join your game (Windows build).

Joining a Game Session

XNA can search for game sessions and retrieve a list of those hosted games as a collection called AvailableNetworkSessionCollection. This is retrieved using the NetworkSession.Find() method:

```
AvailableNetworkSessionCollection games = NetworkSession.Find(
    NetworkSessionType.SystemLink, 1, null);
```

The first parameter is the type of network to search. The second is the maximum number of local gamers. The third is a parameter of type NetworkSessionProperties that can be used to refine the search to a subset of games (null here just searches for all games).

The AvailableNetworkSessionCollection variable should be global to the Game class so it can be retained or reused as needed. To actually join a game, we can use the NetworkSession.Join() method:

```
NetworkSession session = NetworkSession.Join(game);
```

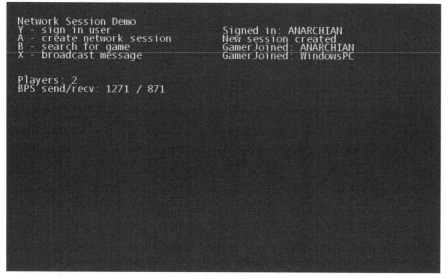

```
Network Session Demo
Y - sign in user                    Signed in: ANARCHIAN
A - create network session          New session created
B - search for game                 GamerJoined: ANARCHIAN
X - broadcast message               GamerJoined: WindowsPC


Players: 2
BPS send/recv: 1271 / 871
```

Figure 14.3
Joining a game hosted by another gamer via system link (Xbox 360 build).

This session variable should also be global (unlike in the code), because if the session variable goes out of scope, the player will be disconnected from the host. In Figure 14.3, you can see that "WindowsPC" has joined a game hosted by an Xbox 360 host (with an Xbox Live gamer profile). There are now two players in the session.

Sending Data (Outgoing Packets)

When you have established a connection to one or more players in a hosted game session, data can be sent and received. A class called `PacketWriter` is used to send packets of data through the network to other players.

```
PacketWriter writer;
```

This `PacketWriter` object can hold many pieces of data like a collection of objects. It can contain almost any data, but nothing complex, like a `Texture2D`— just simple data types, simple classes, and buffers/arrays. Use `PacketWriter`. `Write()` to fill a packet with data to be transmitted to other players:

```
writer.Write( "text data" );
writer.Write( new Vector2(100, 50) );
```

The easiest way to send data is to broadcast it to all players with a simple foreach iteration through the list of local gamers.

```
foreach (LocalNetworkGamer gamer in session.LocalGamers)
{
    gamer.SendData(writer, SendDataOptions.None);
}
```

These are the values in the SendDataOptions enumeration:

- SendDataOptions.Chat
- SendDataOptions.InOrder
- SendDataOptions.None
- SendDataOptions.Reliable
- SendDataOptions.ReliableInOrder

There is potential for the improper use of this parameter to dramatically slow down the performance of the packets in a multiplayer game, so be careful not to abuse them without understanding the impact that options such as InOrder and Reliable have on network traffic. Only use them if the packet order is absolutely necessary. (It usually isn't!)

Receiving Data (Incoming Packets)

When a connection has been established, we can check for incoming packets and respond to them as appropriate in the game based on packet type. A class called PacketReader is used to receive incoming packets of data from other players:

```
PacketReader reader;
```

The same foreach iterator is used again here to retrieve packets:

```
foreach (LocalNetworkGamer gamer in session.LocalGamers)
```

If a packet is waiting from one of the networked gamers, the gamer.IsDataAvailable property will be set to true, so we want to examine this property before trying to receive any data. To actually receive a packet, use the gamer.ReceiveData() method:

```
gamer.ReceiveData(reader, out sender);
```

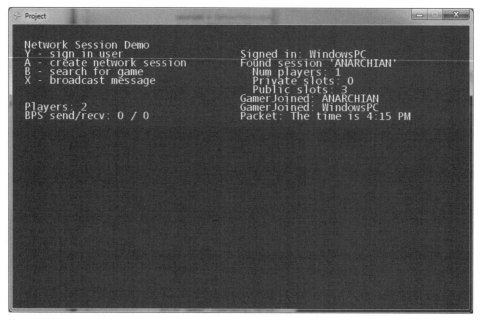

Figure 14.4
This program just sends the current time as a packet (Windows build).

The `reader` object will contain data items that can be pulled out of the collection using one of many read methods, such as `ReadString()`:

```
string data = reader.ReadString();
```

Figure 14.4 shows the Network Session Demo program with a packet being printed on the screen. The current date is used as a simple packet test for this program.

Disconnecting from a Session

A gamer is disconnected from a session when he or she closes the game, loses network connectivity, or powers down his or her Xbox 360 (or Windows PC). Whenever that happens, the `GamerLeft` event is triggered and the player is automatically removed from the list of connected gamers in the session. This is handled automatically by XNA, so we can just worry about responding to the event rather than writing any code to handle the logistics of managing gamers in a networked environment. See Figure 14.5.

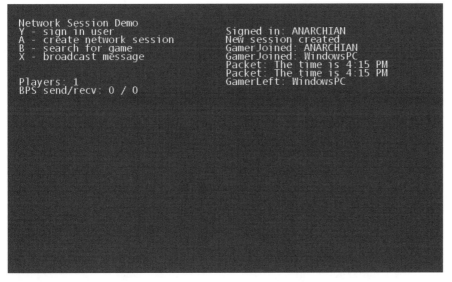

Figure 14.5
The "WindowsPC" gamer has left the session (Xbox 360 build).

Network Session Demo Source Code

Listing 14.1 contains the source code for the Network Session Demo project. We have already gone over the key portions of code in this program, but this pulls all the code together into one cohesive example so you can see it all at once—how to initialize a session, host or join a game, and send and receive data. A complete multiplayer game could be created from just this code!

Listing 14.1   Network Session Demo Project

```
using System;
using System.Collections.Generic;
using System.Linq;
using Microsoft.Xna.Framework;
using Microsoft.Xna.Framework.Audio;
using Microsoft.Xna.Framework.Content;
using Microsoft.Xna.Framework.GamerServices;
using Microsoft.Xna.Framework.Graphics;
using Microsoft.Xna.Framework.Input;
using Microsoft.Xna.Framework.Media;
using Microsoft.Xna.Framework.Net;
using Microsoft.Xna.Framework.Storage;
```

```csharp
namespace Graphics_Demo
{
    //helper class to print scrolling text lines
    public class MessageList
    {
        private Game1 gameObj;
        private string[] messages;
        private int index;

        public MessageList( Game1 game )
        {
            gameObj = game;
            index = 0;
            messages = new string[20];
            for (int n = 0; n < messages.Length; n++)
                messages[n] = "";
        }

        public void Print(string text)
        {
            if (index < messages.Length-1) index++;
            else
            {
                for (int n = 1; n < 20; n++)
                    messages[n - 1] = messages[n];
            }
            messages[index] = text;
        }

        public void Draw(int x, int y)
        {
            for (int n = 0; n < 20; n++)
            {
                if (messages[n] != "")
                    gameObj.print(x, y + n * 15, messages[n]);
            }
        }
    }

    public class Game1 : Microsoft.Xna.Framework.Game
```

```
{
    //the usual suspects
    GraphicsDeviceManager graphics;
    SpriteBatch spriteBatch;
    SpriteFont font;
    KeyboardState keyState;
    GamePadState padState;

    //network objects
    SignedInGamer gamer;
    NetworkSession session;
    AvailableNetworkSessionCollection games;
    PacketReader reader;
    PacketWriter writer;

    //custom scrolling text object
    MessageList status;

    public Game1()
    {
        graphics = new GraphicsDeviceManager(this);
        Content.RootDirectory = "Content";
        Components.Add(new GamerServicesComponent(this));
        gamer = null;
        session = null;
        reader = new PacketReader();
        writer = new PacketWriter();
        status = new MessageList(this);
    }

    protected override void Initialize()
    {
        base.Initialize();
    }

    protected override void LoadContent()
    {
        spriteBatch = new SpriteBatch(GraphicsDevice);
        font = Content.Load<SpriteFont>("font1");
    }
```

```
protected override void UnloadContent() {}

protected override void Update(GameTime gameTime)
{
    keyState = Keyboard.GetState();
    GamePadState oldState = padState;
    padState = GamePad.GetState(PlayerIndex.One);
    if (keyState.IsKeyDown(Keys.Escape) ||
        padState.Buttons.Back == ButtonState.Pressed)
        this.Exit();

    //A button
    if (padState.Buttons.A == ButtonState.Released &&
        oldState.Buttons.A == ButtonState.Pressed)
    {
        CreateSession();
    }

    //B button
    if (padState.Buttons.B == ButtonState.Released &&
        oldState.Buttons.B == ButtonState.Pressed)
    {
        FindGame();
    }

    //X button
    if (padState.Buttons.X == ButtonState.Released &&
        oldState.Buttons.X == ButtonState.Pressed)
    {
        BroadcastMessage();
    }

    //Y button
    if (padState.Buttons.Y == ButtonState.Released &&
        oldState.Buttons.Y == ButtonState.Pressed)
    {
        GamerSignIn();
    }
```

```
    //handle incoming packets
    GetIncomingData();

    //keep things moving
    oldState = padState;
    GamerServicesDispatcher.Update();
    if (session != null) session.Update();
    base.Update(gameTime);
}

void session_GamerJoined(object sender, GamerJoinedEventArgs e)
{
    status.Print("GamerJoined: " + e.Gamer.Gamertag);
}

void session_GamerLeft(object sender, GamerLeftEventArgs e)
{
    status.Print("GamerLeft: " + e.Gamer.Gamertag);
}

void session_GameStarted(object sender, GameStartedEventArgs e)
{
    status.Print("GameStarted: " + e.ToString());
}

void session_GameEnded(object sender, GameEndedEventArgs e)
{
    status.Print("GameEnded: " + e.ToString());
}

void session_SessionEnded(object sender,
    NetworkSessionEndedEventArgs e)
{
    status.Print("SessionEnded: " + e.EndReason.ToString());
}

void GamerSignIn()
{
```

```
        if (gamer == null)
        {
            if (Gamer.SignedInGamers[PlayerIndex.One] == null)
                Guide.ShowSignIn(1, false);
            gamer = Gamer.SignedInGamers[PlayerIndex.One];
        }
        if (gamer != null)
            status.Print("Signed in: " + gamer.Gamertag);
    }

    void CreateSession()
    {
        if (gamer == null)
        {
            status.Print("No local gamer found--sign in first");
            return;
        }

        if (session != null) session.Dispose();
        session = null;

        int maxGamers = 4;
        int maxLocalGamers = 4;

        // Create the session
        session = NetworkSession.Create(NetworkSessionType.SystemLink,
            maxLocalGamers, maxGamers);
        status.Print("New session created");

        session.AllowHostMigration = true;
        session.AllowJoinInProgress = true;

        session.GamerJoined += new EventHandler<
            GamerJoinedEventArgs>(session_GamerJoined);
        session.GamerLeft += new EventHandler<
            GamerLeftEventArgs>(session_GamerLeft);
        session.GameStarted += new EventHandler<
            GameStartedEventArgs>(session_GameStarted);
        session.GameEnded += new EventHandler<
            GameEndedEventArgs>(session_GameEnded);
```

```
        session.SessionEnded += new EventHandler<
            NetworkSessionEndedEventArgs>(session_SessionEnded);
}
void FindGame()
{
    if (session != null) session.Dispose();
    session = null;

    if (games!=null) games.Dispose();
    games = null;

    if (games == null)
    {
        games = NetworkSession.Find(NetworkSessionType.SystemLink,
            1, null);
        if (games.Count == 0)
        {
            status.Print("No System Link games were found");
        }
        else
        {
            AvailableNetworkSession game = games[0];
            status.Print("Found session '" +
                game.HostGamertag + "'");
            status.Print("   Num players: " +
                game.CurrentGamerCount.ToString());
            status.Print("   Private slots: " +
                game.OpenPrivateGamerSlots.ToString());
            status.Print("   Public slots: " +
                game.OpenPublicGamerSlots.ToString());

            session = NetworkSession.Join(game);
            session.GamerJoined += new EventHandler<
                GamerJoinedEventArgs>(session_GamerJoined);
            session.GamerLeft += new EventHandler<
                GamerLeftEventArgs>(session_GamerLeft);
            session.GameStarted += new EventHandler<
                GameStartedEventArgs>(session_GameStarted);
            session.GameEnded += new EventHandler<
                GameEndedEventArgs>(session_GameEnded);
```

```
                          session.SessionEnded += new EventHandler<
                              NetworkSessionEndedEventArgs>(session_Session
Ended);
                }
            }
        }

        void BroadcastMessage()
        {
            string data = "The time is " + System.DateTime.Now.
                ToShortTimeString();
            writer.Write(data);
            foreach (LocalNetworkGamer gamer in session.LocalGamers)
            {
                gamer.SendData(writer, SendDataOptions.None);
            }
        }

        void GetIncomingData()
        {
            if (session == null) return;
            foreach (LocalNetworkGamer gamer in session.LocalGamers)
            {
                while (gamer.IsDataAvailable)
                {
                    NetworkGamer sender;

                    //get a packet
                    gamer.ReceiveData(reader, out sender);

                    if (!sender.IsLocal)
                        status.Print("Packet: " + reader.ReadString());
                }
            }
        }

        protected override void Draw(GameTime gameTime)
        {
            GraphicsDevice.Clear(Color.DarkSlateBlue);
            spriteBatch.Begin();
```

```
        int y = 20;
        print(20, y, "Network Session Demo"); y += 15;
        print(20, y, "Y - sign in user"); y += 15;
        print(20, y, "A - create network session"); y += 15;
        print(20, y, "B - search for game"); y += 15;
        print(20, y, "X - broadcast message"); y += 30;

        //print active session info
        if (session != null)
        {
            print(20, y, "Players: " + session.AllGamers.
                Count.ToString()); y += 15;
            print(20, y, "BPS send/recv: " + session.
                BytesPerSecondSent.ToString() + " / " +
                session.BytesPerSecondReceived.ToString()); y += 15;
        }

        //draw scrolling text lines
        status.Draw(400, 20);

        spriteBatch.End();
        base.Draw(gameTime);
    }

    public void print(int x, int y, string text)
    {
        print(x, y, text, Color.White);
    }

    public void print(int x, int y, string text, Color color)
    {
        try {
            spriteBatch.DrawString(font, text, new Vector2(
                (float)x, (float)y), color);
        }
        catch (Exception e) { }
    }
  }
}
```

SUMMARY

That wraps up networking in a nutshell! This was a pretty quick romp through the networking features of XNA (via the `Microsoft.Xna.Framework.Net` namespace). All the parts that make up a networked game can be a bit daunting to sort out, especially if you're just going off of the MSDN documentation online. That is why it is helpful to see all of it step by step as we have in this chapter. I'm confident that with some rendering code, we could create a multiplayer game with the code in this chapter plus the reference information in Chapter 10, "`Net`," as a backup. Onward!

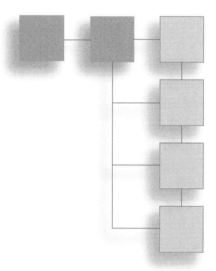

CHAPTER 15

MESHES

The title of this chapter is a bit misleading because it implies that just one subject is covered: meshes. However, there are many concepts we must learn in order to load and render a mesh, from fundamental rendering with a camera and lighting to calculating transformations. These concepts are challenging to grasp at first, so this chapter takes it slow, building a simple example that demonstrates how to render a mesh with lighting and transforms. We will skirt the theory and use the rendering classes provided in the XNA Framework without deriving any of the concepts on our own. For a reference, refer to Chapter 7, "Graphics," which includes detailed information on the Graphics namespace.

These are the topics in this chapter:

- Mesh file formats
- Loading a mesh
- Rendering a mesh
- Mesh Demo project

WORKING WITH MESHES

I have never been crazy about the name "mesh." This is the technical term for a 3D model, but it's too imprecise of a term to describe all that a mesh represents. In short, a mesh is an optimized list of vertices that make up a shape. A mesh in its truest definition does not include textures or materials, just a list of vertices.

All the most relevant mesh formats in use today, however, include these as part of the mesh definition, stored in one or another of the mesh file formats. A mesh in XNA is handled by a class called `Model`, which is a bit ironic. The `Model` class can handle any kind of mesh, from a simple static mesh to a fully animated skeletal model containing separate mesh groups.

Mesh File Formats

The most common mesh formats are Maya and 3DS Max, but most game studios use their own proprietary mesh format optimized for their game engine. Because XNA was built around Direct3D, one built-in mesh format is X (sometimes referred to as XOF). Most modeling software packages like Maya and Max do not support X without a custom exporter. The second mesh file that XNA supports is FBX. This is an older format used originally in a software package called FiLMBOX, now owned by Autodesk.

Loading a Mesh

We will use the namespace `Microsoft.Xna.Framework.Graphics`, which was covered in detail in Chapter 7. I'll forego any further reference information here and refer you to that chapter for the list of classes and methods within `Graphics` and get right down to business. Within the `Graphics` namespace is a class called `Model` that we will use for loading and rendering a mesh file. The `Model` class is fairly well self-contained, containing four key components: `Bones`, `Meshes`, `Root`, and `Tag`. `Bones` is filled with `ModelBone` objects, used to render a skeletal mesh. `Meshes` is filled with `ModelMesh` objects, used for normal rendering.

Before we can load a model file with the content manager, the model file must be added to the project. This is done in the usual way, by right-clicking the content project and selecting Add, selecting Existing Item, and then choosing the mesh file. If a texture is required by the mesh (and most meshes do have textures), then be sure to add the texture to the content project as well.

First, declare a `Model` variable:

```
Model model;
```

Then, from inside the `LoadContent` event method, we load the `Model`:

```
model = Content.Load<Model>("filename");
```

Rendering a Mesh

There is often more code involved in creating the camera than in rendering a mesh, but in the case of XNA, rendering the mesh is a bit involved. Let's start with the camera. A basic rendered scene needs three matrices:

- Projection matrix
- View matrix
- World matrix

Projection Matrix

The projection matrix, often called "perspective," defines the perspective or field of view. We can use a method in the `Matrix` class called `CreatePerspective-FieldOfView()` to create the projection matrix:

```
Matrix projection = Matrix.CreatePerspectiveFieldOfView(
    MathHelper.ToRadians(45.0f),
    graphics.GraphicsDevice.Viewport.AspectRatio,
    0.1f, 10000.0f);
```

This method requires some explanation. The first parameter is the field of view, which is the amount of the scene you wish to see, sort of like the type of lens attached to the camera. Next is the aspect ratio, which should be based on the resolution of the window, calculated by dividing the width by the height. The last two parameters define the near plane and far plane for the purpose of clipping.

View Matrix

The view matrix literally is the viewport created by the camera. It is what you "see" on the screen, based on the projection matrix (the rasterization properties), the camera's position, and the camera's target, or where the camera is pointed. It defines the camera's location and orientation. The position will usually move around quite a bit in a game. For instance, in a car-racing game, the camera will be the driver's view out the window of the car or in chase of the car for third-person view.

```
Vector3 position = new Vector3(0.0f, 10.0f, 10.0f);
Vector3 lookat = new Vector3(0.0f, 3.0f, 0.0f),
Matrix view = Matrix.CreateLookAt( position, lookat, Vector3.Up);
```

World Matrix

The world matrix defines the transforms of the current object to be rendered. The world matrix needs to take into account the rotation, scaling (if any), and translation of a model so that it is oriented correctly in the scene. To create the world matrix, the three transformation matrices (rotation, scaling, and translation) are multiplied together into a new combined matrix, which is the world. Because of the way matrix multiplication affects the elements of a matrix, we must perform multiplication in this specific order:

1. Rotation

2. Scaling

3. Translation

If you mix up the ordering of the matrix multiplication (when combining them all into the world matrix), then an object will show up in very strange places!

```
Matrix world = matRotation * matScaling * matTranslation;
```

Drawing a Model

A model contains transforms for the bones (if any) as well as meshes that are rendered together for each type of material and/or texture used by the mesh. To render a whole model, we have to render each of the meshes in the Model.Meshes collection, using an effect to render each one. Here is a reusable function that will accomplish the task. This method uses global matrices to simplify the code a bit, but a more reusable version would allow you to pass the matrices to the method to render a model without using the global Matrix variables.

```
private void DrawModel(Model m)
{
    Matrix[] transforms = new Matrix[m.Bones.Count];
    m.CopyAbsoluteBoneTransformsTo(transforms);
    foreach (ModelMesh mesh in m.Meshes)
    {
        foreach (BasicEffect effect in mesh.Effects)
        {
            effect.EnableDefaultLighting();
            effect.View = view;
            effect.Projection = projection;
            effect.World = gameWorldRotation *
```

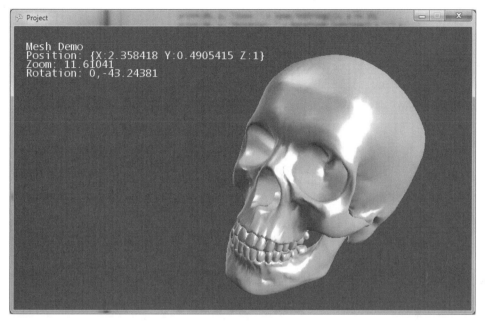

Figure 15.1
Rendering a mesh using the BasicEffect shader.

```
                transforms[mesh.ParentBone.Index] *
                Matrix.CreateTranslation(Position);
        }
        mesh.Draw();
    }
}
```

Mesh Demo

The Mesh Demo project, shown in Listing 15.1, loads a skull mesh (sourced from the DirectX SDK) and is shown in Figure 15.1.

Listing 15.1   Mesh Demo Project

```
using System;
using System.Collections.Generic;
using System.Linq;
using Microsoft.Xna.Framework;
using Microsoft.Xna.Framework.Audio;
using Microsoft.Xna.Framework.Content;
```

```csharp
using Microsoft.Xna.Framework.GamerServices;
using Microsoft.Xna.Framework.Graphics;
using Microsoft.Xna.Framework.Input;
using Microsoft.Xna.Framework.Media;
using Microsoft.Xna.Framework.Net;
using Microsoft.Xna.Framework.Storage;

namespace Graphics_Demo
{
    public class Game1 : Microsoft.Xna.Framework.Game
    {
        GraphicsDeviceManager graphics;
        SpriteBatch spriteBatch;
        SpriteFont font;
        KeyboardState keyState;
        GamePadState padState;

        Model model;
        Vector3 Position = Vector3.One;
        float Zoom = 10.0f;
        float RotationY = 0.0f;
        float RotationX = 0.0f;
        Matrix gameWorldRotation;
        Matrix projection, view;

        public Game1()
        {
            graphics = new GraphicsDeviceManager(this);
            Content.RootDirectory = "Content";
        }

        protected override void Initialize()
        {
            base.Initialize();

            //get the aspect ratio from the Viewport
            float aspectRatio = graphics.GraphicsDevice.Viewport.
                AspectRatio;

            //create the projection matrix
```

```
    projection = Matrix.CreatePerspectiveFieldOfView(
        MathHelper.ToRadians(45.0f),
        aspectRatio, 0.1f, 10000.0f);

    //create the view matrix
    view = Matrix.CreateLookAt(new Vector3(0.0f, 10.0f, Zoom),
        new Vector3(0.0f, 3.0f, 0.0f), Vector3.Up);
}


protected override void LoadContent()
{
    spriteBatch = new SpriteBatch(GraphicsDevice);
    font = Content.Load<SpriteFont>("font1");
    model = Content.Load<Model>("skullocc");
}

protected override void UnloadContent() {}

protected override void Update(GameTime gameTime)
{
    keyState = Keyboard.GetState();
    padState = GamePad.GetState(PlayerIndex.One);
    if (keyState.IsKeyDown(Keys.Escape) ||
        padState.Buttons.Back == ButtonState.Pressed)
        this.Exit();

    //move the model with left thumbstick
    Position.X += padState.ThumbSticks.Left.X * 1.01f;
    Position.Y += padState.ThumbSticks.Left.Y * 1.01f;

    //rotate and zoom with the right thumbstick
    Zoom += padState.ThumbSticks.Right.Y * 1.01f;
    RotationY += padState.ThumbSticks.Right.X;

    //recreate the view matrix due to the Zoom
    view = Matrix.CreateLookAt(new Vector3(0.0f, 10.0f, Zoom),
        new Vector3(0.0f, 3.0f, 0.0f), Vector3.Up);

    //recalculate the world matrix rotation
```

```
            gameWorldRotation = Matrix.CreateRotationX(
                MathHelper.ToRadians(RotationX)) *
                Matrix.CreateRotationY(MathHelper.ToRadians(RotationY));

            base.Update(gameTime);
        }

        protected override void Draw(GameTime gameTime)
        {
            GraphicsDevice.Clear(Color.DarkSlateBlue);

            //restore render states messed up by SpriteBatch
            GraphicsDevice.BlendState = BlendState.Opaque;
            GraphicsDevice.DepthStencilState = DepthStencilState.Default;

            //draw the model
            DrawModel(model);

            //sprite drawing code
            spriteBatch.Begin(SpriteSortMode.Deferred, BlendState.
                AlphaBlend);
            int y = 20;
            print(20, y, "Mesh Demo"); y += 15;
            print(20, y, "Position: " + Position.ToString()); y += 15;
            print(20, y, "Zoom: " + Zoom.ToString()); y += 15;
            print(20, y, "Rotation: " + RotationX.ToString() + "," +
                RotationY.ToString()); y += 15;
            spriteBatch.End();

            base.Draw(gameTime);
        }

        private void DrawModel(Model m)
        {
            Matrix[] transforms = new Matrix[m.Bones.Count];
            m.CopyAbsoluteBoneTransformsTo(transforms);

            foreach (ModelMesh mesh in m.Meshes)
            {
                foreach (BasicEffect effect in mesh.Effects)
```

```
        {
            effect.EnableDefaultLighting();
            effect.View = view;
            effect.Projection = projection;
            effect.World = gameWorldRotation *
                transforms[mesh.ParentBone.Index] *
                Matrix.CreateTranslation(Position);
        }
        mesh.Draw();
    }
}

public void print(int x, int y, string text)
{
    print(x, y, text, Color.White);
}
public void print(int x, int y, string text, Color color)
{
    try {
        spriteBatch.DrawString(font, text, new Vector2(
            (float)x, (float)y), color);
    }
    catch (Exception e) { }
}
    }
}
```

Summary

That wraps up mesh loading and rendering in fairly short order. There are many more advanced ways that a mesh can be rendered—for example, by using custom shaders and even performing animation on a skinned mesh. These are extremely advanced topics that require add-ons from MSDN, which are unfortunately not built in to the XNA Framework. This book will limit our use of meshes to just fixed, non-animated, non-bone meshes. After you have learned all you can about mesh rendering with the simple technique shown here and moved on to the slightly more advanced method of rendering with a custom shader, you should be ready for mesh animation. When you're ready, head over to http://create.msdn.com/en-US/education/catalog/sample/skinned_model for the example.

Chapter 16

Sprites

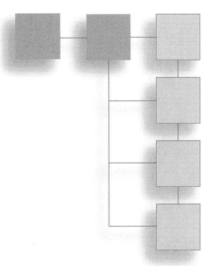

Sprite animation is made possible with the SpriteBatch class, part of the Graphics namespace (refer to Chapter 7, "Graphics," for a quick reference). We need to learn how to render sprites, a process called *rasterization*, which describes the rendering of an object onto a 2D screen. Technically, the video card rasterizes all rendered output based on projection matrix settings. Sprite rasterization is an appropriate term because SpriteBatch renders rectangular shapes using orthogonal projection. This new functionality, combined with rectangles and vectors, will result in a highly usable sprite engine fairly quickly. Not merely for 2D games, a sprite engine is often used to render particles and bitmapped fonts as well.

There are two ways to render sprite objects in XNA. First, we could create a quad (or rectangle) comprised of two triangles with a texture representing the 2D image to be drawn. This technique works fairly well, bringing transparency, lighting, and Z buffering to a sprite engine, but it is complicated. The second technique for drawing sprites is to rasterize an image directly onto the frame buffer as a rectangle. Fortunately, SpriteBatch handles sprite rasterization for us. A *sprite* is a 2D representation of a game entity that usually must interact with the player in some way. A tree or rock might be rendered in 2D and interact with the player by simply getting in the way, stopping the player by way of collision physics. We must also deal with game characters that interact with the player's character, whether it's an arrow fired from a bow or a missile fired from a spaceship. Rather than trying to dig into the technique and derive our own sprite rasterizer, we will just use the `SpriteBatch` class.

Here are the key topics:

- Sprite programming
- Drawing with transparency
- Drawing animated sprites
- The `Sprite` class
- The Animation Demo program

SPRITE PROGRAMMING

`SpriteBatch` doesn't care whether your sprite's source image uses a color key or an alpha channel for transparency; it just renders the image as requested. If you have an image with an alpha channel—for instance, a 32-bit Targa image—then it will be rendered with alpha, including translucent blending with the background. This is the technique used to render a sprite with transparent pixels. Looking at sprite functionality at a lower level, you can tell the sprite renderer (`SpriteBatch`) what color you want to use when drawing the image.

Transparency

The image file should have an alpha channel if you want to use transparency (which is almost always the case). Most artists will prefer to define their own translucent pixels for best results rather than leaving it to chance in the hands of a programmer. The main reason to use alpha rather than color-key transparency is better quality. An alpha channel can define pixels with shades of translucency. In contrast, a color key is an all-or-nothing, on/off setting with solid edges and pixelized edges, because such an image will have discrete pixels. We can do alpha blending at runtime to produce some awesome special effects (such as particle emitters), but for maximum quality it's best to prepare artwork in advance.

Rather than using a black border around a color-keyed sprite (the old-school way of highlighting a sprite), an artist will usually blend a border around a sprite's edges using an alpha level for partial translucency (which looks fantastic

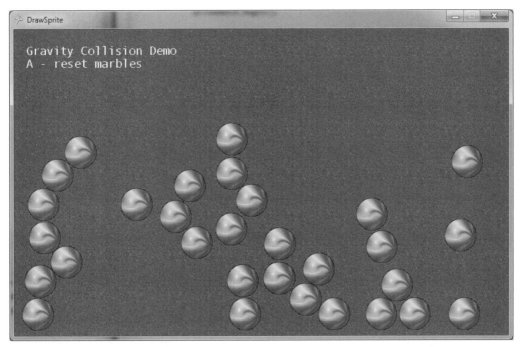

Figure 16.1
The Gravity Collision Demo program demonstrates sprite drawing and collision detection.

in comparison!). To do that, you must use a file format that supports 32-bit RGBA images. TGA and PNG files both support an alpha channel.

Gravity Collision Demo Program

The program in Listing 16.1, the results of which are shown in Figure 16.1, draws a bunch of marble sprites. This is an interesting program because all of the marble sprites are influenced by simulated gravity, and will collide with each other realistically. As they fall down the screen, they will stack up on each other.

Here is the source code for the Gravity Collision Demo program.

Listing 16.1   Gravity Collision Demo Program

```
using System;
using System.Collections.Generic;
using System.Linq;
```

```
using Microsoft.Xna.Framework;
using Microsoft.Xna.Framework.Content;
using Microsoft.Xna.Framework.Graphics;
using Microsoft.Xna.Framework.Input;

namespace DrawSprite
{
    class Marble
    {
        public Texture2D image;
        public Vector2 size;
        public Vector2 position;
        public Vector2 velocity;
    }

    public class Game1 : Microsoft.Xna.Framework.Game
    {
        GraphicsDeviceManager graphics;
        SpriteBatch spriteBatch;
        SpriteFont font;
        GamePadState padState;
        Random random;
        Texture2D background;
        Texture2D imgMarble;
        List<Marble> marbles;
        const float VELY = 4.0f;

        public Game1()
        {
            graphics = new GraphicsDeviceManager(this);
            Content.RootDirectory = "Content";
        }

        protected override void Initialize()
        {
            base.Initialize();
        }

        protected override void LoadContent()
        {
```

```
spriteBatch = new SpriteBatch(GraphicsDevice);
font = Content.Load<SpriteFont>("font1");
random = new Random();

//load background image
background = Content.Load<Texture2D>("background");

//load marble image
imgMarble = Content.Load<Texture2D>("marble");

//create marbles list
marbles = new List<Marble>();
for (int n = 0; n < 30; n++)
{
    Marble marble = new Marble();
    marble.size.X = 64;
    marble.size.Y = 64;
    marble.image = imgMarble;
    marble.velocity = new Vector2(0.0f, VELY);
    marbles.Add(marble);
}
ResetMarbles();

}

protected override void UnloadContent() { }

protected override void Update(GameTime gameTime)
{
    padState = GamePad.GetState(0);

    //end game
    if (Keyboard.GetState().IsKeyDown(Keys.Escape) ||
        padState.Buttons.Back == ButtonState.Pressed)
            this.Exit();

    //A - reset marbles
    if (padState.Buttons.A == ButtonState.Pressed)
        ResetMarbles();
```

```
                //animate explosion1
                foreach (Marble marble in marbles)
                {
                    //apply gravity
                    marble.velocity.Y = 2.0f;
                    marble.position += marble.velocity;

                    //collide with floor
                    if (marble.position.Y > Window.ClientBounds.Height - 64)
                    {
                        marble.position.Y = Window.ClientBounds.Height - 64;
                        marble.velocity.Y = 0;
                    }

                    //collide with other marbles
                    foreach (Marble other in marbles)
                    {
                        if (marble != other)
                        {
                            while (Collision(marble,other))
                                marble.position.Y -= 1.0f;

                            marble.velocity.Y = VELY;
                        }
                    }
                }
            base.Update(gameTime);
        }

        /**
         * Collision test with distance
         **/
        bool Collision(Marble A, Marble B)
        {
            double diffX = A.position.X - B.position.X;
            double diffY = A.position.Y - B.position.Y;
            double dist = Math.Sqrt(Math.Pow(diffX,2)+Math.Pow(diffY,2));
            double radii = A.size.X / 2 + B.size.X / 2;
            return (dist < radii * 0.8);
        }
```

```
void ResetMarbles()
{
    foreach (Marble marble in marbles)
    {
        marble.position = new Vector2(
            random.Next(Window.ClientBounds.Width - 64),
            0 - random.Next(Window.ClientBounds.Height));
    }
}

protected override void Draw(GameTime gameTime)
{
    GraphicsDevice.Clear(Color.CornflowerBlue);
    spriteBatch.Begin();

    //draw the background
    spriteBatch.Draw(background, new Vector2(0,0), Color.White);

    //draw the marbles
    foreach (Marble marble in marbles)
        spriteBatch.Draw(marble.image,marble.position,Color.White);

    print(20, 20, "Gravity Collision Demo");
    print(20, 40, "A - reset marbles");

    spriteBatch.End();
    base.Draw(gameTime);
}

public void print(int x, int y, string text)
{
    print(x, y, text, Color.White);
}

public void print(int x, int y, string text, Color color)
{
    try
    {
        spriteBatch.DrawString(font, text, new Vector2(
```

```
                        (float)x, (float)y, color);
            }
        catch (Exception e) { }
    }
}
}
```

DRAWING ANIMATED SPRITES

Let's talk about sprite animation. A *sprite animation sheet* is an image containing many frames for an animation sequence laid out in tiles that are arranged into rows and columns, as shown in Figure 16.2. In this sprite sheet, there are six columns across and 30 total frames of animation.

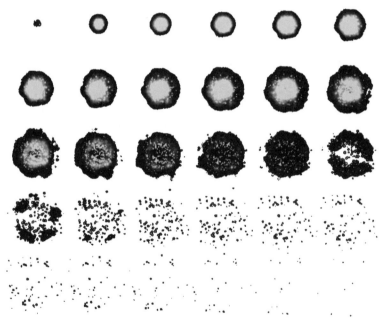

Figure 16.2
Animated explosion sprite stored on a sheet of rows and columns.

The Sprite Class

We're going to create a class to encapsulate all the properties and methods needed to effectively use sprites in a game. The Vector2 class will greatly simplify the code in the Sprite class, which otherwise would have to calculate things such as velocity on its own. In some cases, we'll use Vector2 just for a simple X-Y position.

What do we want to do with sprites? When it comes right down to it, the answer is *almost everything* involving 2D graphics. Sprites are at the very core of 2D games. We need to load and draw simple sprites (with no animation, just a single image), as well as the more complex animated sprites (with frames of animation). There is a need for both static and animated sprites in every game. In fact, most game objects are animated. For starters, Listing 16.2 contains the source code for a reusable Sprite class.

Listing 16.2   A Reusable Sprite Class

```
using System;
using System.Collections.Generic;
using System.Linq;
using Microsoft.Xna.Framework;
using Microsoft.Xna.Framework.Content;
using Microsoft.Xna.Framework.Graphics;
using Microsoft.Xna.Framework.Input;

namespace DrawSprite
{
    class Sprite
    {
        public Texture2D image;
        public bool image_loaded;
        public Vector2 size;
        public int columns;
        public int frame, totalframes;
        public Vector2 position;
        public Vector2 velocity;
        private SpriteBatch spriteBatch;
        private double starttime;

        public Sprite(SpriteBatch sb)
        {
```

```
        spriteBatch = sb;
        image = null;
        image_loaded = false;
        size.X = size.Y = 0;
        columns = 1;
        frame = 0;
        totalframes = 1;
        position = Vector2.Zero;
        velocity = Vector2.Zero;
        starttime = 0;
    }

    public Rectangle getBounds()
    {
        return new Rectangle( (int)position.X, (int)position.Y,
            (int)size.X, (int)size.Y);
    }

    /**
     * This should only be called from Load_Content
     **/
    public bool Load(ContentManager Content, string filename)
    {
        image = Content.Load<Texture2D>(filename);
        image_loaded = true;
        size.X = image.Width;
        size.Y = image.Height;
        return true;
    }

    public void Draw()
    {
        Rectangle src_rect = new Rectangle();
        src_rect.X = (frame % columns) * (int)size.X;
        src_rect.Y = (frame / columns) * (int)size.Y;
        src_rect.Width = (int)size.X;
        src_rect.Height = (int)size.Y;
        spriteBatch.Draw(image, position, src_rect, Color.White);
    }
```

```
    public void Animate(double elapsedTime)
    {
        Animate(0, totalframes, elapsedTime, 30);
    }

    public void Animate(int startframe, int endframe,
        double elapsedTime, double animrate)
    {
        double time = starttime + elapsedTime;
        if (time > animrate)
        {
            starttime = time;
            if (++frame > endframe) frame = startframe;
        }
    }

}
}
```

The Animation Demo Program

The results of the Animation Demo program in Listing 16.3 is shown in Figure 16.3. This example is fairly short thanks to the helpful Sprite class!

Listing 16.3 Animation Demo Program

```
using System;
using System.Collections.Generic;
using System.Linq;
using Microsoft.Xna.Framework;
using Microsoft.Xna.Framework.Content;
using Microsoft.Xna.Framework.Graphics;
using Microsoft.Xna.Framework.Input;

namespace DrawSprite
{
    public class Game1 : Microsoft.Xna.Framework.Game
    {
        GraphicsDeviceManager graphics;
        SpriteBatch spriteBatch;
```

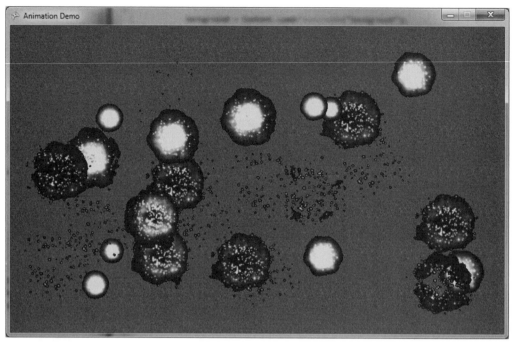

Figure 16.3
The Animation Demo program draws random animated explosion sprites.

```
GamePadState padState;
KeyboardState keyState;
Texture2D background;
Texture2D imgKaboom;
List<Sprite> kabooms;
Random rand;

public Game1()
{
    graphics = new GraphicsDeviceManager(this);
    Content.RootDirectory = "Content";
    rand = new Random();
}

protected override void Initialize()
{
    base.Initialize();
}
```

```
protected override void LoadContent()
{
    spriteBatch = new SpriteBatch(GraphicsDevice);

    //load background image
    background = Content.Load<Texture2D>("background");

    //load explosion sprite sheet
    imgKaboom = Content.Load<Texture2D>("explosion_30_128");

    //create list of explosions
    kabooms = new List<Sprite>();
    for (int n = 0; n < 30; n++)
    {
        Sprite boom = new Sprite(spriteBatch);
        boom.image = imgKaboom;
        boom.size = new Vector2(128,128);
        boom.columns = 6;
        boom.totalframes = 30;
        boom.frame = rand.Next(30);
        boom.position = new Vector2(
            rand.Next(Window.ClientBounds.Width-128),
            rand.Next(Window.ClientBounds.Height-128));
        kabooms.Add(boom);
    }
}

protected override void UnloadContent() { }

protected override void Update(GameTime gameTime)
{
    padState = GamePad.GetState(0);
    keyState = Keyboard.GetState();

    //end game
    if (padState.Buttons.Back == ButtonState.Pressed ||
        keyState.IsKeyDown(Keys.Escape))
            this.Exit();
```

```
        //animate sprites
        foreach (Sprite sprite in kabooms)
            sprite.Animate(gameTime.TotalGameTime.Milliseconds);

        base.Update(gameTime);
    }

    protected override void Draw(GameTime gameTime)
    {
        GraphicsDevice.Clear(Color.CornflowerBlue);
        spriteBatch.Begin();
        spriteBatch.Draw(background, new Vector2(0, 0), Color.White);

        //draw explosion sprites
        foreach (Sprite sprite in kabooms)
            sprite.Draw();

        spriteBatch.End();
        base.Draw(gameTime);
    }
}
}
```

Summary

Sprite animation is another key game programming tool that we cannot do without! This chapter ran through the code to draw a sprite sheet with timed animation fairly quickly, but only because the simplest approach to animation tends to handle most situations called for in a typical 2D game. We'll use this class in the next and final chapter to create a multiplayer *Tank Battle* game!

CHAPTER 17

MULTIPLAYER GAME ENGINE

This final chapter draws on all of the knowledge of the past 16 chapters to build a multiplayer game engine suitable for small arcade-style games. There are many books on the market covering advanced graphics engine programming; the focus here is on gameplay, and especially gameplay via system link and online with the Xbox Live network. This "little engine that could" is barely a layer wrapped around the usual XNA code, but it is enough to simplify the code a bit and provide reusable classes and methods that streamline the whole process of coding a new game. Overall, this chapter covers these topics:

- Integrating the engine
- Font support
- Engine source code
- Building the *Tank Battle* game
- Artwork
- Gameplay classes
- Game source code

BUILDING A SIMPLE XNA ENGINE

Why do we need a so-called "game engine" for a meager game demo such as the cliché tank game in this chapter? The answer can be summarized in one word: *concepts.* Don't think of a game engine as always on par with those found in commercial game-development packages, such as the engines behind *Unreal 3, Neverwinter Nights, Doom, Far Cry, Crysis*, and the like; products such as Garage Games' *Torque Game Engine*; or open-source options such as *Illright* (http://irrlicht.sourceforge.net/) and *Ogre* (http://www.ogre3d.org/).

We will base the source code for a game built with XNA Game Studio on the `Microsoft.Xna.Framework.Game` class. We will create a new class called `Engine` that inherits from `Microsoft.Xna.Framework.Game` to encapsulate all the functionality of that base `Game` class—and in the process tuck away all the methods in the `Game` class, replaced with our own, more gameplay-friendly code. This will greatly simplify and standardize our XNA code, making it easier to modify and use for any type of game you wish to create. As the previous 16 chapters have demonstrated, XNA is *not* a tool for beginners. Although it may be marketed toward beginners, XNA is not suitable for beginners, and therefore you have no usable gameplay code in an XNA project unless you *write* that code. Such is the purpose of a so-called XNA engine: to encapsulate or wrap the core XNA code inside your own class, and then transform that code into a more gameplay-friendly interface. That, then, is the essential goal of a so-called "game engine": to provide *gameplay* services.

The sample game in this chapter is composed of the usual gameplay source code as well as an `Engine` class that encapsulates much of the usual XNA code. To learn how the engine works, we will create a multiplayer *Tank Battle* game, putting as much engine code as possible in the engine project so that the game code doesn't even look like XNA any longer. Of course, we're not trying to get away from XNA by any means; no, the goal is not to abstract away any semblance of XNA, but to provide services in the engine that our gameplay project can consume, thus making game development with XNA faster and easier.

Integrating the Engine

During early development, it is more convenient to include the engine project in the solution with the gameplay project, because changes will be ongoing in the engine as the game is developed. This is a small enough game that a separated engine is not even necessary. The idea is not to create an engine template and then force gameplay code to follow it in a rigid manner, but rather to *support* the gameplay code with as many useful and friendly features as possible to make the code easier to write and update. When the engine project reaches a level of development where it can be compiled and used as a component, then both the engine and its content projects can be moved into a new solution, compiled, and closed. As the theory goes, the compiled engine will result in a DLL file that can be added to the gameplay project. The DLL will contain the .NET Framework assembly information needed to list it in the References list so that it can be added to the *gameplay project* as a referenced library. At that point, the engine library is compiled once again with the game, and the DLL must be distributed *with* the game. I won't go into building a library project in this short chapter, other than to just make the suggestion. To keep the project simpler, the source code for the engine files and gameplay files will be combined. But, should you wish to explore the concept of a separate library project, all the source files will be available!

Font Support

One of the first things we're going to do with the engine is provide several reusable fonts, so we don't have to keep creating them! Rather than require the gameplay programmer to create a new font object in every new project, we will create a bunch of fonts in the engine and make them available as an enumerated list and used as a parameter to the text-output functions. Each of these fonts is included in the Engine class and the content project with several point-size variations for each one. This greatly simplifies printing text, since the Print method now accepts a font name from an enumeration rather than a SpriteFont object! Wait until you see the code—it's great! Here are the fonts that are supported:

- Segoe UI Mono
- Kootenay
- Lindsey
- Miramonte
- Pericles
- PericlesLight
- Pescadero

Engine Source Code

Listing 17.1 contains source code for the Engine class. This is not an "engine" by any means; it is simply descriptive of what the code herein tries to accomplish.

Do not confuse the term "engine" here with a commercial engine like *Unreal*. The little engine here was designed to make it relatively easy to throw together 2D multiplayer arcade-style games, as the *Tank Battle* example later in the chapter demonstrates.

Listing 17.1   Engine Source Code

```
using System;
using System.Collections.Generic;
using System.Linq;
using Microsoft.Xna.Framework;
using Microsoft.Xna.Framework.Audio;
using Microsoft.Xna.Framework.Content;
using Microsoft.Xna.Framework.GamerServices;
using Microsoft.Xna.Framework.Graphics;
using Microsoft.Xna.Framework.Input;
using Microsoft.Xna.Framework.Media;
using Microsoft.Xna.Framework.Net;
using Microsoft.Xna.Framework.Storage;

namespace XNAEngine
{
    public enum Fonts
    {
        Kootenay8,
        Kootenay12,
        Kootenay14,
        Lindsey14,
        Lindsey18,
        Lindsey24,
        Segoe8,
        Segoe12,
        Miramonte8,
        Miramonte12,
        Pericles14,
        Pericles18,
        Pericles24,
        PericlesLight18,
        Pescadero14,
        Pescadero18
    }
```

```
public abstract class Engine : Microsoft.Xna.Framework.Game
{
    /**
     * ENGINE OBJECTS
     **/
    protected GraphicsDeviceManager graphics;
    protected SpriteBatch spriteBatch;
    private float lastTime=0;
    private SpriteFont[] fonts;
    private Fonts defaultFont=Fonts.Miramonte12;
    private Texture2D line;
    public Random random = new Random();
    public GamePadState gamePad;
    public GamePadState oldPad;
    public KeyboardState keys, oldKeys;
    public MouseState mouse;

    //network objects
    public SignedInGamer gamer;
    public NetworkSession session;
    private AvailableNetworkSessionCollection games;
    public string NetworkStatusMessage;

    private bool paused;
    double drawCount = 0, drawTime = 0, drawRate = 0;
    double updateCount = 0, updateTime = 0, updateRate = 0;
    public bool Use720HD = true;
    private Rectangle workBounds;

    /**
     * ENGINE VIRTUAL FUNCTIONS TO BE IMPLEMENTED IN SUB-CLASS
     **/
    public abstract bool Load();
    public abstract void Update(float deltaTime);
    public abstract void Draw2D();
    public abstract void Draw3D();
    public abstract void NetworkReceive(LocalNetworkGamer gamer,
        ref PacketReader packet);
    public bool IsPaused() { return paused; }
```

```
public double GetUpdateRate() { return updateRate; }
public double GetDrawRate() { return drawRate; }

/**
 * ENGINE CONSTRUCTOR
 **/
public Engine()
{
    graphics = new GraphicsDeviceManager(this);
    Components.Add(new GamerServicesComponent(this));
    paused = false;

    //set the desired resolutions
    Vector2 screen = new Vector2(640, 480);
    if (Use720HD)
        screen = new Vector2(1280, 720);
    graphics.PreferredBackBufferWidth = (int)screen.X;
    graphics.PreferredBackBufferHeight = (int)screen.Y;
    graphics.ApplyChanges();

    //usable TV resolution is about 95%
    int bx = (int)(screen.X * 0.05);
    int by = (int)(screen.Y * 0.05);
    workBounds = new Rectangle(bx, by,
        (int)screen.X - bx, (int)screen.Y - by);

    //initialize game pads
    gamePad = new GamePadState();

    //initialize networking
    gamer = null;
    session = null;
}

/**
 * Microsoft.Xna.Framework.Game BASE METHODS
 **/
protected override void Initialize()
{
```

```
        base.Initialize();
        IsFixedTimeStep = true;
        long ticks = 10000000L / 100L;
        TargetElapsedTime = new TimeSpan(ticks);
        IsMouseVisible = true;
    }

    protected override void LoadContent()
    {
        spriteBatch = new SpriteBatch(GraphicsDevice);
        Content.RootDirectory = "Content";

        //line drawing point texture
        line = Content.Load<Texture2D>("dot");

        //load engine fonts
        fonts = new SpriteFont[16];
        fonts[(int)Fonts.Kootenay8] = Content.Load<SpriteFont>
            ("Fonts/Kootenay8");
        fonts[(int)Fonts.Kootenay12] = Content.Load<SpriteFont>
            ("Fonts/Kootenay12");
        fonts[(int)Fonts.Kootenay14] = Content.Load<SpriteFont>
            ("Fonts/Kootenay14");
        fonts[(int)Fonts.Lindsey14] = Content.Load<SpriteFont>
            ("Fonts/Lindsey14");
        fonts[(int)Fonts.Lindsey18] = Content.Load<SpriteFont>
            ("Fonts/Lindsey18");
        fonts[(int)Fonts.Lindsey24] = Content.Load<SpriteFont>
            ("Fonts/Lindsey24");
        fonts[(int)Fonts.Segoe8] = Content.Load<SpriteFont>
            ("Fonts/Segoe8");
        fonts[(int)Fonts.Segoe12] = Content.Load<SpriteFont>
            ("Fonts/Segoe12");
        fonts[(int)Fonts.Miramonte8] = Content.Load<SpriteFont>
            ("Fonts/Miramonte8");
        fonts[(int)Fonts.Miramonte12] = Content.Load<SpriteFont>
            ("Fonts/Miramonte12");
        fonts[(int)Fonts.Pericles14] = Content.Load<SpriteFont>
            ("Fonts/Pericles14");
```

```
            fonts[(int)Fonts.Pericles18] = Content.Load<SpriteFont>
                ("Fonts/Pericles18");
            fonts[(int)Fonts.Pericles24] = Content.Load<SpriteFont>
                ("Fonts/Pericles24");
            fonts[(int)Fonts.PericlesLight18] = Content.Load<SpriteFont>
                ("Fonts/PericlesLight18");
            fonts[(int)Fonts.Pescadero14] = Content.Load<SpriteFont>
                ("Fonts/Pescadero14");
            fonts[(int)Fonts.Pescadero18] = Content.Load<SpriteFont>
                ("Fonts/Pescadero18");

            //give game code a chance to load assets
            Load();
        }

        protected override void UnloadContent() { }

        protected override void Update(GameTime gameTime)
        {
            //calculate update fps
            updateCount++;
            if (Environment.TickCount > updateTime + 1000)
            {
                updateRate = updateCount;
                updateCount = 0;
                updateTime = Environment.TickCount;
            }

            if (paused == false)
            {
                //get status of input devices
                gamePad = GamePad.GetState(PlayerIndex.One);
                keys = Keyboard.GetState();
                mouse = Mouse.GetState();

                //call update function in sub-class
                float delta = Environment.TickCount - lastTime;
                lastTime = Environment.TickCount;
                Update(delta);
```

```
        //save input states
        oldPad = gamePad;
        oldKeys = keys;

        //update network
        GetIncomingData();
    }

    GamerServicesDispatcher.Update();
    if (session != null) session.Update();
    base.Update(gameTime);
}

protected override void Draw(GameTime gameTime)
{
    //calculate draw fps
    drawCount++;
    if (Environment.TickCount > drawTime + 1000)
    {
        drawRate = drawCount;
        drawCount = 0;
        drawTime = Environment.TickCount;
    }

    //begin rendering
    GraphicsDevice.Clear(Color.DarkBlue);

    //render
    GraphicsDevice.BlendState = BlendState.Opaque;
    GraphicsDevice.DepthStencilState = DepthStencilState.Default;
    Draw3D();

    //begin 2D
    spriteBatch.Begin();
    Draw2D();
    spriteBatch.End();
    //end 2D

    base.Draw(gameTime);
    //end rendering
}
```

```
protected override void OnActivated(object sender, EventArgs args)
{
    paused = false;
    base.OnActivated(sender, args);
}

protected override void OnDeactivated(object sender, EventArgs args)
{
    paused = true;
    base.OnDeactivated(sender, args);
}

/**
 * ENGINE HELPER FUNCTIONS
 **/
public Texture2D LoadTexture(string filename)
{
    Texture2D texture = Content.Load<Texture2D>(filename);
    return texture;
}

public void DrawImage(Texture2D texture, Vector2 position)
{
    spriteBatch.Draw(texture, position, Color.White);
}

public void Print(int x, int y, string text)
{
    Print(fonts[(int)defaultFont], x, y, text, Color.White);
}

//Print using font identified via the Enum
public void Print(Fonts font, int x, int y, string text,
    Color color)
{
    Print(fonts[(int)font], x, y, text, color);
}

//Base Print function that does all the real work
public void Print(SpriteFont font, int x, int y, string text,
    Color color)
```

```
{
    try
    {
        spriteBatch.DrawString(font, text, new Vector2(
            (float)x, (float)y), color);
    }
    catch (Exception e) { }
}

public void DrawVLine(int x, int y1, int y2, Color color)
{
    spriteBatch.Draw(line, new Rectangle(x, y1, 1, 1+y2-y1), color);
}

public void DrawHLine(int x1, int x2, int y, Color color)
{
    spriteBatch.Draw(line, new Rectangle(x1, y, 1+x2 - x1, 1),
        color);
}

public void DrawBox(Rectangle rect, Color color)
{
    DrawBox(rect.X, rect.Y, rect.X + rect.Width, rect.Y +
        rect.Height, color);
}

public void DrawBox(int x1, int y1, int x2, int y2, Color color)
{
    DrawVLine(x1, y1, y2, color);
    DrawVLine(x2, y1, y2, color);
    DrawHLine(x1, x2, y1, color);
    DrawHLine(x1, x2, y2, color);
}

public bool Collision(Sprite A, Sprite B)
{
    float radius = (A.size.X + B.size.X) / 2;
    return Collision(A.position, B.position, radius);
}
```

```
public bool Collision(Vector2 first, Vector2 second, float radius)
{
    double diffX = first.X - second.X;
    double diffY = first.Y - second.Y;
    double dist = Math.Sqrt(Math.Pow(diffX, 2) +
        Math.Pow(diffY, 2));
    return (dist < radius);
}

/**
 * NETWORKING CODE
 **/
void session_GamerJoined(object sender, GamerJoinedEventArgs e)
{
    NetworkStatusMessage = "GamerJoined: " + e.Gamer.Gamertag;
}

void session_GamerLeft(object sender, GamerLeftEventArgs e)
{
    NetworkStatusMessage = "GamerLeft: " + e.Gamer.Gamertag;
}

void session_GameStarted(object sender, GameStartedEventArgs e)
{
    NetworkStatusMessage = "GameStarted: " + e.ToString();
}

void session_GameEnded(object sender, GameEndedEventArgs e)
{
    NetworkStatusMessage = "GameEnded: " + e.ToString();
}

void session_SessionEnded(object sender,
    NetworkSessionEndedEventArgs e)
{
    NetworkStatusMessage = "SessionEnded: " + e.EndReason.
        ToString();
}

public void GamerSignIn()
```

```
{
    if (gamer == null)
    {
        if (Gamer.SignedInGamers[PlayerIndex.One] == null &&
            Guide.IsVisible == false)
        {
            Guide.ShowSignIn(1, false);
        }
        gamer = Gamer.SignedInGamers[PlayerIndex.One];
    }
    if (gamer != null)
    {
        NetworkStatusMessage = "Signed in: " + gamer.Gamertag;
    }
}

public void CreateSession()
{
    if (gamer == null)
    {
        NetworkStatusMessage = "No local gamer--sign in first";
        return;
    }

    if (session != null) session.Dispose();
    session = null;

    int maxGamers = 4;
    int maxLocalGamers = 4;

    // Create the session
    session = NetworkSession.Create(NetworkSessionType.SystemLink,
        maxLocalGamers, maxGamers);
    NetworkStatusMessage = "New session created";

    session.AllowHostMigration = true;
    session.AllowJoinInProgress = true;

    session.GamerJoined += new EventHandler<
        GamerJoinedEventArgs>(session_GamerJoined);
```

```
        session.GamerLeft += new EventHandler<
            GamerLeftEventArgs>(session_GamerLeft);
        session.GameStarted += new EventHandler<
            GameStartedEventArgs>(session_GameStarted);
        session.GameEnded += new EventHandler<
            GameEndedEventArgs>(session_GameEnded);
        session.SessionEnded += new EventHandler<
            NetworkSessionEndedEventArgs>(session_SessionEnded);
    }

    public void FindGame()
    {
        if (session != null) session.Dispose();
        session = null;

        if (games != null) games.Dispose();
        games = null;

        if (games == null)
        {
            games = NetworkSession.Find(NetworkSessionType.SystemLink,
                1, null);
            if (games.Count == 0)
            {
                NetworkStatusMessage = "No System Link games found";
            }
            else
            {
                AvailableNetworkSession game = games[0];
                NetworkStatusMessage = "Found session '" +
                    game.HostGamertag + "'";

                session = NetworkSession.Join(game);
                session.GamerJoined += new EventHandler<
                    GamerJoinedEventArgs>(session_GamerJoined);
                session.GamerLeft += new EventHandler<
                    GamerLeftEventArgs>(session_GamerLeft);
                session.GameStarted += new EventHandler<
                    GameStartedEventArgs>(session_GameStarted);
```

```
            session.GameEnded += new EventHandler<
                GameEndedEventArgs>(session_GameEnded);
            session.SessionEnded += new EventHandler<
                NetworkSessionEndedEventArgs>(session_SessionEnded);
        }
    }
}

public void NetworkSendPacket(PacketWriter writer)
{
    if (session == null) return;
    foreach (LocalNetworkGamer gamer in session.LocalGamers)
    {
        gamer.SendData(writer, SendDataOptions.None);
    }
}

private void GetIncomingData()
{
    if (session == null) return;
    PacketReader reader = new PacketReader();
    foreach (LocalNetworkGamer gamer in session.LocalGamers)
    {
        while (gamer.IsDataAvailable)
        {
            NetworkGamer sender;

            //get a packet
            gamer.ReceiveData(reader, out sender);
            if (!sender.IsLocal)
            {
                NetworkReceive(gamer, ref reader);
            }
        }
    }
}
```

BUILDING THE *TANK BATTLE* GAME

Figure 7.1 shows the finished game. The game functions similarly to the Network Demo program from Chapter 14, "Multiplayer Networking," where a single code base is used and any player may host or join another hosted game at any time. This is one of the greatest pros of the XNA networking library: It can seamlessly transition from host to client and vice versa, as well as run with much the same code as a LAN (System Link) game or an Xbox Live game played online against other remote players. Speaking of which, anyone who has an App Hub account can play the tank game against you! To make the game work over Xbox Live, a minor change must be made to the code. You'll note that the SystemLink option is used to create the network sessions. If you want to switch to playing on Xbox Live, that single option is all that must be changed.

This game is intended to be a launching point for any number of potential games. It is an *infrastructure template* for a networked tank game for two players. Of course we could adapt it for more than two, but for the sake of learning, this chapter focuses on just two players at this point. If you pore over

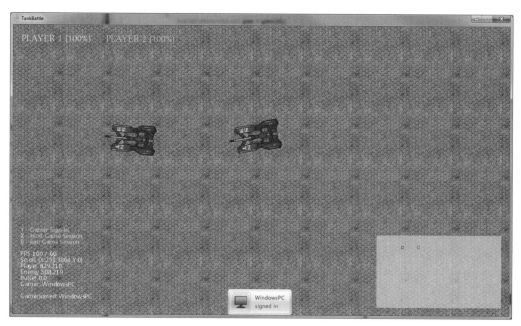

Figure 17.1
The Xbox 360 account is hosting, while the Windows PC build is joining the game.

the source code and examine how it works for just two players, I am confident you will have no problem adapting it for three, four, or eight! As a matter of fact, I had the game running with four players early on, and had to simplify it because the code was a bit unwieldy—in other words, it grew in complexity beyond the goal I had for this chapter! I want *you* to build a great game, so I can't supply you with one up front. I need to take a step back and just show you how, give you the tools, and let you make a game out of it.

Artwork

The artwork for the game comes from several places. First, the tank sprite and artwork were created by Mark Simpson (Prinz Eugn at Gamedev.net). The ground texture was sourced from an asset collection called DarkMatter by The Game Creators (www.thegamecreators.com). As you can see in Figure 17.2, the tank chassis and turret are moved independently, so it's possible to drive in one direction while shooting in another.

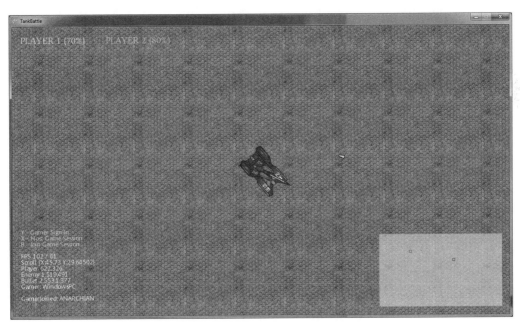

Figure 17.2
Shots can be fired at long range, beyond the boundary of the screen.

Gameplay Classes

There are some helper classes in the *Tank Battle* project to help organize the source code, which would otherwise become quite complicated due to the lists and custom properties needed for the tanks and shell/bullet sprites. The base `Sprite` class is extended for these custom game objects with the additional things needed to make the game work.

Hint

When starting up the Windows build of the networked *Tank Battle* game, it will often take several seconds before the game window appears due to the gamer services component.

The game keeps track of each player's health, but doesn't enforce game state. That is, there is no "win" or "lose" screen or notification. The damage dealt is 10 percent per shot, so you can adjust this to suit the needs of your own game. When the health drops to 0 percent, the player should lose the game—or get respawned, if you want to make it more fun! I would really like to see obstacles, spawn points, A.I. bot tanks, and destructible terrain added to this game. It has some real potential with just a few gameplay features that would be relatively easy to add now that the framework has been created.

Ground Class

The `Ground` class, shown in Listing 17.2, implements a scrolling background to allow the tanks a larger battlefield, since obviously the screen resolution alone is too small for any kind of effective gameplay! We don't necessarily want a *huge* battlefield, but one that is just large enough to give the players some room to chase and evade. In a polished and more highly playable version of this game, we would expect to find obstacles such as walls, buildings, perhaps even destructible objects, A.I. players, and other things (based on the game mode). How about a capture-the-flag mode? The possibilities truly are endless. I think it would be really fun to give each player an A.I. ally tank to help them fight against their opponent. The A.I. tanks would add a bit of uncertainty to the game! Another gameplay idea that usually nets a good result with players is the addition of power-up items that the player can pick up. How about different weapons with which the player can equip his or her tank?

Listing 17.2   The Ground Class

```
using Microsoft.Xna.Framework;
using Microsoft.Xna.Framework.Content;
using Microsoft.Xna.Framework.Graphics;

namespace XNAEngine
{
    class Ground
    {
        private GraphicsDevice device;
        private ContentManager content;
        private SpriteBatch spriteBatch;
        private Texture2D tile;
        private Texture2D buffer;
        private Vector2 oldPos;
        private RenderTarget2D renderTarget;
        public Rectangle Boundary;
        public Vector2 Position;
        public Microsoft.Xna.Framework.Graphics.Viewport
            Viewport { get; set; }

        public Ground(ContentManager _content, SpriteBatch _spriteBatch)
        {
            content = _content;
            spriteBatch = _spriteBatch;
            device = spriteBatch.GraphicsDevice;
            buffer = null;
            tile = null;
            oldPos = Vector2.One;
            renderTarget = null;

            //if object is created inside LoadContent, then lock & load!
            if (content != null)
                Load();
        }

        public void Load()
        {
```

```
        Viewport = device.Viewport;
        tile = content.Load<Texture2D>("tile");
        CreateScrollBuffer();
    }

    public void Draw()
    {
        //keep view inside the buffer boundary
        if (Position.X < 0)
            Position.X = 0;
        else if (Position.X > buffer.Width - Viewport.Width)
            Position.X = buffer.Width - Viewport.Width;
        if (Position.Y < 0)
            Position.Y = 0;
        else if (Position.Y > buffer.Height - Viewport.Height)
            Position.Y = buffer.Height - Viewport.Height;

        //draw the ground scroll buffer
        Vector2 pos = Position;
        Rectangle sourceRect = new Rectangle((int)pos.X, (int)pos.Y,
            Viewport.Width, Viewport.Height);
        spriteBatch.Draw(buffer, Vector2.Zero, sourceRect, Color.White);
    }

    private void CreateScrollBuffer()
    {
        //create scroll buffer (4x total size of screen)
        buffer = new Texture2D(spriteBatch.GraphicsDevice,
            Viewport.Width * 2, Viewport.Height * 2);
        Boundary = new Rectangle(0, 0, buffer.Width, buffer.Height);

        //create new render target
        renderTarget = new RenderTarget2D(device, buffer.Width,
            buffer.Height);

        //set render target to scroll buffer
        device.SetRenderTarget(renderTarget);

        //fill buffer with tiles
        Vector2 tiles;
```

```
            tiles.X = buffer.Width / tile.Width;
            tiles.Y = buffer.Height / tile.Height;

            spriteBatch.Begin();
            for (int y = 0; y < tiles.Y; y++)
            {
                for (int x = 0; x < tiles.X; x++)
                {
                    Vector2 pos = new Vector2(x * tile.Width, y *
                        tile.Height);
                    spriteBatch.Draw(tile, pos, null, Color.White);
                }
            }
            spriteBatch.End();

            //copy texture to buffer
            buffer = (Texture2D)renderTarget;
            //restore default render target
            device.SetRenderTarget(null);
        }

        public Rectangle GetBoundary()
        {
            return new Rectangle(0, 0, buffer.Width, buffer.Height);
        }
    }
}
```

Tank **Class**

The Tank class, shown in Listing 17.3, might be considered an extension of the Sprite class, but while implementing the class for this game I found it more helpful to have two Sprite variables defined in the class instead—one for the tank's main body (called the chassis) and one for the turret (the gun). The chassis is used for things like collision detection because it's the largest piece, while the turret sprite just follows along in a relative position, drawn over the top of the chassis every time the Tank.Draw method is called. While developing any game, even a fairly simple game like this two-player *Tank Battle*, it is helpful

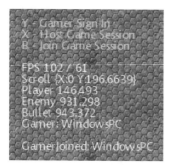

Figure 17.3
The information panel in the lower-left corner shows vital data (essential when debugging a networked game).

to have debugging information on the screen. Figure 17.3 shows some debug messages printed to the lower-left corner of the game window.

Listing 17.3   The Tank Class

```
using System;
using Microsoft.Xna.Framework;
using Microsoft.Xna.Framework.Graphics;
using Microsoft.Xna.Framework.Content;

namespace XNAEngine
{
    public class Tank
    {
        private SpriteBatch sb;
        public Sprite Chassis;
        public Sprite Turret;
        public Vector2 Position;
        public bool Firing { get; set; }
        public float MoveTimer { get; set; }
        public float FireTimer { get; set; }
        public int Health { get; set; }
        public bool Moving { get; set; }

        //this should be called from LoadContent
        public Tank(ContentManager content, SpriteBatch spriteBatch)
        {
```

```
        sb = spriteBatch;
        Chassis = new Sprite(spriteBatch);
        Chassis.Load(content, "chassis");
        Chassis.pivot = new Vector2(64, 64);
        Turret = new Sprite(spriteBatch);
        Turret.Load(content, "turret");
        Turret.pivot = new Vector2(32, 80);
        Position = new Vector2(0, 0);
        MoveTimer = 0;
        FireTimer = 0;
        Firing = false;
        Health = 100;
    }

    public void Update(float delta) { }

    public void Draw()
    {
        Chassis.position = new Vector2(Position.X + 64,
            Position.Y + 64);
        Chassis.Draw();
        Turret.position = new Vector2(Chassis.position.X,
            Chassis.position.Y);
        Turret.Draw();
    }

    public void MoveTurret(float degs)
    {
        if (degs < -5.0) degs = -5.0f;
        else if (degs > 5.0) degs = 5.0f;
        Turret.rotation += MathHelper.ToRadians(degs);
    }

    public void Turn(float degs)
    {
        if (degs < -5.0) degs = -5.0f;
        else if (degs > 5.0) degs = 5.0f;
        Chassis.rotation += MathHelper.ToRadians(degs);
        MoveTurret(degs);
        Moving = true;
    }
```

```
        public void Drive(float dir)
        {
            float angle = Chassis.rotation - MathHelper.ToRadians(90);
            Vector2 vel = new Vector2(
                dir * (float)Math.Cos(MathHelper.WrapAngle(angle)),
                dir * (float)Math.Sin(MathHelper.WrapAngle(angle)));
            Position += vel;
            Moving = true;
        }
    }
}
```

Shell **Class**

The Shell class, shown in Listing 17.4, is a very basic extension class that inherits from Sprite and just adds one new property: an Owner property, which identifies which tank fired the shot. Speaking of shooting, Figure 17.4 shows what happens if you aren't careful with that fire button! Just make sure you can avoid incoming fire as fast as you dish it out.

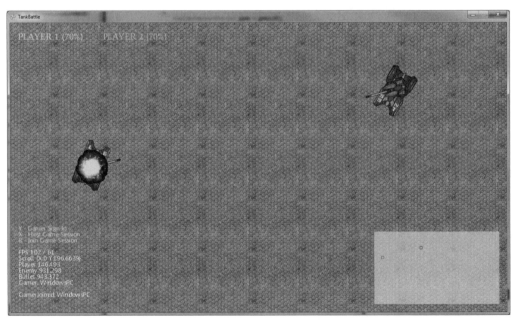

Figure 17.4
The enemy scores a hit on our tank!

Listing 17.4   The `Shell` Class

```
using Microsoft.Xna.Framework;
using Microsoft.Xna.Framework.Graphics;
namespace XNAEngine
{
    class Shell : Sprite
    {
        public int Owner { get; set; }
        public Shell(SpriteBatch sb) : base(sb)
        {
        }
    }
}
```

Game Source Code

The complete source code for the `Game` class is shown in Listing 17.5, representing the majority of the gameplay code for *Tank Battle*. Remember, much of the helper code was encapsulated in the `Engine` class so we're at a slightly higher level of coding here as a result. Note also that this `MyGame` class inherits from `XNAEngine.Engine`, which has its own abstract methods that must be implemented in the subclass. Gone are the default XNA events such as `LoadContent`, replaced with our own (in this case, it is simply called `Load`). Similarly, we have replaced `Update()` and `Draw()` with our own methods that are implemented by any class that inherits from `Engine`. The advantage is a cleaner source-code file that is at least somewhat protected from future changes to the XNA Framework. If the folks at Microsoft makes any changes—and odds are, they will—we can make most of the changes in `Engine` rather than in `MyGame`. Speaking of the game, let's see another screenshot—Figure 17.5 shows the game running on an Xbox 360, as host, ready to receive a connection from another player.

Listing 17.5   The Complete Source Code for the `Game` Class

```
using System;
using System.Collections.Generic;
using Microsoft.Xna.Framework;
```

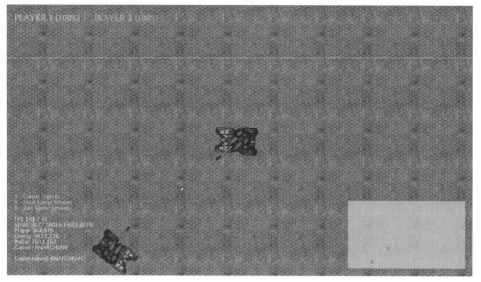

Figure 17.5
The game hosted on an Xbox 360.

```
using Microsoft.Xna.Framework.Audio;
using Microsoft.Xna.Framework.Content;
using Microsoft.Xna.Framework.GamerServices;
using Microsoft.Xna.Framework.Graphics;
using Microsoft.Xna.Framework.Input;
using Microsoft.Xna.Framework.Media;
using Microsoft.Xna.Framework.Net;
using Microsoft.Xna.Framework.Storage;

namespace XNAEngine
{
    public class MyGame : XNAEngine.Engine
    {
        const int FIRE_DELAY = 1500;
        const float SHELL_VEL = 12.0f;

        Tank[] tanks;
        List<Shell> shells;
        List<Shell> enemyShells;
        Texture2D shellImage;
        Sprite explosion;
```

```
Ground ground;
Sprite radar;
Vector2 bulletPos;

SoundEffect tankFire;
SoundEffectInstance tankFireInst;
SoundEffect explosionSound;
SoundEffectInstance explInst;

/**
 * Engine constructor
 **/
public MyGame() { }

/**
 * Implements Engine.Load
 **/
public override bool Load()
{
    //create ground scroller
    ground = new Ground(Content, spriteBatch);

    //create tank sprites
    tanks = new Tank[2];
    for (int n = 0; n < 2; n++)
    {
        tanks[n] = new Tank(Content, spriteBatch);
        int x = random.Next(ground.Boundary.Width - 128);
        int y = random.Next(ground.Boundary.Height - 128);
        tanks[n].Position = new Vector2(x ,y );
        tanks[n].Chassis.rotation = MathHelper.ToRadians(
            random.Next(360));
        tanks[n].Turret.rotation = tanks[0].Chassis.rotation;
        tanks[n].Health = 100;
        tanks[n].Firing = false;
        tanks[n].Moving = false;
    }

    tanks[0].Position = new Vector2(640-64,360-64);
```

```
            //create shell sprites
            shells = new List<Shell>();
            shellImage = Content.Load<Texture2D>("shell");

            //create enemy shell sprites
            enemyShells = new List<Shell>();

            //create explosion sprite
            explosion = new Sprite(spriteBatch);
            explosion.Load(Content, "explosion_30_128");
            explosion.columns = 6;
            explosion.totalframes = 30;
            explosion.size = new Vector2(128, 128);
            explosion.alive = false;

            //load sound clips
            tankFire = Content.Load<SoundEffect>("tankfire");
            tankFireInst = tankFire.CreateInstance();
            explosionSound = Content.Load<SoundEffect>("explosion");
            explInst = explosionSound.CreateInstance();

            //create radar image
            radar = new Sprite(spriteBatch);
            radar.Load(Content, "radar");
            radar.position = new Vector2(1280 - radar.size.X - 20, 720 -
                radar.size.Y - 20);

            return true;
        }

        /**
         * Implements Engine.Update
         **/
        public override void Update(float delta)
        {
            if (gamePad.Buttons.Back == ButtonState.Pressed
                || keys.IsKeyDown(Keys.Escape) ) this.Exit();
            if (gamePad.Buttons.Y == ButtonState.Pressed)
            {
                GamerSignIn();
```

```
    }
    else if (gamePad.Buttons.X == ButtonState.Pressed)
    {
        CreateSession();
    }
    else if (gamePad.Buttons.B == ButtonState.Pressed)
    {
        FindGame();
    }
    UpdatePlayerTank(delta);
    UpdateFiring(delta);
    UpdateBullets();
    UpdateExplosions(delta);
    UpdateNetworking();
}

void UpdatePlayerTank(float delta)
{
    //control the tank
    tanks[0].MoveTimer += (int)delta;
    if (tanks[0].MoveTimer > 1)
    {
        tanks[0].MoveTimer = 0;

        //turn chassis
        float stickx = gamePad.ThumbSticks.Right.X;
        if (stickx != 0)
            tanks[0].MoveTurret(stickx);

        //rotate turret
        stickx = gamePad.ThumbSticks.Left.X;
        if (stickx != 0)
            tanks[0].Turn(stickx);

        //apply throttle
        float sticky = gamePad.ThumbSticks.Left.Y;
        if (sticky == 0)
            tanks[0].Moving = false;
        else
            tanks[0].Moving = true;
```

```
            if (tanks[0].Moving)
            {
                //calculate velocity from tank's direction
                float rot = tanks[0].Chassis.rotation;
                rot -= MathHelper.ToRadians(90);
                rot = MathHelper.WrapAngle(rot);
                float velx = 2.0f * sticky;
                float vely = 2.0f * sticky;
                tanks[0].Chassis.velocity = new Vector2(
                    velx * (float)Math.Cos(rot),
                    vely * (float)Math.Sin(rot) );

                //scroll ground with tank velocity
                ground.Position += tanks[0].Chassis.velocity;
                //move tank
                tanks[0].Position += tanks[0].Chassis.velocity;

                /**
                 * THIS IS NOT WORKING RIGHT!
                 **/
                if (ground.Position.X >= 0 &&
                    ground.Position.X <= ground.Boundary.Width -
                        ground.Viewport.Width &&
                    ground.Position.Y >= 0 &&
                    ground.Position.Y <= ground.Boundary.Height -
                        ground.Viewport.Height)
                {
                    tanks[0].Position.X = ground.Position.X + 640 - 64;
                    tanks[0].Position.Y = ground.Position.Y + 360 - 64;
                }
            }
        }
    }

    void UpdateFiring(float delta)
    {
        tanks[0].FireTimer += (int)delta;
        if (tanks[0].FireTimer > FIRE_DELAY)
        {
```

```
            if (gamePad.Triggers.Right > 0)
                tanks[0].Firing = true;
        }

        if (tanks[0].Firing)
        {
            tanks[0].FireTimer = 0;
            tanks[0].Firing = false;
            FireShell();
        }
    }


    void UpdateBullets()
    {
        //test for bullet collisions
        foreach (Shell shell in shells)
        {
            if (shell.alive)
            {
                //is this shell out of bounds?
                if (shell.position.X < 0 ||
                    shell.position.X > ground.Boundary.Width ||
                    shell.position.Y < 0 ||
                    shell.position.Y > ground.Boundary.Height)
                {
                    shell.alive = false;
                }
                else
                {
                    //did this shell hit a target?
                    Vector2 tankCenter = tanks[1].Position;
                    tankCenter.X += tanks[1].Chassis.size.X / 2;
                    tankCenter.Y += tanks[1].Chassis.size.Y / 2;
                    if (Collision(shell.position, tankCenter, 64))
                    {
                        explInst.Play();
                        shell.alive = false;
                        tanks[1].Health -= 10;
                        explosion.alive = true;
                        explosion.position = tanks[1].Position;
```

```
                                explosion.frame = 0;
                                SendHitPacket();
                        }
                        bulletPos = shell.position;
                }
            }
        }
    }

    void UpdateExplosions(float delta)
    {
        //update explosion
        if (explosion.alive || explosion.frame < 30)
        {
            explosion.Animate(0, 29, delta, 30);
            if (explosion.frame >= 29)
                explosion.alive = false;
        }
    }

    /**
     * Implements Engine.Draw3D
     **/
    public override void Draw3D() { }

    /**
     * Implements Engine.Draw2D
     **/
    public override void Draw2D()
    {
        ground.Draw();
        DrawShells();
        DrawEnemyShells();
        DrawTanks();
        DrawExplosions();
        DrawRadar();

        //clear out all enemy shell sprites
        enemyShells.Clear();
```

```
    Print(Fonts.Pescadero18, 20, 20, "PLAYER 1 (" +
        tanks[0].Health.ToString() + "%)", Color.Yellow);
    Print(Fonts.Pescadero18, 240, 20, "PLAYER 2 (" +
        tanks[1].Health.ToString() + "%)", Color.LightBlue);

    int y = 500;
    Print(Fonts.Kootenay12,20,y,"Y - Gamer Sign-In",
        Color.Yellow); y += 15;
    Print(Fonts.Kootenay12,20,y,"X - Host Game Session",
        Color.Yellow); y += 15;
    Print(Fonts.Kootenay12,20,y,"B - Join Game Session",
        Color.Yellow); y += 30;

    Print(Fonts.Kootenay12,20,y,"FPS " + GetUpdateRate().ToString()
        + " / " + GetDrawRate().ToString(), Color.White); y += 15;
    Print(Fonts.Kootenay12,20,y,"Scroll " + ground.Position.
        ToString(), Color.White); y += 15;
    Print(Fonts.Kootenay12,20,y,"Player " + tanks[0].Position.X.
        ToString("N0") + "," + tanks[0].Position.Y.ToString("N0"),
        Color.White); y += 15;
    Print(Fonts.Kootenay12,20,y,"Enemy " + tanks[1].Position.X.
        ToString("N0") + "," + tanks[1].Position.Y.ToString("N0"),
        Color.White); y += 15;
    Print(Fonts.Kootenay12,20,y,"Bullet "+bulletPos.X.ToString("N0")
        + "," + bulletPos.Y.ToString("N0"), Color.White); y += 15;
    if (gamer != null)
    {
        Print(Fonts.Kootenay12, 20, y, "Gamer: " + gamer.Gamertag,
            Color.White); y += 15;
    }
    else
        Print(Fonts.Kootenay12, 20, y, "No Gamer profile loaded",
            Color.White); y += 15;
    Print(Fonts.Kootenay12,20,y,NetworkStatusMessage,Color.White);
}

void DrawShells()
{
    //draw shells
    foreach (Sprite shell in shells)
    {
```

```
            if (shell.alive)
            {
                //move shell
                shell.position += shell.velocity;
                //remember position
                Vector2 oldPos = shell.position;
                //make position relative to screen for drawing
                float x = shell.position.X - ground.Position.X;
                float y = shell.position.Y - ground.Position.Y;
                shell.position = new Vector2(x, y);
                if (shell.position.X > -16 &&
                    shell.position.X < ground.Viewport.Width + 16 &&
                    shell.position.Y > -16 &&
                    shell.position.Y < ground.Viewport.Height + 16)
                {
                    shell.Draw();
                }
                //restore position
                shell.position = oldPos;
            }
        }
    }

    void DrawEnemyShells()
    {
        //draw enemy shells
        foreach (Sprite shell in enemyShells)
        {
            if (shell.alive)
            {
                //remember position
                Vector2 oldPos = shell.position;
                //make position relative to screen for drawing
                float x = shell.position.X - ground.Position.X;
                float y = shell.position.Y - ground.Position.Y;
                shell.position = new Vector2(x, y);
                if (shell.position.X > -16 &&
                    shell.position.X < ground.Viewport.Width + 16 &&
                    shell.position.Y > -16 &&
                    shell.position.Y < ground.Viewport.Height + 16)
```

```
            {
                shell.Draw();
            }
            //restore position
            shell.position = oldPos;
        }
    }
}

void DrawTanks()
{
    //draw the tanks
    for (int n = 0; n < 2; n++)
    {
        //remember position
        Vector2 oldPos = tanks[n].Position;
        //set relative position on screen
        float x = tanks[n].Position.X - ground.Position.X;
        float y = tanks[n].Position.Y - ground.Position.Y;
        tanks[n].Position = new Vector2(x, y);
        if (tanks[n].Position.X > -128 &&
            tanks[n].Position.X < ground.Viewport.Width + 128 &&
            tanks[n].Position.Y > -128 &&
            tanks[n].Position.Y < ground.Viewport.Height + 128)
        {
            //draw the tank
            tanks[n].Draw();
        }
        //restore position
        tanks[n].Position = oldPos;
    }
}

void DrawExplosions()
{
    //draw explosions
    if (explosion.alive)
    {
        //save position
        Vector2 oldPos = explosion.position;
```

```
            //set relative position
            float x = explosion.position.X - ground.Position.X;
            float y = explosion.position.Y - ground.Position.Y;
            explosion.position = new Vector2(x, y);
            if (explosion.position.X > -16 &&
                explosion.position.X < ground.Viewport.Width + 16 &&
                explosion.position.Y > -16 &&
                explosion.position.Y < ground.Viewport.Height + 16)
            {
                explosion.Draw();
            }
            //restore position
            explosion.position = oldPos;
        }
    }

    void FireShell()
    {
        Shell shell=null;
        tankFireInst.Play();
        //find unused shell
        foreach (Shell s in shells)
        {
            if (s.alive == false)
            {
                shell = s;
                break;
            }
        }

        //...or create a new one
        if (shell == null)
        {
            shell = new Shell(spriteBatch);
            shells.Add(shell);
        }
        shell.Owner = 0;
        shell.alive = true;
        shell.image = shellImage;
        shell.size = new Vector2(shellImage.Width, shellImage.Height);
```

```
        float x = tanks[0].Position.X + 64;
        float y = tanks[0].Position.Y + 64;
        shell.position = new Vector2(x, y);
        shell.rotation = tanks[0].Turret.rotation;
        float angle = shell.rotation - MathHelper.ToRadians(90);
        angle = MathHelper.WrapAngle(angle);
        shell.velocity.X = SHELL_VEL * (float)Math.Cos(angle);
        shell.velocity.Y = SHELL_VEL * (float)Math.Sin(angle);
        shell.pivot = new Vector2(4, 8);
}


void DrawRadar()
{
        radar.Draw();
        int rx = (int)radar.position.X;
        int ry = (int)radar.position.Y;

        //show player's position
        int x = rx + (int)tanks[0].Position.X/8;
        int y = ry + (int)tanks[0].Position.Y/8;
        DrawBox(x, y, x + 6, y + 6, Color.Green);

        //show enemy tank position
        x = rx + (int)tanks[1].Position.X / 8;
        y = ry + (int)tanks[1].Position.Y / 8;
        DrawBox(x, y, x + 6, y + 6, Color.Blue);

        //show shells
        foreach (Shell shell in shells)
        {
            if (shell.alive)
            {
                x = rx + (int)shell.position.X / 8 - 4;
                y = ry + (int)shell.position.Y / 8 - 4;
                DrawBox(x, y, x + 1, y + 1, Color.Red);
            }
        }

        //show enemy shells
        foreach (Shell shell in enemyShells)
```

```
        {
            if (shell.alive)
            {
                x = rx + (int)shell.position.X / 8 - 4;
                y = ry + (int)shell.position.Y / 8 - 4;
                DrawBox(x, y, x + 1, y + 1, Color.Red);
            }
        }
    }

    /**
     * Implements Engine.NetworkReceive
     **/
    public override void NetworkReceive(LocalNetworkGamer gamer,
        ref PacketReader packet)
    {
        Int16 id = packet.ReadInt16();
        switch(id)
        {
        case 1: //enemy tank
            tanks[1].Position = packet.ReadVector2();
            tanks[1].Chassis.rotation = (float)packet.ReadDouble();
            tanks[1].Turret.rotation = (float)packet.ReadDouble();
            break;
        case 2: //shell
            Shell shell = new Shell(spriteBatch);
            shell.image = shellImage;
            shell.size = new Vector2(shellImage.Width, shellImage.
                Height);
            shell.Owner = 1;
            shell.pivot = new Vector2(4, 8);
            shell.position = packet.ReadVector2();
            shell.rotation = (float)packet.ReadDouble();
            enemyShells.Add(shell);
            break;
        case 3: //hit
            explInst.Play();
            explosion.alive = true;
            explosion.frame = 0;
            explosion.position = tanks[0].Position;
```

```
            tanks[0].Health -= 10;
            break;
        }
    }
}

/**
 * Send tank data to other player
 **/
void UpdateNetworking()
{
    SendTankPacket();
    SendShellPackets();
}

void SendTankPacket()
{
    PacketWriter writer = new PacketWriter();
    //add packet id
    Int16 id = 1;
    writer.Write(id);
    //add tank data
    writer.Write(tanks[0].Position);
    writer.Write((double)tanks[0].Chassis.rotation);
    writer.Write((double)tanks[0].Turret.rotation);
    //send
    NetworkSendPacket(writer);
}

void SendShellPackets()
{
    PacketWriter writer = new PacketWriter();
    if (shells.Count == 0) return;
    foreach (Shell shell in shells)
    {
        //add packet id
        Int16 id = 2;
        writer.Write(id);
        //add shell data
        writer.Write(shell.position);
        writer.Write((double)shell.rotation);
```

```
                //send
                NetworkSendPacket(writer);
            }
        }

    void SendHitPacket()
    {
        PacketWriter writer = new PacketWriter();
        //add packet id
        Int16 id = 3;
        writer.Write(id);
        //no data--just notification
        //send
        NetworkSendPacket(writer);
        }
    }
}
```

Improving the Game

Even a relatively simple two-player networked game involves a lot of work, as the source code in this chapter shows! There are so many things I would have liked to add to the game, had time permitted. There are a few known bugs because—let's face it—this is a quick and dirty sample game. I think it's got huge potential, though!

First of all, there's a scrolling battlefield, which we might have easily made into a whole chapter on its own! The scroller could be used for any number of other game genres, from side-scrolling platformers to vertical-scrolling shooters. The tanks have rotating turrets, while the RADAR screen shows the tanks and bullets flying. There really is no reason this game can't support many more players, but one-on-one was necessary, in my opinion, to make the code easier to follow—and as a result, it allows for a better learning experience. The important thing is, you can use this game as a learning tool to build your own networked Xbox 360 games.

In any event, here are some features you may wish to add to the game:

▪ Add support for four, eight, or 16 players.

▪ Add a title screen with menu.

- Add a lobby feature so players can join before combat begins.

- Allow players to send text messages so they can talk smack!

- Add more tanks and allow players to choose one.

- Start players off with a little walking guy and allow them to get into a tank or jump out.

- Allow players to keep track of the score, and add conditions for winning the game.

- Improve the user interface with controls, borders, etc.

SUMMARY

It's a wrap! The *Tank Battle* game fulfills the goals we set out to achieve back in Chapter 1, "Introduction to XNA Game Studio 4.0," of making an Xbox 360 networked game! It's been a very long haul. The book definitely could have spent more time on rendering, but shader-based rendering with DirectX 9 is now a well-established subject with many scores of books to support the technology. Yes, that's a bit of a cop out, but the purpose here was not to try to outdo anyone with rendering effects, but to show primarily indie and hobby developers how to make a networked game for the Xbox 360. In the end, we can also run this code on Windows, and with some changes, on Zune or Windows Phone 7... but that is a subject for another day. Meanwhile, I'm working with some friends to port our game, *Starflight - The Lost Colony*, to XNA. To quote a friend of mine, "It must be done!" With that in mind, I leave with you the task of making something cool out of this *Tank Battle* game. I look forward to seeing what you come up with!

APPENDIX

RESOURCES FOR FURTHER STUDY

The following resources will help the reader who wishes to continue his or her education in video-game development. Not merely a list of random resources, the Web sites and books listed are highly recommended by the author, from his personal collection.

WEB RESOURCES FOR FURTHER STUDY

The casual developer will usually need quick solutions to programming problems, which means a good list of online resources both for the C# language and for XNA Game Studio. The following Web sites are educational, informative, and perhaps even funny and off topic, but all will be worth visiting.

Book Support Web Sites

The publisher's Web site is at http://www.cengage.com. Book resources can be downloaded from http://www.cengage.com/downloads.

The author's Web site also has resource files available at http://www.jharbour .com/forum. The main site is a Web log, and the forum is a discussion as well as a source for news and updates, and a repository of solutions and links to files such as the sources for this book.

Game-Development Sites

Here are some excellent-game development sites on the Web that I visit frequently, most of which are directly related to XNA Game Studio.

- App Hub for XNA Game Studio: http://create.msdn.com
- App Hub Forums: http://forums.create.msdn.com/forums
- App Hub Education: http://create.msdn.com/en-us/education/roadmap
- App Hub Academia: http://create.msdn.com/en-US/education/academia
- Microsoft Faculty Connection: http://www.microsoft.com/education/facultyconnection/default.aspx?c1=en-us&c2=0
- App Hub Indie Games Catalog: http://catalog.create.msdn.com/en-US/gamescatalog.aspx
- XNA Dream.Build.Play Competition: http://www.dreambuildplay.com
- MSDN Main: http://msdn.microsoft.com
- MSDN Visual C# 2010: http://msdn.microsoft.com/en-us/library/dd831853.aspx
- MSDN XNA 4.0: http://msdn.microsoft.com/en-us/library/bb200104.aspx
- RB Whitaker's XNA Tutorials: http://rbwhitaker.wikidot.com/xna-tutorials
- Riemer's XNA Tutorials: http://www.riemers.net
- XNA Development: http://www.xnadevelopment.com
- GameDev.net: http://www.gamedev.net
- Game Development Search Engine: http://www.gdse.com
- CodeGuru: http://www.codeguru.com
- Programmers Heaven: http://www.programmersheaven.com
- AngelCode: http://www.angelcode.com

News, Reviews, and Downloads

Keeping up with all that is happening in the world of game development and beyond is a daunting task, to say the least. New things occur every minute all over the world. Hopefully, the next set of links will help you keep up to date with it all.

- Course Technology: http://www.courseptr.com
- Yahoo! Games: http://www.videogames.yahoo.com
- Blue's News: http://www.bluesnews.com
- Download.com: http://www.download.com
- Tucows: http://www.tucows.com
- Slashdot: http://slashdot.org
- Imagine Games Network (IGN): http://www.ign.com

Industry

If you want to be in the business, you need to know the business. Reading magazines, viewing sites related to the industry, and visiting association meetings, and attending conferences will help you in this endeavor.

- *Game Developer* magazine: http://www.gdmag.com
- GamaSutra: http://www.gamasutra.com
- International Game Developers Association: http://www.igda.org
- Association of Software Professionals: http://www.asp-software.org
- Game Developers Conference: http://www.gdconf.com
- GameHouse (formerly RealArcade): http://www.gamehouse.com

Humor

Here are some great sites to visit when you are looking for a break from coding.

- Homestar Runner: http://www.homestarrunner.com
- Off the Mark: http://www.offthemark.com/computers.htm
- Player Versus Player: http://www.pvponline.com

PRINT RESOURCES FOR FURTHER STUDY

I've provided a short description for each of the books in this list because they are either books I have written (plug!) or that I highly recommend and have found useful, relaxing, funny, or essential on many an occasion. You will find this list of recommended books useful as references to the C# language and as complementary titles and references to subjects covered in this book.

Books by This Author

If you enjoyed this book and would like to look into other books written by me, here is a list of my programming books currently in print that are at least *somewhat* related to the topic at hand.

Advanced 2D Game Development

Jonathan S. Harbour; Course Technology PTR; ISBN 1598633422

Get ready to build a complete, professional-quality 2D game engine from start to finish! This is your comprehensive guide to 2D game development using DirectX in the C++ programming language. Each chapter of the book covers one major component of the game engine, including 2D and 3D rendering, DirectInput, FMOD audio, game math, multi-threading, Lua scripting, and more, and the game engine is built upon chapter by chapter. Through the creation of the game engine, you'll learn step by step how to write solid code for multiple compilers, adding to the code as you work through each chapter. And every chapter includes a sample game that illustrates the new techniques being taught. Perfect for game-programming students and professionals alike, this book is your ultimate guide to awesome 2D game development.

Beginning Game Programming, 3rd Edition

Jonathan Harbour; Course Technology PTR; ISBN 1435454278

This book shows budding game developers how to take their game ideas from concept to reality. Requiring only a basic understanding of the C++ language, this unique guide covers all the skills needed to create 2D and 3D games using code written in DirectX. Each element of a game is taught step by step, from learning how to create a simple Windows program, to using the key DirectX components to render 2D and 3D, to adding sound to your game. Using the skills taught within each chapter, readers will develop their own game library, which they can build upon for future game projects. And this updated, new edition includes end-of-chapter quizzes and projects to help you practice your new skills! At the end of the book, you will put newfound skills to use as you create your own complete, fully functional game.

Beginning Java Game Programming, 2nd Edition

Jonathan S. Harbour; Course Technology PTR; ISBN 1598634763

Are you serious about learning how to create real, Java-based games for fun and sharing? Do you have a basic understanding of the Java programming language? If you've answered yes, then you are ready to get started building Web-based 2D games from scratch using the latest version of the Java Development Kit! This hands-on guide is perfect for beginner-level game programmers who want to quickly and easily learn how to create games using Java. Written in simple language, the book teaches each new skill using engaging tutorials, followed by end-of-chapter questions and exercises to help reinforce what you've just learned. Each chapter builds upon the previous ones, allowing you to repeat and practice the techniques covered. You'll begin with the basics of writing a simple 2D game using vector graphics, move on to utilizing Java's advanced 2D library to add animation and sound effects, and end by creating a professional, sprite-based game full of interesting artwork and details that you can share with others on your own Web site!

DarkBASIC Pro Game Programming, 2nd Edition

Jonathan S. Harbour and Joshua R. Smith; Course Technology PTR; ISBN 1598632876

Learn to write 2D and 3D games without any programming experience by harnessing the advanced 2D/3D graphics features of DarkBASIC Professional. This easy-to-use language handles the entire game engine for you, so you are free to focus on designing and playing your own games. Written for beginners with no programming experience, *DarkBASIC Pro Game Programming, 2nd Edition* is a welcome change of pace from traditional game-programming books. You won't need to spend time figuring out how the game engine works, but only what the game is supposed to do. You will be able to create self-contained executable games with the graphics and sound files stored inside the EXE file. No DarkBASIC runtime library is needed; compiled programs are self-contained and require only that DirectX be installed. Finally, a book for complete beginners who want to learn to write games!

Game Programming All in One, 3rd Edition

Jonathan S. Harbour; Course Technology PTR; ISBN 1598632892

This book gives aspiring game programmers the skills they need to create professional-quality games. If you have a working knowledge of C and you are ready to expand your skills into the field of game programming, then get ready to begin your journey with this latest edition! It doesn't cover the topic of programming in general, but rather the specifics of programming for games. Using the cross-platform Allegro game library, you'll learn how to write complete games that will run on almost any operating system. Both Windows and Linux screenshots are displayed throughout. Using the techniques taught within this book and the tools included on the CD-ROM, you'll be able to write standard Windows and DirectX programs without the cost of an expensive compiler.

Multi-Threaded Game Engine Design

Jonathan S. Harbour; Course Technology PTR; ISBN 1435454170

This book shows experienced game developers how to apply multi-thread techniques to game-programming technology to improve game performance. Using Direct3D and C++, a sample game engine is created step by step throughout the course of the book, and numerous examples illustrate the concepts presented. Detailed screenshots and well-documented source code help readers understand the techniques being presented throughout the book. Multi-threading is one of the hottest game-development topics today; this book shows students how to add advanced, cutting-edge techniques to their game-programming skill set.

Visual Basic Game Programming for Teens, 3rd Edition

Jonathan S. Harbour; Course Technology PTR; ISBN 1435458109

This book teaches teens and other beginners how to create their own 2D role-playing game (RPG) using the free-to-download and easy-to-use Visual Basic 2008 Express. The game is built step by step throughout the book as readers learn new skills and build upon them. This new edition features almost entirely new content from the previous edition. With it, readers will also learn game-tool creation, animation skills, and graphics programming.

Visual C# Game Programming for Teens

Jonathan S. Harbour; Course Technology PTR; ISBN 1435458486

This book teaches teens and other beginners how to create games using C# and Windows Forms (GDI+). A true beginner's guide, this book covers each essential step for creating your own complete role-playing game (RPG), including a character-creation screen and a combat system. This book serves as a comprehensive introductory guide for readers who are new to programming or new to programming for games. The reader is shown how to load and draw bitmaps, create sprites, render a game world, keep track of inventory and character stats, and build tools, including a level editor, character editor, item editor, and monster editor. Every chapter contributes toward a growing game library that is used to improve and add new and more advanced features to the game. When the reader finishes with the book, he or she will have created a complete game.

Additional Books

These books were chosen for their support of DirectX 9 shaders (which can be used in an XNA project), as well as other topics of interest in game development. This list includes the "best of the best" books currently in this author's own library.

AI Techniques for Game Programming

Mat Buckland; Course Technology PTR; ISBN 193184108X

This book explains the difficult topics of genetic algorithms and neural networks in plain English. Gone are the tortuous mathematic equations and abstract examples found in other books. Each chapter takes you through the theory a step at a time, clearly explaining how you can incorporate each technique into your own games.

Artificial Intelligence for Games, 2nd Edition

Ian Millington and John Funge; Morgan Kaufmann; ISBN 0123747317

Creating robust artificial intelligence is one of the greatest challenges for game developers, yet the commercial success of a game often depends on the quality of the AI. In this book, the authors bring extensive professional experience to the problem of improving the quality of AI in games. They describe numerous examples from real games and explore the underlying ideas through detailed case studies. They go further to introduce many techniques little used by developers today. The book's associated Web site contains a library of C++ source code and demonstration programs, and a complete commercial source-code library of AI algorithms and techniques.

Best of Game Programming Gems

Mark DeLoura; Charles River Media; ISBN 1584505710

Welcome to a collection of the most valuable and timeless articles from the essential reference series for game developers. This book combines the greatest cutting-edge, ready-to-use techniques contributed by industry experts to volumes 1–6 of the *Game Programming Gems* series. Each article was carefully chosen by the editors and compiled into one best-of-the-best volume in an effort to share 49 timeless gems of game-programming wisdom with you and to save you time and effort with a plethora of reliable methods to add to your developer's toolbox. The articles are organized into six sections covering the topics of general information, math and physics, artificial intelligence, graphics, networking, and audio. Whether you are new to game development or a practiced veteran, you're sure to find inspiration and insight to make more entertaining and satisfying games.

Microsoft C# Programming for the Absolute Beginner

Andrew Harris; Course Technology PTR; ISBN 1931841160

If you are new to programming with C# and are looking for a solid introduction, this is the book for you. Developed by computer-science instructors, books in the *For the Absolute Beginner* series teach the principles of programming through simple game creation. You will acquire the skills that you need for more practical C# programming applications and will learn how these skills can be put to use in real-world scenarios. Best of all, by the time you finish this book you will be able to apply the basic principles you've learned to the next programming language you tackle.

Character Animation with Direct3D

Carl Granberg; Charles River Media; ISBN 1584505702

This is *the* book to get on 3D mesh animation techniques with Direct3D—currently the only up-to-date book (i.e., with *working* source-code examples) on the market. I highly recommend it! Just be forewarned: This is an extremely advanced book that should, at minimum, be read after one has read Granberg's RTS book (or another intermediate DirectX book).

Character Development and Storytelling for Games

Lee Sheldon; Course Technology PTR; ISBN 1592003532

This book begins with a history of dramatic writing and entertainment in other media. It then segues to writing for games, revealing that while proven techniques in linear media can be translated to games, games offer many new challenges of their own such as interactivity, non-linearity, player input, and more. It then moves beyond linear techniques to introduce the elements of the craft of writing that are particularly unique to interactive media. It takes us from the relatively secure confines of single-player games to the vast open spaces of virtual worlds and examines player-created stories, and shows how even here writers on the development team are necessary to the process, and what they can do to aid it.

Data Structures and Algorithms for Game Developers

Allen Sherrod; Charles River Media; ISBN 1584504951

This book teaches the fundamentals of the data structures and algorithms used in game development. It provides programmers with a detailed reference to what data structures and algorithms are, and why they are so critical in game development. It teaches new game programmers, students, and aspiring game developers how to create data structures and write algorithms using C++. All key features of C++ are also covered, especially those related to game development. Additionally, a demo application is included in each chapter focusing on the data structure and/or algorithms presented in that chapter. The book covers many modern topics that game and graphics programmers must know to be successful, including geometry-management techniques as well as data structures and algorithms such as KD-Trees, Binary Space Partitioning Trees, Sphere Trees, etc. The code written in this book is not dependent on any specific hardware or operating system. Each chapter ends with questions, exercises, and challenges for the reader to complete in order to help them better understand and apply what they learn.

Emergence in Games

Penny Sweetser; Charles River Media; ISBN 1584505516

The future direction of game development is toward more flexible, realistic, and interactive game worlds. However, current methods of game design do not allow for anything other than pre-scripted player exchanges and static objects and environments. An emergent approach to game development involves the creation of a globally designed game system that provides rules and boundaries for player interactions, rather than prescribed paths. *Emergence in Games* provides a detailed foundation for applying the theory and practice of emergence in games to game design. Emergent narrative, characters and agents, and game worlds are covered and a hands-on tutorial and case study enable the reader to put the skills and ideas presented into practice.

Game Coding Complete, 3rd Edition

Mike McShaffry; Charles River Media; ISBN 1584506806

Welcome to the newest edition of the essential, hands-on guide to developing commercial-quality games. Written by a veteran game programmer, this book examines the entire game-development process and all the unique challenges associated with creating a game. In this excellent introduction to game architecture, you'll explore all the major subsystems of modern game engines and learn professional techniques used in actual games. This third edition features expanded content and coverage of the latest and most exciting game-programming techniques including AI, multiprogramming, working with scripting languages such as Lua, and writing C# tools like your level editor. All the code and examples presented have been tested and used in commercial video games, and the book is full of invaluable best practices, professional tips and tricks, and cautionary advice.

Game Engine Architecture

Jason Gregory; A K Peters; ISBN 1568814135

A 2009 *Game Developer* Front Line Award finalist, this book covers both the theory and practice of game-engine software development, bringing together complete coverage of a wide range of topics. The concepts and techniques described are the actual ones used by real game studios like Electronic Arts and Naughty Dog. Many of the examples are grounded in specific technologies, but the discussion extends way beyond any particular engine or API. The references and citations make it a great jumping-off point for those who wish to dig deeper into any particular aspect of the game-development process. Intended as the text for a college-level series in game programming, this book can also be used by amateur software engineers, hobbyists, self-taught game programmers, and existing members of the game industry. Junior game engineers can use it to solidify their understanding of game technology and engine architecture. Even senior engineers who specialize in one particular field of game development can benefit from the bigger picture presented in these pages.

Going to War: Creating Computer War Games

Jason Darby; Course Technology PTR; ISBN 1598635662

Do you want to learn how to create computer war games, but don't know how to get started or don't have any experience with game programming? *Going to War: Creating Computer War Games* shows you how to use the drag-and-drop game engine, Multimedia Fusion 2, to make your very own computer war games to play and share. After an introduction to the Multimedia Fusion 2 interface and the basics of how to use it, you'll get started on the game that you'll create throughout the course of the book. You'll begin by making your game map, using a system of hexagon tiles to create the terrain and the different units you want to include in your game such as soldiers and tanks. Then you'll learn how to set rules for player movement, different types of terrain, and combat. You'll even find more advanced techniques such as how to implement officers, fortifications, and even a simple monetary system in your games. The book even discusses how to track and find bugs in your games and how to create an editor that allows you to easily apply data you've already created to new games. Everything you need to build your own war games is included with the book. By the time you've worked your way through it, you'll have designed your very own working and playable war game.

Introduction to 3D Game Programming with DirectX 9.0c: A Shader Approach

Frank Luna; Jones & Bartlett Publishers; ISBN 1598220160

This is a comprehensive book on 3D graphics programming with Direct3D 9. It is not intended for beginners, however. You will need a solid grasp of C++ and at least a working knowledge of DirectX before this book will be beneficial to you. As an intermediate- to advanced-level book, it will teach you the most useful techniques used in game projects today such as 3D terrain, character animation, and shader programming.

Mathematics for 3D Game Programming and Computer Graphics, 2nd Edition

Eric Lengyel; Charles River Media; ISBN 1584502770

This completely updated second edition illustrates the mathematical concepts that a game programmer needs to develop a professional-quality 3D engine. Although the book is geared toward applications in game development, many of the topics appeal to general interests in 3D graphics. It starts at a fairly basic level in areas such as vector geometry and linear algebra, and then progresses to more advanced topics in 3D game programming such as illumination and visibility determination. Particular attention is given to derivations of key results, ensuring that the reader is not forced to endure gaps in the theory. The book assumes a working knowledge of trigonometry and calculus, but also includes sections that review the important tools used from these disciplines, such as trigonometric identities, differential equations, and Taylor series.

Mathematics for Game Developers

Christopher Tremblay; Course Technology PTR; ISBN 159200038X

This book explores the branches of mathematics from the game developer's perspective, rejecting the abstract, theoretical approach in favor of demonstrating real, usable applications for each concept covered. Use of this book is not confined to users of a certain operating system or enthusiasts of particular game genres; the topics covered are universally applicable.

Programming an RTS Game with Direct3D

Carl Granberg; Charles River Media; ISBN 1584504986

The real-time strategy game developed in this book is an extraordinary example of the genre and a fantastic learning tool for any intermediate- to advanced-level DirectX programmer. The chapters on 3D terrain and animation are indispensable. Although the shader code is presented in HLSL 2.0 file format, the shader programs still compile and run, and can easily be copied into an FX file for 3.0 support.

Real-Time Rendering, 3rd Edition

Tomas Akenine-Moller, Eric Haines, and Naty Hoffman; A K Peters; ISBN 1568814240

Because software and hardware are constantly and rapidly evolving due to the insatiable need for more realistic and complex graphics, the book avoids getting too specific. To quote the authors, "The field is rapidly evolving, and so it is a moving target." This lack of specificity doesn't detract from the usefulness of the book, though. Instead, it works at a higher, more abstract level, describing approaches to rendering techniques using generic algorithms. It is up to the programmer to apply these methods to the specific program or system on which they are to be implemented. This book describes some very complex methods, and this book is not for the average computer-graphics creator. However, if you are working in an industry that depends on real-time rendered animation—like the gaming, medical, or military fields—or you are building the next-generation, real-time render engine, this book will offer insight and concepts you can use to build some impressive software.

INDEX